An Investor's Guide to Understanding and Mastering Options Trading

An Investor's Guide to Understanding and Mastering Options Trading

Generating Steady Profits of 100% in a 10% World

Second Edition

Bill Johnson
with James DiGeorgia and David Nichols

21st Century Investor Publishing, Inc.

Published by 21st Century Investor Publishing, Inc.
1900 Glades Road Suite 441 Boca Raton FL 33431

ISBN 0-9718048-2-6

Library of Congress Control Number: 2002111643

Printed in the United States of America.

This publication is designed to provide accurate and authoritative information in regard to the subject matter covered. It is provided with the understanding that the publisher is not engaged in rendering legal, accounting or other professional services. If legal advice is required, the services of a competent professional person should be sought. — From a Declaration of Principles, jointly adopted by Committee of American Bar Association and Committee of Publishers and Associations

Although both the author and 21st Century Investor Publishing, Inc. believe the information, data, and contents presented are accurate, they neither represent or guarantee the accuracy and completeness nor assume any liability. It should not be assumed that the methods, techniques, or indicators presented in this book will be profitable or that they will not result in losses. Trading involves the risk of loss, as well as the potential for profit. Past performance is not a guarantee of future results.

CONTENTS

PREFACE

Equity options are perhaps one of the most innovative and important tools in modern financial times. They allow investors a means to transfer risk from one investor to another, just as most of us tranfer the financial risk of car accidents to insurance companies. Depending on how they are used, options can also provide tremendous financial leverage.

It is undoubtedly the leverage aspect of options that has made them so popular. They allow investors and speculators ways to participate in otherwise risky stocks without putting much money at risk. I have seen, on two occasions, $70,000 accounts each explode to over $1 million the very next day strictly due to options. This type of leverage is not possible with stocks alone.

With all their shining qualities, though, options still manage to mystify people. They leave investors with losses even though it appears they should have made money. Their value can be cut in half even though there is no change in the stock price. Conservative strategies can create hidden risks. Options can be dangerous because they are deceptively simple to learn, and many novices jump in with big investments only to watch them erode to nothing.

However, these are not reasons to avoid options; they are reasons why investors should learn about them. This book is designed to take you through aspects of option trading you will not find in any other book. It is based on my real experiences as a broker and options and risk management trainer for the largest option retailer in the world. You'll learn the basics of options as well as practical applications such as placing trades, analyzing and drawing profit and loss diagrams, avoiding volatility traps, and why you shouldn't exercise a call option early. But most of all, you'll have a thorough understanding of the basic, intermediate and advanced concepts and strategies used by most retail investors along with their hidden risks — the risks most investors cannot explain.

Can you get 100% returns in a 10% world? Yes, it is certainly possible, but it's outright dangerous to attempt unless you understand options. In fact, if you do not understand deltas and gammas — to which we dedicate an entire chapter — it is almost certain that you will end up on the losing side of the trade. One small misunderstanding in the mechanics or terminology can cause profits to immediately evaporate. We'll even tell you about an investor who lost $4,000 instantly because he used one wrong word.

This book will give you the ins and outs, the pros and cons, and attempt to answer most of the questions you could ever have about options.

INTRODUCTION

Options are growing in popularity at an exponential rate. There is a good reason for this, as you will find, and investors are quick to cash in on all the advantages they have to offer. At the same time, there has never been more negative publicity surrounding any financial asset.

Imagine an account worth $70,000 one day that becomes worth more than $1 million the next. This has happened on more than one occasion, all from the use of options. This type of leverage is impossible to achieve through stocks alone. Conversely, we saw Baring's Bank, an historic 233-year-old institution that helped finance the Napoleonic Wars, brought down *single-handedly* because of an options trader. It may seem to the unsuspecting eye that options are nothing more than a form of legalized gambling and serve no beneficial purpose for the financial markets. In addition, the financial press is quick to point out that no new equity is created with options as when shares of stock are issued.

So why is there so much commotion over options? Why are they so popular, yet seemingly so dangerous?

The reason is that options are insidiously simple. You can learn everything you need to know in a matter of minutes to place an order. You will be naively confident that you know all the risks and possible outcomes and even be lured into placing "sure bets" with large amounts of money. But later, instead of the expected windfall you expected, you see a large loss staring you in the face.

It is much like playing the game of blackjack, a popular casino game that is very easy to learn, at least on a basic level. Essentially, all you have to do is bet that your hand is closer to 21 points in value than the dealer's hand. Because it is so easy to understand, you will always see the blackjack tables among the most crowded — with nearly everyone losing. Just like blackjack, options are incredibly tough to understand at a level necessary to make money.

The main purpose of this book is to make the difficult, subtle risks and concepts of options easy to understand. Once these are understood, you will then be on your way to using options effectively. This book is divided into two sections. The first section covers the most commonly misunderstood options topics and terminology, and is designed to give you a solid foundation and understanding of these assets. They are explained in simple, everyday language with limited mathematics. The second section covers strategies. We will look at basic, intermediate, and advanced strategies in depth. The strategies covered are those you will most likely use to trade, and those you will often hear about throughout your investment career.

This book differs from others because you will learn the most challenging concepts of options from a different perspective. I have spent nearly nine years actively trading options; many were with the brokerage firm that clears more than 40% of all option trades — more than any other firm. I gained firsthand experience by advising and trading for investors, speculators, and fund managers from around the globe. I have seen what works and what does not. I have seen million dollar accounts go bust because of "conservative" option strategies, and have even seen a client jailed for trying to avoid Regulation T requirements.

It has been my experience that most options guidebooks are written from one of two perspectives: academic or market making — neither of which apply to the retail investor. None of these books shows you the in-depth side of the risks involved with retail investing.

Once you understand options at this level, you will be well informed and able to make the appropriate trades based on your risk tolerances. Although advanced knowledge of this subject does not guarantee profits, it will never leave you with a surprise loss you were unwilling to take.

Options are a wonderful management tool. Strategies range between ultraconservative to high-risk gambles, which means there are strategies for nearly everyone. Unfortunately, many traders immediately delete the word "options" from their investing vocabulary because of some bad press or a bad experience. These traders are missing opportunities — or accepting unnecessary risks — that come from *not* using options. In fact, it is quite ironic that these "risky" assets can be constructed to behave like a risk-free bond. Investors who understand and use these instruments will have a distinct advantage over those who do not.

Options can be difficult if you want to advance further with them. Volumes of books have been written about options, and a Nobel Prize was even awarded for a formula that calculates their theoretical values. However, it is often the simple concepts that are overlooked and misunderstood, which makes the advanced topics that much more difficult to comprehend. It is our goal to help you understand these assets in an easy-to-read format. We want to show you the simplicity of options.

So to begin, it is important to understand options at the most simplistic levels — what they are and why they were created. If you are new to options, forget everything you have heard about them, and start right by reading this book with an open mind. Learn what they are and how they can be used for your benefit. Options may not be useful for everyone, but they are certainly more useful to more investors than they are given credit. It is up to you to discover the strategies that are right for you, learn to use them to your advantage, and become a better investor through your understanding of them.

PART I
Topics and Terminology

Chapter 1: Option Basics

What is an Option?

Although options may initially seem mysterious to most investors, the basics are actually quite simple to understand.

Options are simply legal *contracts* between two people to buy and sell stock for a fixed price over a given time period.

These contracts are standardized, meaning they control a fixed amount of shares and expire at the same time. Because of this standardization, they are traded on an exchange, just like shares of stock. The contracts are usually highly liquid, which means many buyers and sellers are standing by who are willing to buy or sell. You can buy an option contract with the same speed it takes you to call your broker and buy stock.

There are two types of options: **calls** and **puts**.

Long Call Options

A call option gives the owner the right, but not the obligation, to <u>buy</u> stock ("call" it away from the owner) at a specified price over a given time period.

In trading lingo, any asset that you buy is called a long position. If you buy a call option, you are the owner, and are long the contract. Notice that the owner, the long position, has the right, *but not the obligation,* to buy stock. You are allowed to purchase the stock for a fixed price, but are not required to do so. In other words, you have the *option* to buy, which is where these financial assets get their name.

The price at which you can buy the stock is called the *strike* price, which is a slang term that got its use because that is the price at which the deal — the contract — was *struck*. Generally, each contract controls 100 shares of stock, called the *underlying* stock.

We will discuss this more in depth later. For now, just understand that unless otherwise stated, each contract controls 100 shares.

Each contract is good for only a certain amount of time. Usually you can find contracts good for as little as a couple of weeks and as long as three years. However, these are standardized time frames, so you do not pick the exact date you want it to expire.

Just as stock is traded in shares, options are traded in units called *contracts*.

If you buy one IBM March $100 call option (one contract), you have the right, but not the obligation, to buy 100 shares of IBM (the underlying stock) for $100 per share (the strike price) through the expiration date in March, which is usually the third Friday of the month[1].

If you think about the definition of a call option, you have probably encountered similar agreements outside the financial markets. Your local pizza place may have a coupon good for the next thirty days that allows you to buy a large pizza for $10. That is similar to a *call* option. It is like a contract that locks in the purchase price over a fixed time period. After that time period, the option to buy at that price expires. Although the pizza shop may make an exception and allow you to use the coupon after the expiration date, there is no such thing with a call option. Once it is expired, it is gone.

Think of a call option as a coupon giving you the right to buy stock at a fixed price through an expiration date. The big difference between a coupon and a call option is that you must pay for the option, while coupons are generally handed out free of charge.

Long Put Options

A put option allows owners to <u>sell</u> their stock ("put" it back to someone else) for the strike price within a given time. As with call

---

[1] Technically, options expire on the Saturday following the third Friday of the expiration month. However, this is for clearing purposes, and there is nothing the option trader can do with an option on Saturday. The third Friday of expiration month is the last trading day so, for practical purposes, it is the day you want to consider as expiration.

options, the put buyer (long position) has the right, but not the obligation. If you buy an IBM March $100 put, you have the right, but not the obligation, to *sell* 100 shares of IBM for $100 per share through the third Friday in March.

Buying a put option is similar to buying an auto insurance policy. You can buy a policy for a premium and collect the insurance value if you wreck your car. If you do not wreck your car, you are out the amount of only the premium. Likewise, you can buy a put option for a premium and turn it back to the insurer (the put seller) if your stock should crash (fall below the strike price). If the stock stays above the strike, you would let the "insurance" expire and lose only the premium you paid.

Short Calls and Puts

Notice that with both calls and puts, the buyers (the "long" positions) have the right, but not the obligation, to buy or sell. The investor on the other side (the seller of the option, also called the "short" position) has the *obligation* to fulfill the contract; he or she has no choice. If a long call owner decides to buy the stock, the short call trader must oblige and sell. Likewise, if long put owners decide to sell their stock, the short put traders must purchase the stock. *Regardless of whether the short option seller is forced to buy or sell stock, the premium received from the initial short trade is theirs to keep.* That is their compensation for accepting the risk.

	Call Option	**Put Option**
Long position (the buyer)	Right, but not the obligation, to buy stock at the strike price	Right, but not the obligation, to sell stock at the strike price
Short position (the seller)	Possible obligation to sell stock at the strike price	Possible obligation to buy stock at the strike price

The Options Clearing Corporation (OCC)

Many traders new to options may be concerned that the short side will not deliver. In other words, if you want to use your option to either buy or sell shares, is there a risk of the short seller refusing?

There is no need to worry about contract performance from the short seller. For example, if you decide you want to purchase 100 shares of IBM at $100 with your call option, there is no need to worry about the seller of the call (the short call position) not delivering the shares. This is because an intermediary called the Options Clearing Corporation (OCC) is really the buyer to every seller and the seller to every buyer. The function of the OCC is to provide investor confidence, thereby providing better prices and liquidity.

The OCC is well capitalized and does not run the risk of default. As a result, investors do not even need to know who is on the other side of the trade because the OCC guarantees contract performance. Ever since the inception of the OCC in 1973, no investor has ever lost money due to default by the other party. This does not mean that the OCC guarantees contract *profitability*; instead, it means only that you are guaranteed to buy or sell shares with your long option position if you decide to do so.

How Are Options Similar to Stocks?

- Options are securities.

- Options trade on national SEC (Securities Exchange Commission)-regulated exchanges.

- Option orders are transacted through market makers and retail participants with bids to buy and offers to sell and can be traded like any other security.

How Do Options Differ from Stocks?

- Options have an expiration date, whereas common stocks can be held forever(unless the company goes bankrupt). If an option is not exercised on or before expiration, it no longer exists and expires worthless.

- Options exist only as "book entry," which means they are held electronically. There are no certificates for options like there are for stocks.

- There is no limit to the number of options that can be traded on an underlying stock. Common stocks have a fixed number of shares outstanding.

- Options do not confer voting rights or dividends. They are strictly contracts to buy or sell the underlying stock or index. If you want a dividend or wish to vote the proxy, you need to exercise the call option.

Chapter 2: Option Specifications and Terms

Before you can understand trading strategies, it is important to understand many of the terms you will hear when trading options. Options, like many other fields, have their own colorful lingo to communicate important terms and concepts. If you do not understand these terms, it will be difficult to follow the trading strategies that follow. In addition, it could be a costly lesson once you do start trading. A slight misunderstanding in the terms can land you on the wrong side of the trade in a hurry!

Margin Accounts, Fed Calls, and Maintenance Calls

Whenever you buy stocks, bonds, or other specific types of assets in the financial markets, you are not necessarily required to pay for them in full. Under Regulation T pursuant to the Exchange Act of 1934, the Federal Reserve Board regulates the extension of credit to brokerage firms. Regulation T, or Reg T for short, states that brokerage firms are required to collect only 50% of the purchase price (subject to a $2,000 minimum), and the brokerage firm may lend the additional amount, provided you have signed a *margin account agreement* form. Once you have a margin account, you may purchase any marginable security simply by paying the required Reg T amount, and the brokerage firm will provide the rest. The Reg T amount varies based on the assets. Stocks are currently 50%, but bonds may be much lower depending on the maturity date. To buy securities with borrowed funds or "on margin," the security must be marginable per the SEC. While the intricacies of margin account are well beyond the scope of this book, it is important to have a basic understanding when dealing with options.

Technically, the rules allow options with more than nine months remaining before expiration to be purchased on margin; however, you will probably never find a single firm that allows it. This is because individual firms are allowed to make the regulations stricter if they desire; they just cannot make them looser. For example, while Reg T states that only 50% payment is required for stocks, your brokerage firm is free to require 60% or any amount higher than 50% but could not allow something less. Most firms do not want to lend money for options because of risks you will soon understand as you read this book.

The Reg T amount is due within three business days of the trade, not counting the trade date. For example, if you buy a marginable stock on Monday, you are required to have a check to your broker by close of business on Thursday — three full business days after the trade date. The amount you are required to send is called the Fed call.

For example, assume you buy 100 shares of a marginable $100 stock for a total of $10,000. Your account will show a Fed call in the amount of $5,000 (50% of the purchase price). Of course, you are always free to send more than this amount; this is just the minimum amount due. Once you do, your account will look like this:

Market Value Long: $10,000
Debit: $5,000
Equity: $5,000

The market value long will change with fluctuations in the stock price. The debit amount (borrowed funds) will never change (unless you send in more money). Although this may seem confusing, it is no different from any asset you buy with borrowed funds. If you buy a $100,000 house and pay $20,000 down, your "market value long" is $100,000 and the "debit" is $80,000, which leaves you with $20,000 equity. If the value of your home rises, your equity increases, but the amount you owe the bank stays the same (assuming you do not have an adjustable rate mortgage). Likewise if the value of the home falls, you lose equity. Just like the bank, your brokerage firm will charge you interest on these debit balances. Debit balances are typically a couple of points above prime, so they can be a great source of loans over credit cards. However, unlike banks, you are not necessarily locked in to a guaranteed rate. The amount you pay will likely rise or fall with changes in interest rates.

Let's assume your stock position is now worth $12,000, which makes your equity increase by $2,000 to $7,000 as follows:

Market Value Long: $12,000
Debit: $5,000
Equity: $7,000

If you sell your stock, $5,000 will cover the debit, and the remaining $7,000 is yours to keep. Speculators tend to buy stocks on margin because it provides greater leverage. As we will find out later, options provide even more leverage but without the dollar amounts at risk as with stocks. For example, if you had originally paid for the $10,000 of stock in full, your return would be a $2,000 gain divided by $10,000 principal for a 20% return. Notice how the margin investor made the same $2,000 return, but for only $5,000 down for a 40% return, which is exactly double. This is because they could buy twice the amount of shares for the same amount of money. Of course, leverage works both ways. If the stock falls to $8,000, the investor who pays in full is down 20%, while the margin investor is down 40%.

Margin Cash

Although certain options are technically marginable, you would probably never see it allowed by any firm. So why include margin basics when discussing options? Although it may seem contradictory, options are not marginable, but you can be on margin when buying options.

Let's assume you bought the $10,000 in stock but paid for it in full. Your account would then show:

Market Value Long: $10,000
Debit: $0
Equity: $10,000

Margin cash: $5,000

The brokerage firm is therefore saying that you have $5,000 in "margin cash" and are allowed to take out this amount as a loan. Think of the margin cash as a maximum credit line on your account.

Let's say you request a check to be sent to you for $5,000. Your account now looks like this:

Market Value Long: $10,000
Debit: $5,000
Equity: $5,000

Margin cash: $0

Notice that by taking out the maximum amount, you didn't fall below the 50% mark. You have $5,000 equity per $10,000 in assets, which is 50%. Had your broker allowed you to take out one additional dollar, you would fall below the Reg T amount. Do not worry about the mechanics of this, because it can be incredibly difficult. Your brokerage firm will take care of these values for you.

Instead of requesting a *check* for $5,000, you can use this money to buy options or even more stock. Whether you accept a check or buy options, you are now "on margin" and will pay interest on the debit balance. This is how you can be on margin with options even though options are generally not marginable. Using your margin cash from securities in the account to buy options will create a debit balance.

You could also buy stock with this cash. If so, the same 50% rule still applies, which means you could actually buy another $10,000 worth of stock. Assuming you paid for the $10,000 of stock in full, you could use the $5,000 margin cash to purchase another $10,000, and your account would look like this:

Market Value Long: $20,000
Debit: $10,000
Equity: $10,000

Margin cash: $0

And again you are at 50% equity, because you now have $20,000 in assets and $10,000 equity.

Margin cash used to buy stocks is usually put in its own category called buying power and is often double the amount of margin cash available. However, it is possible that *buying power* can be more than double the margin cash amount, but it's beyond our scope as to why that happens.

Maintenance Calls

You are allowed to post 50% of the cost and still be within the regulations. What happens if the stock drops afterward? Recall the previous example where you bought $10,000 in stock on margin and your account looks like this:

Market Value Long: $10,000
Debit: <u>$5,000</u>
Equity: $5,000

Margin cash: $0

Now assume the stock falls to a value of $9,000:

Market Value Long: $9,000
Debit: <u>$5,000</u>
Equity: $4,000

Margin cash: $0

Now you have $4,000 equity for $9,000 in assets, or 44%. As long as your account does not fall below your firm's required minimum amount, you will be within regulations. In other words, you cannot initiate a position for less than 50% of the cost; however, once you do, you have a "cushion," and the account can actually fall to a lower level called the maintenance level. The maintenance level is technically 25%, but most firms require a stricter amount, which is usually 30% or 35%. If your firm requires a minimum of 35%, your account could fall to:

Market Value Long: $7,692
Debit: <u>$5,000</u>
Equity: $2,692

Margin cash: $0

If your stocks fall to $7,692, you will have $2,692 in equity, or 35%. At this point if the value of the stocks fall any more, you will receive a *maintenance call*, which is a request by your broker to get your account back to a minimum of 35%. Generally, maintenance calls are due immediately, and there is no three-day settlement. However, most brokerage firms will try to work with you depending on the severity of the maintenance call. You can usually meet the maintenance call by depositing funds or marginable securities or selling stock, all of which will change the equity percentage of your account.

For example, if the stock falls to a value of $7,000, your equity will be $2,000, or 28%. Because you are below the house requirement of 35%, in this example, you are required to bring the account back up to that minimum level. Your account will look like this:

Market Value Long:	$7,000
Debit:	$5,000
Equity:	$2,000
Margin cash:	$0
Maintenance call:	$450

If you deposit $450 into your account, it will then look like this:

Market Value Long:	$7,000
Debit:	$4,550
Equity:	$2,450
Margin cash:	$0
Maintenance call:	$0

The $450 deposit will reduce the total debit by this amount, and your new equity percentage is $2,450/$7,000 = 35%. Therefore, the maintenance call has been met.

We just saw how falling stock values can lead to maintenance calls. What if the stock moves up? If the stock in your account moves up past the 50% level, you will start to increase your margin cash and buying power figures.

All Stock Purchases Generate Fed Calls

Fed calls are generated even if you sell the stock the same day or shortly thereafter. For instance, if you buy $50,000 worth of stock in the morning and sell in the afternoon for $52,000, you will still be required to show your "good faith deposit" for at least $25,000 by the third business day. Keep in mind you can certainly use the buying power in the account to meet Fed calls. Just because a Fed call is generated does not mean you must send in a check. Just like maintenance calls, Fed calls can be met by depositing marginable securities, selling marginable securities, or depositing cash. If you buy and sell a security without meeting the Fed call, it is called a *freeride*. After a few freerides, your broker will likely mark your account as "permanent cash upfront," which means you no longer have the privilege of three business days to send in a check. All purchases must have cash in the account first.

The regulators developed this rule to keep people from speculating on the market with money they do not have — and subjecting brokerage firms to potentially large risks. If the rule did not exist, you could, for example, buy one million shares of Intel in the morning, hope for a small move upward, and sell for a nice profit. If the stock fell, you could walk away from your account leaving the firm with large losses. This is exactly what happened with the options trader (mentioned in the introduction of the book) who was jailed. Eventually the scheme caught up to him, and he bounced more than $5 million in checks for Fed calls. If you buy on margin, make sure you can meet the Fed calls. Once the check clears, you can immediately withdraw the funds if you wish. Regulators just want you to demonstrate that you have the resources to pay for stock you are buying and selling.

There is one more margin term you may hear, called *liquidation*. A liquidation occurs if you buy stock and then sell stock *the following day* (or later) to meet the Fed call. The reason regulators want the stock sold in the same day is best shown by the following example. Say you have $10,000 worth of a marginable stock in your account with 50% equity. If you buy $10,000 of another stock and wish to sell your existing stock to cover, that is fine. It just has to be sold in the same day as the purchase. If not, you may find that tomorrow your stock is worth only a fraction of that amount, and you can no longer be sold to meet the Fed call. Again, regulators are trying to protect the markets by making you sell your securities today as if you are relying on today's prices.

These are just the very basics of margin trading, and you should speak to your broker for more details if you are interested. We are covering only the basics here because of references made throughout the book to Fed calls and maintenance calls. The main point to glean

from this section is that you can be on margin even though options
are generally not marginable at most firms. Also, to buy options, you
usually need cleared funds in the account or margin cash. In most
cases, a cashier's check or money order can be used to purchase
options immediately.

Stock and Index Options

Options can be traded on most stocks and indices. Most stocks
traded on a listed exchange such as the New York Stock Exchange
(NYSE) — any ticker symbol with three or fewer letters such as
TXN, BA, T, GM — will usually have options. If a stock has options,
it is said to be *optionable*. Many of the larger, well-known Nasdaq
stocks — tickers with four or more letters such as DELL, INTC,
MSFT — are also optionable. Options are currently traded on more
than 1,400 stocks.

Investors can also trade options on more than 40 indices. The
Dow Jones Industrial Averages (DJX), S&P 500 (SPX), S&P 100
(OEX), and Nasdaq 100 (NDX) are some of the more popular indices.
Because index options are usually among the most expensive, most
investors lean toward equity options — options on specific stocks.

Whether you have an option representing stock or an index, the
option's price is *derived* from this *underlying* asset and, consequently,
options are also known as *derivatives*. Many types of derivatives
exist: options, futures, options on futures, swaps, swaptions, CMOs,
and more. If you hear of someone speaking about derivatives in
relation to stocks, they are most likely talking about options.

Strike Price (Exercise Price)

We mentioned earlier that options give you the right to buy and
sell stock at specified prices called strike prices.

If you have a Microsoft August $70 call, you have the right, but
not the obligation, to purchase 100 shares of Microsoft for a price
of $70 — that is the strike price. It is the buy price you are locked
into through option expiration (for calls) and the sell price for puts.

Strikes are usually available in $5 increments and in $2.50 increments for stocks under $25. Options on more expensive stocks ($200+) will likely trade in $10 increments or higher. You may see unusual increments, such as 0.66, but these are usually the result of a stock split.

If you buy or sell the underlying asset, you can do so by *exercising* the option. This means you simply notify your broker that you want to buy shares with your call option (or sell shares with your put option). We will be talking more about exercising options shortly, but just understand that strike prices are also called *exercise prices*, because that is the price you pay or receive if you exercise your option.

Size of Contracts

One option contract usually covers one round lot (100 shares) of stock. Consequently, the price of an option must be multiplied by 100 to find the total price. This 100 figure is sometimes called the *contract size* or the *multiplier*, because that is the value an option's price (called the *premium*) and it must be multiplied by 100 to find the total purchase price. If an option is trading for $2, then one contract will cost: 1 contract * $2 * 100 = $200 plus commissions. Ten contracts would cost 10 * $2 * 100 = $2,000 (plus commissions) and so forth. You can buy or sell contracts in whole numbers only; you cannot buy or sell fractions of contracts.

An option's multiplier could change. This is usually the result of a stock split or merger. If a stock splits in a whole amount (e.g., 2:1 or 3:1), the number of contracts you hold will increase by that factor, and the price and exercise price will drop by the inverse. To determine the factor, simply divide the two numbers in the ratio that is given by your broker. For instance, a 2:1 split is a multiplier of 2/1 = 2, and a 3:1 has a multiplier of 3/1 = 3. If you hold 10 May $50 contracts trading at $12 and the stock splits 2:1, you would hold 20 May $25 contracts trading for $6 after the split — double the contracts at half the price (and half the exercise price). Notice that this is similar to what happens with a stock split: If a stock splits 2:1, you own twice as many shares at half the price.

But if the stock splits in an amount that is not a whole number (e.g., 3:2 or 5:4), only the multiplier and exercise price will change — the number of contracts you own will stay the same. For example, in a 3:2 split, the multiplier is 3/2 = 1.5, which is not a whole number. If you hold 10 May $50 contracts trading at $12 and the stock splits 3:2, you will still have 10 contracts after the split, but they will be the May $33.33 and trading for $8 after the split, with each contract representing 150 shares (100 shares * the new multiplier of 1.5). In this case, the option's price needs to be multiplied by 150 to determine the total value. Options that have the multiplier changed during their life are called *adjusted* options.

How are the new strikes and prices determined? To find the new values, simply take the strike price and divide by the new multiplier. In this example, the contract was originally a $50 strike so it is now $50/1.5 = $33.33, and the price will be reduced from $12 to $12/1.5 = $8. Notice how the original position was worth $12,000 (10 contracts * $12 * 100) and is still the same value after the split: 10 contracts * $8 * 150 = $12,000.

If adjusted options are confusing for you, there is no need to worry about it, because your account will be adjusted automatically.

Exercise Value

The total cost of exercising an option is called the *exercise value*. Continuing with the last example, if you have 10 May $50 contracts trading for $12, then the total cost of the option is $12,000. However, the exercise value is 10 * $50 * 100 = $50,000. That is how much it would cost if you exercised the contract and actually purchased the shares (plus commissions). Notice that the exercise value does not change after the split. 10 * $33.33 * 150 = $50,000. Now it should be evident why strikes and multipliers change. That is so you do not unfairly gain or lose value in the option just because the stock split.

Moneyness

Options are classified as at-the-money, in-the-money, or out-of-the-money. This is known as the *moneyness* of an option. A strike price equal to the current market price of the underlying stock is said to be at-the-money. For example, if a stock is trading at $100, the $100 strike (call or put) is at-the-money.

For call options, if the stock price is below the strike, the option is out-of-the-money. If the stock price is above the strike, it is in-the-money. With the stock at $100, a $105 call (or higher strike) is out-of-the-money, and a $95 call (or lower) is in-the-money.

When you are long an in-the-money call, you can purchase the stock for less than market price.

The reverse is true for puts. If the stock price is above the strike, the put option is out-of-the-money. If the stock price is below the strike, the put is in-the-money. Any time you are long an in-the-money put, you can sell your stock for more than the market price.

The following chart may help:

	Calls	**Puts**
Stock price ABOVE strike	in-the-money	out-of-the-money
Stock price BELOW strike	out-of-the-money	in-the-money

If you have trouble remembering the differences between in-the-money and out-of-the-money options, just remember that any time you buy or sell stock with your option for more favorable prices than the stock currently trading, you have an in-the-money option.

Incidentally, your broker may consider a slightly in-the-money or slightly out-of-the-money option as at-the-money, and this is perfectly acceptable. This is because it is nearly impossible to find a strike that is exactly the same price as the underlying stock. In the real world of trading, usually the strike that is nearest the current stock price is considered at-the-money.

Intrinsic and Time Values

We learned earlier that the amount you pay for an option is called the premium. The *premium* can be broken down into two component parts: the *intrinsic value* and the *time value*. To understand option strategies, it is important to separate an option's price into intrinsic and time values.

An option that is in-the-money has intrinsic value. This is the value of the option if you were to immediately exercise — the difference between the stock price and the strike. For example, if the stock is trading for $101 and you hold the $100 call, you could realize a $1 gain by exercising the call option; you would receive stock worth $101 but pay only $100*.

For puts, the idea of intrinsic value is the same but in the opposite direction. If the stock were trading for $99, the $100 put would have an intrinsic value of $1. The holder of the put could exercise and sell stock worth $99 but receive $100 — a $1 gain.

Probably the easiest way to understand intrinsic value is to think of it as the number of points the stock is in your favor in relation to the strike price. For example, if you are long a call, you are bullish and want the stock to go up. If you have the $100 strike call with the stock at $103, then your option is 3 points in-the-money; the stock is trading $3 to the bullish side (above) of your option. If you are long the $105 put, you are bearish and want the stock to fall. With the stock at $103, the stock is two points to the bearish side (below) of your strike.

The value of an out-of-the-money option is composed purely of time premium (also called time value); there is no advantage in exercising the option at this time.

Intrinsic value is also defined as the difference between the stock price and the exercise price (stock - exercise) for calls or the difference in the exercise price minus the stock price (exercise - stock) for puts. If this number is positive, the option has intrinsic value; if zero or negative, the option has only time value.

For example, a stock is trading at $105 and you have the $100 call option. Clearly it is better to use the option and pay $100 a share for the underlying stock than to pay the current market price of $105. So this option has $5 intrinsic value or, equivalently, is $5 in-the-money. We can confirm this using the above intrinsic formula for calls: stock - exercise = $105 - $100 = $5.

Depending on how much time is remaining on the option, it may trade for more than intrinsic value. If the above option is trading for $7, then $5 of that value is intrinsic value, and $2 is time value. Time value is what is left over after accounting for intrinsic value. The following formula may help:

Premium - Intrinsic Value = Time Value

To run through an example with puts, if the stock is $100 and you have the $105 put, then you could benefit by exercising the put and selling your stock for $105 instead of the $100 market price. Therefore, this put has intrinsic value. If this option were trading for $8, then $5 is intrinsic value and $3 is time premium. Using the intrinsic value formula for puts: exercise - stock = $105 - $100 = $5 intrinsic value.

An option that trades for exactly the intrinsic amount with no time premium is said to be trading at parity. This usually happens very close to expiration. For example, if the stock is $105, and the $100 call is trading for exactly $5, the option is trading at parity.

Examples:

Call option premium	Stock	Intrinsic Value	Time Value
$50 call = $3	$52	$2	$1
$100 call = $7	$105	$5	$2
$80 call = $5.50	$79	$0	$5.50
$75 call = $4.75	$77	$2	$2.75
Put option premium			
$100 put = $5	$97	$3	$2
$75 put = $2.75	$77	$0	$2.75
$40 put = $3	$38.50	$1.50	$1.50
$85 put = $6.50	$79	$6	$0.50
Notice in these examples that the intrinsic value plus the time value equals the total price (premium) of the option. This will always be the case.			

Expiration Dates

One of the most critical factors in understanding options is that they expire and are consequently known as *wasting assets* — their price can decline solely from the passage of time. This alone makes many investors nervous about using options because it may not seem like an asset if it can decay from time. However, this is no different from your local grocer who purchases produce — assets — at prices that will decline from the passage of time. Even produce can end up worthless. It should be evident that decaying assets are not necessarily bad; if they were, your grocer would not carry them. It just means they need to be managed effectively.

You can usually purchase options that expire in as little as a few weeks or as far out as three years using LEAPS® (Long Term Equity Anticipation Securities, which is a registered trademark of the Chicago Board Options Exchange). LEAPS are simply long-term options that offer a new set of trading opportunities because of their prolonged life.

Technically, options expire on the Saturday following the third Friday of the month. But, the last day to <u>trade</u> them is the third

Friday of the expiration month. Many of the index options will expire one day earlier on Thursday.

Exercise and Assignments

If you own an option, you have the right, but not the obligation, to buy or sell stock. When you exercise your option, you submit instructions to your broker and the transaction is settled on the third business day following exercise. If you exercise one $50 call option today, your account will be debited for $5,000 (plus commissions), and you will receive 100 shares of the stock with both transactions occurring on the third business day from the exercise. If you exercise a $50 put, you will lose 100 shares of your stock and receive a credit of $5,000 (less commissions) to your account on the third business day.

The owner of an option has the right to exercise. The person on the other side, the seller, has the obligation to perform. If a long option holder exercises, the short option position is *assigned* on the option. It is important to know the difference, because many texts will discuss strategies and use the terms *exercise* and *assign*. Unless you know who is initiating the action and who is receiving, it may be difficult to follow along with the strategy.

Index options are a little different because they are settled in cash. If the index's settlement value is 3,025 and you hold the 3,000 strike, your profit is 25 (the difference between the closing price and strike) times the multiplier (again, usually 100). Because index options are settled in cash, you will not receive the shares in the index by exercising an index option.

If you are assigned on an option, your broker will receive notification from the OCC the next business day and should contact you immediately to inform you of the transactions that took place in your account.

Types, Classes, Series, and Styles

There are many ways to classify options, and you will hear the terms *types, classes, series,* and *styles* when trading options.

As you've learned, the two types of options are calls and puts. Within these types are classes of options, which are nothing more than calls or puts on a specific stock. For example, IBM calls and Intel puts are two different classes of options. Within the classes are specific series. A series of options covers the same class and has the same expiration date and strike price. For instance, IBM May $100 calls comprise a series of options.

There are two styles of options: **American** and **European**[2]. An American-style option can be exercised at any time prior to expiration, but its European counterpart can be exercised only at expiration. Do not confuse these terms to mean that options in the United States compare to options in Europe. These are strictly names given to the two styles of options. American and European styles are available in the United States, but you do not get your choice. Any class of options is specified by the exchange as either American-style or European-style.

All equity (stock) options in the United States are American-style and can therefore be exercised at any time prior to expiration (assuming normal business hours). Many index options in the United States however, are European-style and can be exercised only at expiration. The S&P 100 Index (OEX) is probably the biggest exception for the indices — it is an American-style option.

It is usually unwise to exercise a call option early except to capture a dividend, which we will be discussing more in Chapter 12. A trader is usually better off selling the position in the open market to capture any time premium remaining on the option. For example, say a stock is trading at $50, and the $45 call is trading for $7. As explained earlier, this option has $5 intrinsic value and $2 time value. If you exercise the option, you will receive shares worth $50 but pay only $45 — a $5 profit. But if you sell the call to close in the open market, you will receive $7. So if you are planning to exercise a call option, you should usually wait until expiration to do so.

---

[2]Technically, a third style exists called a "capped" option, which is automatically exercised for a pre-determined profit when the underlying stock closes at or above the strike for calls or at or below the strike for puts. Capped options are rarely traded anymore.

Trading Tip:

Exercise instructions do not necessarily have to be given to your broker during market hours. Many firms will allow exercise instructions up until 5:30 p.m. ET, but check with your broker regarding their policies on exercising options. Keep this in mind if you should be holding an otherwise out-of-the-money option with big news announced after the close. You may still be able to place exercise instructions!

For example, say you have a $50 call option on expiration day. The market just closed with the stock at $48 and the option expiring worthless. Several minutes later, a buyout is announced on your stock, which is trading as high as $65 in after-hours trading. In this case, you can still call your broker, submit exercise instructions, take delivery of the shares, and sell them Monday morning (or the first business day after exercise). Of course, there is a risk that the stock will no longer be trading at that price at the open of the following business day. Because of this risk, you may consider selling the shares during after-hours trading to lock in the gain. At any rate, just understand that you usually have some time frame after the market closes on expiration day to submit exercise instructions.

Another interesting point with this strategy is that you do not need to meet the Fed call if the shares are sold the next business day. If you exercise 10 $50 call options, you have purchased $50,000 worth of stock (the exercise value). Under normal stock purchases, you would need to deposit half this amount, or $25,000, within three business days to meet the Fed call. However, if you buy the shares through option exercise and sell them the next business day, you do not need to meet the Fed call!

Put options, on the other hand, should be exercised early when the option is sufficiently deep-in-the-money. One way to determine if it is deep enough in-the-money is to ask yourself if you think there is any chance of the stock being above the exercise price by expiration. If you do not think so, put options represent a cash inflow to the account, so you may as well exercise early and take the cash today rather than waiting until expiration. Exercising puts early can make great financial sense if the conditions are right. We will talk more about this in Chapter 12 on Early Exercise.

Automatic Exercise

Any equity option that is at least 3/4 of a point in-the-money (75 cents) at expiration (one cent in-the-money for index options) will be automatically exercised *unless you submit instructions to your broker telling him or her otherwise.* Be very careful with this procedure, and monitor your positions closely.

There have been many cases where traders think an option is going to expire worthless, but it rallies to 3/4 of a point (75 cents) or more in-the-money at expiration. The following Monday the investor ends up with a large number of shares in the account from the automatic exercise only to watch the stock open way down on negative news, creating large losses. *In cases like these, it is possible to lose more than your original investment on a call option.*

Also, if you have an equity option that is at least 3/4 of a point or more in-the-money, do not assume you do not need to call your broker to exercise it. Here's why: The option will be exercised, but if there is no cash to pay for it (even though you have three business days to bring it in) or if it creates a large debit balance on a margin account, your broker has the right to sell the position if instructions have not been given by you. Always let your broker know your intentions regarding exercise instructions.

Be careful when exercising puts or when holding in-the-money puts near expiration. If you do not have the shares in the account, your exercise instructions (or automatic exercise) will create a short stock position in your account.

What does this mean? It means you will have sold shares that are not in the account, thus creating a short position. Your broker will see this, but in many cases he or she may assume you sold shares and are planning to bring in certificates within the three-business-day time frame, so he may not even contact you. During this time, it is possible for the stock to trade for a much higher price and cause a huge loss when you buy the shares back to close out the short position.

If you *do* want a short stock position in the account — a strategy traders use to speculate on a downturn in stock price — your broker can probably borrow the shares for you. However, you must contact the broker and let them know ahead of time. If your broker is able to borrow the shares, you will not be required to close out the short position after three business days.

Because of these intricacies, it is always a good idea to check with your broker on expiration Friday to see if you have any option positions that may expire in-the-money. If so, either close out the positions or let your broker know your intentions regarding exercise of the option. Also, check the positions in your account the day after option expiration to be sure there are no surprises.

So far, we have covered option basics and terminology. The next step is learning to read option quotes, which will help you continue to build your understanding of the basics.

Option Quotes

The following chart is a typical listing of option quotes you may see online. Newspaper quotes will look similar, except they usually do not print the bid and ask prices. Also, newspapers typically print only three expiration months even though at least four exist at any given time.

These quotes are for Microsoft January calls with the stock trading for about $44. The first call option listed is a January $30, which means the option expires in January (the last trading day will be the third Friday of the month), and it gives the owner the right to purchase 100 shares of Microsoft for a price of $30.

The symbol for that particular option is MAFAF, which is the symbol you would use to trade or get quotes on that particular option. Every option has a unique symbol that designates the underlying stock (or index), expiration month, and strike. In Chapter 4, we will show you how the symbols are determined.

Microsoft Call Options (stock = $43.75)							
Month/Strike	**Symbol**	**Last**	**Chg**	**Bid**	**Ask**	**Vol**	**Op Int**
Jan 30	MAFAF	11.38	-1.50	14.37	14.88	4	708
Jan 32.5	MAFAZ	10.38	-1.63	12.13	12.63	2	138
Jan 35	MAFAG	9.75	+.88	10.13	10.63	14	736
Jan 37.5	MQFAU	6.13	-.50	8.13	8.50	5	432
Jan 40	MQFAH	6.63	+1.38	6.25	6.63	212	2,976
Jan 42.5	MQFAV	4.25	+.25	4.75	5.00	251	1,545
Jan 45	MQFAI	3.25	+.75	3.50	3.88	178	5,951

The "Last" column designates the last trade for that option. The January 30 call last traded at a price of $11.38. How much would it cost to buy the option at this price? We need to multiply the cost by the multiplier of 100, so it would cost $11.38 * 100 = $1,138 plus commissions for one contract.

The "Chg" column shows how much the option is up or down from the last trade that took place other then the current day. So the last trade was $11.38, but that is $1.50 lower than the last time the option traded *prior to today*. That should give you an indication as to just how quickly options can move. The preceding trade was $12.88 (11.38 + 1.50) and the very next trade was $11.38, which is down more than 11.5%. Keep in mind that the "last trade" may have been yesterday but could have been several days or possibly weeks earlier; it is the last price *when that option traded*. This implies that you should never reference the last trade as a gauge of value when trading options; it is virtually worthless information. Rather, reference the asking price if you are buying and the bid if you are selling.

The "Bid" column shows the highest price at which someone is willing to pay for that option, and the "Ask" shows the lowest price at which someone is willing to sell that option. If you want to buy the call, reference the asking price, because that is a seller. If you want to sell the call, reference the bid price, because that is a buyer. In either case, there will be a buyer matched with a seller, and the trade can be executed. Notice how different the bid-ask prices are from the last trade, which shows why you should always reference the bid-ask prices when trading options. The January 30 call is currently $14.88 to purchase, and not $11.38 as the last trade implies.

The "Vol" column shows the current volume for that contract. If you are looking online, it will be the current volume and may change throughout the day. If you are looking in a newspaper, it will be the total volume for the previous trading day. For the January $30 call, only four contracts traded on that day.

The last column, "Opt Int," shows the open interest. This tells us how many open contracts exist. To create an open contract, the buyer and seller need to be opening positions. In other words, the buyer "buys calls to open" while the seller is "selling calls to open." If this happens, open interest will increase. If both parties are closing, then open interest will decrease. If one is opening and the other is closing, open interest will remain unchanged. We will talk more about opening and closing transactions when we discuss how to place trades in Chapter 4.

So if trading were closed for the day, tomorrow's open interest for the January $30 calls may be as low as 704 (if the four contracts were all closing) or as high as 712 (if everybody were opening positions). If some trades were mixed, tomorrow's open interest will be somewhere between 704 and 712.

Open interest helps to determine *liquidity*. In other words, if you need to get out of your option, are there plenty of buyers and sellers, or do you run the risk of moving market prices if you place an order?

For example, say you hold 50 contracts of a particular option that has 60 open interest. If you sell the contracts at market, there is a good chance the price could plummet, because on a relative scale this is a huge sell order. If you sell the 50 contracts with 7,000 open interest, for example, it will probably not even phase the price of the option.

We see the highest open interest is for the January $45 calls, which is understandable since the underlying stock, Microsoft, is trading for $43.75 and the highest open interest contracts are usually found at-the-money.

Be careful when interpreting open interest not to focus on just the number itself. Many times a "high" open interest number may not be that liquid if the price of the option is very low. For instance, the January $30 calls in the chart have an open interest of 708, which in total dollars is 708 * 100 * $14.88 = $1,053,504. But what if the option were trading for 1/16 or $0.63? Now the total dollars would be only 708 * 100 * $.063 = $4,460, which could easily be sitting in one trader's account. A better way to interpret open interest is to multiply the total open interest by 100, and then multiply by the price of the option to get a feel for how much money is actually being traded at that strike.

The exchanges usually try to keep at least one at-the-money and one out-of-the-money option, so they will continually open new contracts as the underlying stock or index trades through the highest or lowest strikes available. In fact, as I write this, Microsoft has strikes ranging from $20 to $140 for the month of January because of the recent fall in the market.

Bullish, Bearish, and Neutral

You will hear the terms *bullish* and *bearish* when you are involved with the financial markets. Because option strategies use the same lingo, it is important to know exactly what investors mean when they say they are either bullish or bearish.

The term bullish actually gets its name from the way a bull attacks; it lowers its horns and then raises its head — from low to high. If you are bullish on a stock, you think it is going higher. The term bearish gets its name from the way a bear attacks; it raises its paws and strikes down — from high to low. If you are bearish on a stock, you think it is going to fall.

If you are not bullish or bearish, then you are neutral; you think the stock will sit still. Believe it or not, there are option strategies that allow you to make money from this outlook as well, which is something you cannot do with stocks.

Chapter 3: Option Expiration Cycles

You may have noticed that not all stocks have the same months available for options. For example, it is now October 2001 and MRVC has April options but SCMR does not. Why is that? When will April options become available for SCMR? To answer these questions, you need to understand option expiration cycles.

When options first started trading in 1973, the Chicago Board Options Exchange (CBOE) decided that only four months of equity options would be traded at any given time. Later, with the advent of LEAPS more than four months could be traded, at least for the more popular securities. To conserve space, your local newspaper probably prints only three of these months. However, there are always <u>at least four</u> different months traded at any given time (more if LEAPS are available).

Originally, stocks were assigned to one of three cycles: a January, February, or March cycle. The assignment had nothing to do with earnings cycles of a company or any other deep-seated reason; it was purely a random assignment.

Option Cycles

A January cycle means that options will be traded on the first month of each quarter. So, if a stock were assigned a January cycle under the original rules, options could be traded <u>only</u> in the following months:

Jan Feb Mar   **Apr** May Jun   **Jul** Aug Sep   **Oct** Nov Dec

A February cycle could trade only in the middle months of each quarter:

Jan **Feb** Mar   Apr **May** Jun   Jul **Aug** Sep   Oct **Nov** Dec

Of course, the March cycle would be traded on the end-months: March, June, September, and December.

Because of these positions, sometimes you will hear the cycles referred to as front-month (January), mid-month (February), and end-month (March) cycles.

As options gained in popularity, investors and floor traders alike were looking for ways to trade or hedge for shorter terms. So around 1984, the CBOE decided to always trade the current month, the following month (called the near-term contract) and then an additional two months from the original cycle. This is a little confusing, so it is best to explain with an example.

Example: Say it is now January and we are looking at a stock that trades options in a January cycle. Which months will be traded?

Jan Feb Mar   **Apr** May Jun   **Jul** Aug Sep   Oct Nov Dec

Looking at the above diagram may help. Remember, under the new rules, the CBOE decided that there would always be the current month plus the following month available. Because it is January in our example, then January and February are available. Because four months must trade, the remaining two months will be from the original cycle, which would be April and July.

What happens when January expires?

When January expires, then the current contract will be February, so we will see the following:

Jan **Feb Mar**   **Apr** May Jun   **Jul** Aug Sep   **Oct** Nov Dec

When February expires, March will be the current contract, so we will see the following:

Jan Feb **Mar**   **Apr** May Jun   **Jul** Aug Sep   **Oct** Nov Dec

However, notice that only three contracts are traded and we need four.

Because a fourth contract must be made available, October will be added because it is the next month available on the January cycle. So when February expires, we will see the following:

Jan Feb **Mar**   **Apr** May Jun   **Jul** Aug Sep   **Oct** Nov Dec

A commonly asked question continuing with the above example is: "When will, say, November contracts be traded?"

This is easy once you understand option cycles. The first thing you want to ask is this: Is November part of the January cycle? No, it is part of the February cycle. Because it is not on the same cycle, the <u>only</u> time it will become available will be when the September contract expires. When September expires, October will be the current contract and November will start trading.

Here is where it can be a little tricky. See if you can answer the following question using the diagram below, still assuming a January cycle.

Jan Feb Mar   **Apr May** Jun   **Jul** Aug Sep   **Oct** Nov Dec

It is now April and we have April, May, July, and October trading as shown. When will the January contracts start trading?

Because we are wondering about a month that <u>does</u> in fact fall on the January cycle, this one may open for trading months in advance.

If you run through the steps above, you will see that the January contract will start trading when May expires. Once May is expired, June will become the current so there will be a June, July, and October for a total of three months. The fourth month will be the addition of January.

Sometimes it helps to solve these by going backwards. Since we are asking when the January contract will start trading, start with January and move backwards. The next month to be trading would be October, then July, and we'd also need a current month to complete the fourth month, which would be June. In order for June to become the current month, May would have to expire, which is the same answer we got above.

LEAPS®

As mentioned earlier, there are always at least four contracts trading at all times. If a stock has LEAPS traded, then more than four months will be available. Once you understand the basic option cycle, adding LEAPS is not difficult.

LEAPS are long-term options and usually trade in January for a maximum of three years (although there are exceptions). If a stock trades LEAPS, then new LEAPS will be issued sometime in late May. When the month of January is "hit" in the normal rotation (other than by default as the current or near-term contract), a new LEAPS contract will be added. The January option will become a normal option and the root symbol will change.

Because this is difficult to explain without the use of examples, let's look at INTC options.

It is currently November and INTC has the following months trading:

Month	Root Symbol
November	INQ
December	INQ
April	INQ
January '01	INQ
January '02	WNL
January '03	WNL

From what we learned earlier, we know there must be a November and December contract and we see that there is. You can never tell which cycle a particular stock is on by looking at the first two months; remember, all options will have these months being traded.

We see that January '01 is the next contract traded. Normally, this would tell us that this stock is on a January cycle. However, INTC has LEAPS too, which means a January option will always be traded, so we still cannot be sure which cycle it is on just because we see January next in line. Looking out to the next month, we see April is trading. Because April is part of the January cycle, we can now be certain that INTC trades on a January cycle.

Jan Feb Mar   **Apr** May Jun   Jul Aug Sep   Oct **Nov Dec**

Based on what we know, the four months highlighted above should be trading for INTC and we see they are when compared to the above table. Now, when November expires, December and January become the current and near-term months respectively and July will be added.

In this case, <u>no</u> LEAPS will be added because the LEAPS are currently out three years to '03.

However, when May expiration comes around, June, July, and October will be trading and January will be added. At this point, the '02 LEAPS will have their root symbol changed to INQ and the '04 LEAPS will be added.

So, depending on which cycle your stock is on, look for new LEAPS to be added sometime in late May, June, or July. Otherwise, the basic option expiration cycle applies.

Let's go back to the questions asked at the very beginning and see if we can determine the answers:

It is now October and MRVC has April options but SCMR does not.

    1) Why is that?
    2) When will April options become available for SCMR?

Looking at the options for MRVC, there are:

November, December, January, April

For SCMR:

November, December, March, June

It is evident there are no LEAPS, because only four contract months are trading. We know there will be November and December for each. For MRVC, the next month is January, so it is on a January cycle. SCMR is on a March cycle.

When will April options become available for SCMR?

Because April is not part of the March cycle, the only time April options will become available is when February expires. At that time, March will be the current month and April will be the near-term contract.

Option expiration cycles can be a little confusing if you are new to them. With a little work, they will become second nature. They are important to know because many strategies require some type of position management during the holding period, yet the proper contracts may not exist. Understanding these cycles can give you an added edge in option trading.

Additional Questions:

1) **It is now August and your stock trades on a March cycle. Which months should you expect to see trading?**

Jan Feb **Mar**   Apr May Jun   Jul **Aug Sep**   Oct Nov **Dec**

We will see the current and near-term months trading (August and September). In addition, we will see two contracts from the original March cycle, which will be December and March.

2) **When will the May contracts start trading?**

Because May is not part of the March cycle, the only time they could trade is when March contracts expire. At that time, April will be the current month and May will be the near-term.

3) **When will the June contracts begin trading?**

Because June is part of the March cycle, it could start trading months in advance, so we need to be careful here. Run through them step by step.

When August expires, we will have September, October, December, and March for a total of four contracts. No June contracts will trade at this point.

When September expires, we will have October, November, December, and March. June still will not trade. When October expires, we will have November, December, and March for a total of three. At this time, June contracts will be rolled out.

Option expiration cycles are very confusing at first. However, it will help you greatly to understand them to make the most of your option strategies. You may, for example, need a particular month trading but not have it available for several months. If you understand the expiration cycles, it will enable you to make better decisions on speculating, investing, or hedging.

Chapter 4: Placing Option Trades

Trading options is tough enough without making senseless mistakes. Unfortunately, many traders learn the hard way what the following definitions really mean. Before we can talk about strategies, it is best if we take some time to talk about some of the terms you will hear when you actually place option trades.

Opening and Closing Transactions

When you enter an option order, you will need to specify whether it is an opening or closing transaction. This information is needed by the OCC to determine the amount of *open interest* in that particular contract.

You can either buy or sell an option and either open or close it. Therefore, only four possibilities exist:

1. **Buy to open:** This means we are purchasing an option as the initial order. We are opening a new position that will allow us to have either the right to buy (call option) or the right to sell (put option). Also, because we are buying, this transaction will result in a net debit to the account — we must pay for the trade.

2. **Sell to close:** This means we are closing a position previously "bought to open." When the order is executed, we will no longer have the right to buy (call) or sell (put) the underlying stock. When we sell to close, we receive money from the trade.

3. **Sell to open:** This means we are selling an option contract as an initial order. We are opening a new position that will create an obligation to sell the stock (short call) or be forced to purchase the stock (short put). Because we are selling, we will receive cash for this transaction.

4. **Buy to close:** This means we are closing a previously "sell to open" option position. Upon execution, we are offsetting

our opening position and will no longer have the potential obligation to buy or sell the stock. Because we are buying, the account will be debited.

If you are <u>initiating</u> a position, whether long or short, you are opening. If you are offsetting a previously "open" position, you are closing.

Notice that option traders can buy and sell options without ever buying or selling the stock. If you buy a call, you have the right to buy stock. If you decide you do not want this call anymore, simply sell the call to close.

Many new traders believe you must buy the stock with the call and then sell the stock, but this is not true. You can simply buy and sell the contracts; in fact, more than 95% of all options are closed in this manner without ever taking delivery of the shares.

Similarly, if you sell a call to open, you have the potential obligation to sell shares if the long position — the person who "bought to open" — decides to exercise. If you no longer want this potential obligation, you can simply buy the call to close and you are out of the contract. Bear in mind that the prices at which you close out your positions may be unfavorable.

Quantity

You must tell your broker how many contracts you are willing to buy or sell. Remember, each contract generally represents 100 shares of the underlying stock. If you buy 10 contracts, you are controlling 10 * 100, or 1,000 shares of stock. It is usually a good idea to trade options only in lots representing the number of shares of stock you would be comfortable holding. For example, if you are comfortable holding 500 shares, you should trade up to 5 contracts.

It is generally not a good idea to trade the same dollar amounts. For example, say a stock is trading for $30 with the $30 call trading for $2 ($200 per contract). While 500 shares of stock would cost $15,000, it is not a good idea to substitute this amount for $15,000/ $200 = 75 contracts. The reason is that as the stock moves higher, call options will start reacting more like stock (the reverse is true for puts). You can end up controlling an uncomfortably large position, which can be dangerous and lead to unforeseen losses.

Option Symbols

You will need to give your broker the option symbol you want to trade. Your broker should be able to look this up for you once you give him or her the underlying stock or index symbol, expiration month, and strike price.

All options have a "root" symbol, and two additional letters designating the month and strike. If a stock is listed on an exchange such as the New York Stock Exchange or American Stock Exchange for example, the root symbol will usually be the same as the ticker symbol. It is easy to spot a listed security — it will always have a symbol of three or fewer letters. So IBM, GE, and T are all listed securities, and their option root symbol will usually be the same as the stock ticker (although it may be different from splits, mergers, or acquisitions).

For any Nasdaq traded stock (any stock with four or more letters in the ticker symbol), the option root symbol will usually be reduced to three letters. In many cases it will be similar to the original symbol but with the addition of the letter "Q." For example, the root symbol for DELL is DLQ, INTC is INQ, and MSFT is MSQ.

Once you have the root symbol, it is fairly easy to designate the month and strike. For call options, the letters A through L (letters 1 through 12) designate the months January through December. For puts, the letters M through X (letters 13 through 24) are used:

Option Month Symbols

	Jan	Feb	Mar	Apr	May	Jun	Jul	Aug	Sep	Oct	Nov	Dec
Calls	A	B	C	D	E	F	G	H	I	J	K	L
Puts	M	N	O	P	Q	R	S	T	U	V	W	X

For the strike prices, A represents $5, B is $10, etc. Once you reach $100 (letter T), a new root symbol is created and you start back at letter A, which is now $105. Here is a list of option strikes:

A	B	C	D	E	F	G	H	I	J	K	L	M	N	O	P	Q	R	S	T
5	10	15	20	25	30	35	40	45	50	55	60	65	70	75	80	85	90	95	100
105	110	115	120	125	130	135	140	145	150	155	160	165	170	175	180	185	190	195	200
205	210	215	220	225	230	235	240	245	250	255	260	265	270	275	280	285	290	295	300

Option Strike Price Symbols

In addition to the above letters strikes, the letters U through Z are usually reserved for $2.50 strike intervals:

U	V	W	C	Y	Z
7.50	12.50	17.50	22.50	27.50	32.50
37.50	42.50	47.50	52.50	57.50	62.50
67.50	72.50	77.50	82.50	87.50	92.50

It looks confusing, but it is actually very easy. Say you want to buy a Microsoft October $45 call. The root symbol is MSQ. The October call symbol is J and the $45 strike symbol is I. So the call option symbol for the option will be MSQJI. You can use this symbol to enter trades and get quotes on the option. Please note that some trading systems will require you to follow the symbol with a ".O" or a "/O" to designate that the symbol is an option. If this occurs, the call option symbol may actually need to be entered as MSQJI.O or MSQJI/O.

Remember, this is only a guideline. You should always check with your broker if you are in doubt about any symbol.

Market Orders Versus Limit Orders

Your broker will ask you if you want the trade entered as a *market order* or as a *limit order*. A market order guarantees the execution, and a limit order guarantees the price. Both the execution and price cannot be guaranteed. If they could, you could place an order to guarantee that you purchase a $100 order for $95 — better yet, you could buy it for $1! You can either specify a price and risk the execution, or guarantee the execution and risk the price moving.

If you enter your trade as a market order, your order will definitely be filled. But you cannot be sure at which price. You will be filled at the best available price *when your order hits the exchange.* In most cases, you will be filled at the asking price if you are buying and at the bid price if you are selling. However, if the stock is in a fast market (which means the prices are not updating with the trades because of heavy volume), you can be filled at prices very different from the quotes you are watching. If you absolutely need to get in or out of a trade, you really have no choice but to go "at market" and guarantee the execution.

Limit orders guarantee the price but not the execution. Buy-limits are placed below the current price while sell-limits are placed above the current price. If you enter a limit order, your trade will be filled at that price (or lower) if you are buying or at your limit price (or higher) if you are selling. To guarantee the price, your broker cannot guarantee that it will be filled. If you are willing to gamble on a more favorable price at the risk of not getting filled, use limit orders.

For example, say an option is trading for $20. You want to own it long-term, but you think it will fall near-term. You can place a limit order to buy, for example, at a limit of $17. If the option trades at that price or lower, you will be filled; otherwise you will not.

Aside from possibly not getting filled, there is another risk in placing buy-limit orders: You are buying into a downtrend. Maybe you get filled on the above order at $17 (or even a little cheaper) only to watch it trade for $12 a short time later.

By the way, if you are placing a limit order on options, be aware of the following rule. Options quoted below $3 may be entered in increments of 5 cents (1/16 before decimalization) and options above $3 must be entered in increments of 10 cents (1/8 before decimalization). Therefore, if you see an option quoting $3.50 to $3.60, do not send in a limit order at $3.55, because the exchange will return your order to be reentered in 10-cent increments. This time delay can be costly in option trading.

Or Better Orders

An "or better" condition is a type of limit order that blends a market order and limit order. With an or better order, you place buy orders *above* the current asking price and sell orders *below* the current bid price.

Say an option is $5 on the ask. You can tell your broker to buy at a limit of $5.50 or *better*, for example. Now, when your order hits the floor, you will be filled as long as it does not exceed $5.50. You would use this type of order if the quotes are moving rapidly and you are afraid of missing the trade. In this example, if the trade is entered quickly, you may get filled at the current price of $5, but you are giving some room for the price to fluctuate up to $5.50. If the price is higher than your limit price when your order reaches the floor, you will not be filled.

Some people think this is a dangerous risk, because the floor will probably fill you at the higher $5.50 price. But this is not true because traders are bound by time-and-sales, which reflect the current prices at the time your order was received. With "or better" orders, your order is still not guaranteed to fill, but the odds are much higher in your favor when compared to a straight limit order.

Stop and Stop-Limit Orders

Because more confusion exists with stop and stop-limit orders than any other type of order, we will explain them thoroughly.

Stop and stop-limit orders are conditional orders stating to buy or sell *if* the stock or option reaches a certain limit. Although these may sound like the limit orders discussed previously, they are markedly different.

Remember, limit orders are used to <u>buy below</u> or <u>sell above</u> the current price. Stop orders will do the opposite and either sell below or buy above the current price. Why would someone want to sell for less or pay more? Stop orders are risk management tools that allow you to hedge your trades.

Say you purchase a stock at $50, and it is now trading at $60. You still think it will move higher, but you want to sell if it starts to fall. A stop order can accomplish this goal.

If you place an order to sell your shares at a stop-price of $58, for example, your order will become a market order, and you will sell your shares *if* the stock trades at <u>or below</u> $58.

Stop orders, if triggered, guarantee the execution but not the price.

It is very important to understand that stop orders are activated for prices below your stop-price, too. For example, say this stock closes at $58.50 one day, and you still have your shares because the stop-price of $58 was never triggered. But the next day, the stock opens at $48 on negative news. Your stop limit of $58 is now triggered and you will be sold at $48 for a $2 loss. The stop-price ($58 in this example) is only the "trigger" point; it is not necessarily the price you will get for your stock. In fact, it is rare that this is exactly the price you receive.

One of the worst cases I ever witnessed was a client who placed a stop order on 3,000 shares on one of the "dot-com" stocks trading at around $120. The stock started to evaporate on no news one afternoon with each tick falling 1/2-point or more. The trader bought the shares at around $100 and had a stop at $110 to "protect" profits. Once his stop-price was triggered, it became a market order, which sat in line behind a stack of tickets with the market makers, waiting to be filled. He got his confirmation back with the 3,000 shares filled at $87! His $30,000 profit he thought was protected turned out to be a $39,000 loss.

Stop orders used to be called *stop-loss* orders (and you still may hear the term). But, as just shown, it is possible to still end up with a loss. Because of this, the SEC no longer allows stop orders to be called stop-loss orders by professionals.

Stop orders can also be used to buy stock. Most of the time, traders who are short stock use buy-stops. For example, say you short 100 shares of stock at $50. You will profit if it falls, and you will lose if it rises. To protect yourself, you may elect to place a buy-stop at $53, for example, which will buy the shares back if the stock should trade at $53 or higher. Sure, this is still a loss, but the buy-stop forces traders to be disciplined and get out if the trade moves against them.

Buy-stops can also be used to initiate a long position (not just to close out short positions). Say you have been looking at a stock that has been trading for a long time at $20. Rumors are spreading about a new product that, if launched, could send this stock to $100 or higher. You do not want to purchase this now, because it may still sit there; in fact, it may even fall if the product is not launched. This is a great scenario for a buy-stop.

You can place your order to buy the shares at a stop-price of $24, for example. Now, the only way you will be filled is if the stock is, in fact, moving higher. This keeps you from having to constantly watch the news on the stock. Again, this does not guarantee you a price of $24, it guarantees only that you will be filled if the stock is $24 or higher. However, if you are filled, it is likely due to the market pricing in the effects of the new product. If your prediction is correct, you now have shares to profit from.

Option stop orders work the same way with one little quirk. With stock, buy-stops and sell-stops are triggered from the last trade. With options, sell-stops are triggered on the asking price but sold at the bid price. Buy-stops are triggered at the bid price but purchased at the asking price.

For example, say you bought an option at $10 and it is now trading at $20. You want to place a sell-stop order at $17. The option starts to fall and is soon quoted with bid $16.25 and ask $17. Your order is triggered because the asking price is at your stop of $17; however, you will be filled at the bid price of $16.25. This can lead to disappointing fills — especially if the bid-ask spreads get very wide. Be very careful when using stops with options.

We said earlier that stop orders guarantee the execution but not the price. Is there a way to guarantee the price? Yes, and that is with stop-limit orders. But the risk is that you may not get filled.

Stop-limit orders, if triggered, guarantee the price but not the execution.

Let's go back to the example where you purchased stock at $50 but it is currently trading for $60. Again, you think it will continue higher, so you prefer to hold it, but you want to get out if it should fall. However, you want to sell only if it trades at $58 and you can be assured of getting $58. If the stock trades lower, you would prefer to hold it. This is the time for stop-limit orders.

With stop-limit orders, you need to designate <u>two</u> prices with your order: One is the stop-price, and the other is the limit price. You would, in this example, place a stop-limit order to sell at a stop-price of $58 with a limit of $58. If the stock trades at $58 (the stop-price), the order is "triggered" as with a regular stop order. But instead of becoming a market order, it now becomes a limit order to sell only if you can get $58 or higher. Now if the stock opens at $48, you will still own the shares. Notice that a loss was still not prevented.

Stop-limit prices may be less than or equal to the stop-price. In the previous example, you could place the order to sell at a stop-price of $58 with a stop limit of $57.50 thereby giving you a little room if the stock should fall once triggered.

Which is better, the stop or stop limit? That all depends on the situation, and you may use either at one time or another. Here is a little test to determine which is right for you at that time. If the stock starts to fall, is your goal to get out regardless of price? If so, use a stop order, because that is the only way to be sure you are out.

Now ask yourself if there is <u>any</u> stock price at which you would rather hold than sell. If there is, use that price as your limit on a stop-limit order.

	Guarantee Execution?	Guarantee Price?	Prevent Loss?	To Place Order:
Stop orders	Yes	No	No	Use one number: the stop price
Stop limit orders	No	Yes	No	Use two numbers: the stop price and the stop-limit price

Time Limits

When you place a limit order, you will need to specify a time limit. Remember, because limit orders are not guaranteed to fill, your broker will need to know how long you want the order to stand. If you select a day order, the order will be canceled at the end of the trading day if it is not filled.

Good 'Til Canceled (GTC) orders are allowed to stand for <u>up to</u> six months or until it is filled. Make sure to ask your broker how long a GTC order lasts with his company. The exchanges allow for up to six months, but any brokerage firm has the right to make the rule more restrictive.

If you place a market order, you have no choice but to make it a day order. In fact, if you place it over the Internet, your trade will probably default to a day order and not even give you the choice. Why? Remember, market orders are guaranteed to fill.

There are other time limits such as "Fill or Kill" and "Immediate or Cancel," but these are rarely used. Most of your orders will be either day or GTC. Please see our Web site, www.21stcenturyoptions.com, for more information about these other types of orders.

Trading Example: Say you are bullish on Intel trading at $34.75 and you want to purchase 5 January $40 call options. The quote is bid $2.75 and the ask is $3. Your instructions to your broker would be:

Buy calls to open, 5 contracts of the INQAH at market.

That's it. In a matter of seconds, you are the owner of a contract giving you the right, but not the obligation, to buy 500 shares of Intel at a price of $40.

The previous example trade is guaranteed to fill because it is a market order, but you cannot be totally sure of the price. It will most likely fill at the asking price of $3, but it could be higher or lower depending on the conditions when your order is received. The trade will cost 5 contracts $*$ $3 $*$ 100 shares per contract = $1,500 + commissions.

Trading Tip:

You should get in the habit of jotting down some basic information if you place your trade with a broker. Write down the date, time, broker's name (or "rep code"), and confirmation number. Remarkably, one of the biggest mistakes in the brokerage industry is for the broker to fail in sending the order. If you have the order information, it is much easier to track and can save your trade. There have been numerous instances where customers were given backdated trades (in large dollar amounts at that) for no reason other than they had detailed information and seemed credible. Think about how much more credible you sound if you say, "I spoke to Mr. Smith on January 10th at 2:15 in the afternoon when I placed the INQAH option order." It certainly carries more weight than "I spoke to one of your brokers last week sometime."

If you place your trades over the Internet, get in the habit of writing down the confirmation number. This will prevent you from thinking you sent the order when you were actually only in the "verify" stage. If you have a confirmation number, you can be assured the order has been received.

Note: It is a good idea to specify to your broker that you are trading the **Intel January $40** call as well, just to prevent any misunderstanding about the symbol. If you place the trade over the Internet, you will need to enter only the symbol, but the full description of the option will appear in the "verify" stage. Make sure to read it carefully before sending the order!

Chapter 5: "Show or Fill Rule"

This is a great little tip for all option investors — especially those who trade smaller numbers of contracts, say 1 to 5.

It is known as the "Limit Order Display Rule," sometimes called the "Show or Fill Rule" (the official name is "Exchange Act Rule 11Ac1-4"). It is not a rule that the market makers make very well known for obvious reasons, as we shall soon see. However, knowing this rule can make a big difference in your option profits.

Before we look at the rule, we need to understand some basics to the quoting system used for stocks and options.

Let's say you get a quote on an option as follows:

BID $5   **ASK** $5.75

What exactly does this mean? It means the market makers are "bidding" $5 for the option; this is the price they are willing to pay. They are "asking" $5.75; this is the price they are willing to sell. There is often a lot of confusion with these terms, but they are really quite simple if you think of the following analogy. If you sell your house, you are "asking" a certain price, right? If you are buying a house, you put in a "bid" for it. Bid means buy, ask (sometimes called the offer) means sell.

The reason for the confusion is this: Retail investors who buy options are used to paying the "asking" price, so they often think the ask price represents the buyers. Similarly, if they sell their option, they are used to receiving the bid price, so they think the bid price represents the sellers.

But think about this. If you are buying the option, you need a seller to take the other side of the trade. The reason you can buy the option at the ask price is because the market maker, the person on the other side of the trade, is willing to sell for that price. Now you have a buyer matched with a seller and the trade can be executed. Likewise, if you sell your option, you can be matched with the buyer at the bid.

When you get a quote, the bid price represents the highest bidder and the ask price represents the lowest offer or seller[*]. This makes sense, because we are not concerned with the person who is willing to sell that same option for some higher amount, say $10, or the one who is willing to buy it for a lower amount such as $1.

Trading Between the Bid-Ask Spread

Let's go back to the original quote:

BID $5   **ASK** $5.75

Say you wanted to buy the option and did not want to pay $5.75, but you were willing to pay $5.50. You could put in a *bid* (remember, you are buying the option, so you would be a bidder) simply by instructing your broker to buy at a limit of $5.50.

Prior to the "show or fill rule," the market maker could leave the quote unchanged, letting your high bid of $5.50 not be shown as follows:

BID $5   **ASK** $5.75

Under the "show or fill rule," the market maker must take one of two actions: **either fill your order or show your order as follows:**

BID $5.50   **ASK** $5.75

You are now posted as the highest bidder, have narrowed the spread, and have given someone the incentive to sell because of the now higher bid. The markets always benefit from narrow spreads.

Let's say another trader comes along who does not want to sell at the $5.50 bid price but is willing to receive $5.65. This trader could

---

[*]Technically, the BID and ASK represent the best bid and offer at the margin, the point where price is determined. For example, someone could come in and bid $6 but would be filled at $5.75 because they are outside the margin. The quote would not jump to $6 on the bid even though they are, technically, the highest bidder. It is a technical point but, for our purposes, think of the BID as the highest bidder and the ASK as the lowest offer.

put in an order to sell his contracts at a limit of $5.65. Assuming the market maker does not fill the trade, the quote now looks like this:

BID $5.50   **ASK** $5.65

Again, the spread has been narrowed further, and a stronger incentive is now given to the market to buy because the asking price has just been reduced from $5.75 to $5.65.

KEY POINT: It is an exchange policy (at least for the major ones) to have all quotes good for <u>at least 20</u> contracts.

Here is how you can benefit from this knowledge:

Going back to the original quote:

BID $5   **ASK** $5.75

Say you want to buy a small number of contracts such as 3. If you put in a bid of $5.50, the market maker needs to either fill you or show you.

Now, obviously, the market maker does not want to sell you the option at $5.50, because he is asking $5.75. But if he does not fill you, he must show your order and change the quote to:

BID $5.50   **ASK** $5.75

Here is the benefit: The market maker is thinking, "If I show the order and post the bid at $5.50, I may have to buy another 17 contracts because my quotes must be good for at least 20 contracts. I am really willing to bid only $5, so let me fill this order to get it out of the way!"

How can you profit from this? Think of all the times you bought at the ask price or sold at the bid. Those 1/4- and 1/2-point spreads (or much more) on both sides really start to add up. Placing trades "in between" the bid and ask can make all the difference in your profits, especially for smaller numbers of contracts.

Chapter 6: Profit and Loss Diagrams

As the saying goes, a picture is worth a thousand words. This is especially true regarding profit and loss diagrams on options. By looking at a picture, you can immediately see where your max profit and loss is, feel how the position will behave, and know where the danger zones are for any strategy.

However, the vast majority of options traders do not know how to read profit and loss diagrams. Many do not even understand what the diagrams mean. Consequently, options traders are greatly limiting their use and understanding of options. Understanding profit and loss diagrams is vital for understanding options.

So, what exactly is a profit and loss diagram? Let's start with the simplest one — a long stock position.

If you are long stock (meaning you own it), you will make one point of profit for every point increase in the stock above your cost. Likewise, for every point drop below your cost, you will lose exactly one point. This is easy to show on a spreadsheet. Assume we buy one share of stock at a price of $50:

If the stock price is:	Your profit/loss will be:
$45	-$5
$46	-$4
$47	-$3
$48	-$2
$49	-$1
$50	$0 (the breakeven point)
$51	+$1
$52	+$2
$53	+$3
$54	+$4
$55	+$5

Assuming you paid $50 for the stock, the preceding table shows that you will have a loss of $5 if the stock is trading at $45. If the stock is trading for say, $53, you will have a profit of $3 per share. If the stock is trading for $50, you will have no profit and no loss — you will just break even.

Even though this is a relatively simple position, its behavior is not readily apparent. So let's take the above numbers and put them in a picture — a profit and loss diagram. All we have to do is plot the stock prices from the preceding table on the horizontal axis (the x-axis) and the profit/loss numbers on the vertical axis (the y-axis). Once we do, we are presented with the following picture:

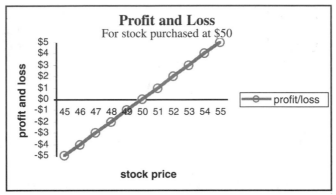

How do you read the chart? Using the chart below, look at any stock price along the horizontal axis such as $53, for example. Now trace a line to the profit/loss line and see where that point lines up with the vertical axis to the left. It lines up with $3 profit, which is exactly what we calculated in the spreadsheet previously. In other words, if the stock price is $53, we will have a $3 profit. At a stock price of $46, we see the profit/loss line shows a $4 loss.

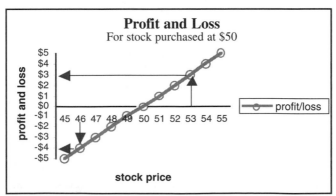

It is much easier to look at the picture rather than the spreadsheet to see how a long stock position at $50 will behave. We know immediately that the breakeven point is at $50 — the point at which the profit/loss line crosses zero on the profit and loss line (the vertical axis). We can also immediately see that there is unlimited loss (at least all the way down to a stock price of zero because you can never lose more than what you paid), and an unlimited upside potential because the profit and loss line continues up to the right without bounds.

What if you are short the stock? Shorting stock involves borrowing the shares and selling them with the intent of buying them later at a cheaper price. You are, in essence, doing the reverse of the traditional "buy low, sell high" strategy. You are trying to "sell high, buy low." Short sellers are attempting to profit if the stock falls. The profit and loss diagram for short stock looks like this:

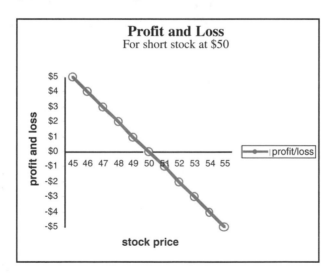

A short position will always behave the opposite of the corresponding long position. In this case, we see that profit is made as the stock falls and unlimited losses occur as the stock rises. The unlimited loss part is what makes the short stock position so dangerous.

Let's try something a little more complicated and see what a long call position looks like.

Long Call

Before we look at profit and loss diagrams for options, there is one very important point that needs to be made. When we speak of profit and loss diagrams for options, we are talking about the profit and losses *at expiration of the option*. Prior to expiration, it is very difficult to say what the profit/loss diagrams will look like because of the many factors that affect an option's price.

What does a profit and loss diagram look like for a long $50 call? Assume a trader pays $3 per share for the call and, consequently, that is all that can be lost. So, no matter how low the stock falls, this trader's maximum loss is just the premium of $3.

However, if the stock closes at $52 for example, the $50 call will be worth exactly $2 at expiration. A stock price of $50 or below produces a $3 loss, while a stock price above $50 produces the intrinsic value of the option. If we plot these results on a chart, we get the following picture:

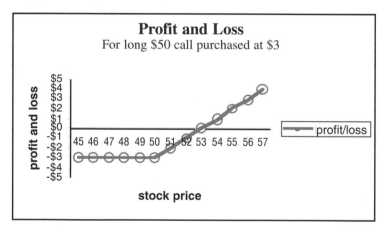

The picture shows us what we already inferred. The trader cannot lose more than the $3 premium regardless of how far the stock falls below $50. But if the stock rises above $50 at expiration, the trader makes point-for-point with the stock. Notice that the profit and loss curve bends upward at the strike price. When looking at profit and loss diagrams for options, a bend will always occur at each strike price involved in the strategy. It may bend up, down, or flatten out to the side, but one of those three movements will always occur at the strikes.

Look at the chart below. We see the call option trader has limited the downside risk below $50, as compared to the long stock position, but still retained all of the upside potential. All the downside risk has been removed (as shown by the crossed-off portion of the downward curve), so the curve flattens out and never falls below -$3. Of course, this does not come for free. If you notice, the breakeven has been moved upward by $3, the price of the call option, to $53. This is the most powerful benefit of options; they allow you to customize the profit/loss profiles to suit your exact needs.

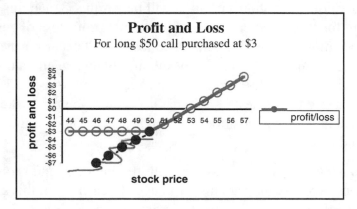

Profit and Loss
For long $50 call purchased at $3

Short Call

Let's see what a short call looks like. Remember, we said that a short position is exactly the opposite of the corresponding long position.

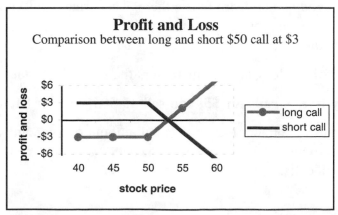

Profit and Loss
Comparison between long and short $50 call at $3

The profit and loss diagram for the short call (solid line) is telling us that the maximum profit is $3, the amount of the premium. This will be made for any stock price (at expiration) below $50. Because the $50 call will be worthless to the owner (the long position) at expiration, the short position will profit by the entire premium of $3.

Notice how this short call is the mirror image of the long call position (dotted line). For the long call, $3 is the maximum loss, which is the amount of the short call's maximum gain. The short call's breakeven point is at $53 because, at this point at expiration, the option will be trading for $3 (remember, this is the profit for the long position). The short's position will be worth -$3, and this is the amount for which the call was sold for a net profit/loss of zero. If the stock moves above $53, unlimited losses will occur for the short call beyond this point. Because of the highly leveraged nature of options, the short call (also called a naked or uncovered call) position is among the riskiest of all. That is because you can make only a limited gain on the position, but you're assuming an unlimited risk to do so.

Look again at the above chart with the long call and short call positions. Because they are mirror images of each other, this shows that no *net* flow of cash is created from the options markets. In other words, any option trader's gain is exactly somebody else's loss; the money merely changes hands.

Let's look at a more complicated position: the ratio spread. This is being shown to demonstrate the power of profit and loss diagrams and why you should learn to use them. The strategy will not even be discussed, but you can learn about it just by looking at a profit and loss diagram.

First of all, let's say a trader enters the following trade:

Buy 10 $50 calls for $5, and sell 35 $65 calls for $1.75

Because the trader has an unequal amount of long and short contracts (bought 10 and sold 35), it is called a ratio spread or ratio-write with calls.

Now, think about this for a minute. Just by looking at the above ratio spread, can you tell what the trader wants the stock to do? Where the maximum profit and loss is? Where the danger zones are?

Now let's use the profit and loss diagram for this ratio spread to see if we can answer those questions more easily:

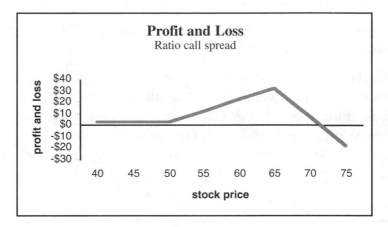

Much easier, isn't it? We can now see that the trader will make money if the stock either falls below $50 or rises up to $65, which is the point of maximum profit. After $65, the trader starts to lose some profits and will reach a breakeven point at around $72 (the exact answer is $71.45). Beyond $72, unlimited losses will occur.

Would you have been able to analyze the trade in this way just knowing that the trader bought 10 $50 calls at $5 and sold 35 $65 strikes at $1.75? Most people cannot. That is what profit and loss diagrams are for.

Because we will be using these tools throughout this book to drive home points about option strategies, it is crucial that you become comfortable with them. If you learn to use them, they will greatly help your understanding of options and can expose areas of risk on your next — and existing — positions that you may never have considered.

How to Create Profit and Loss Diagrams

To draw a profit and loss diagram, pick a range of stock prices that are relevant for the option(s) you want to draw. For example, if you are interested in a $50 put option, use a couple of strikes below and above this strike.

Let's assume we want to draw a profit and loss diagram for a $50 put option purchased for $2:

Start by writing down the values for the option, at expiration, for various stock prices (column 2 in the following chart). Then write the cost of the option, which will be the same number ($2), for the various stock prices (column 3). The profits or losses in column 4 are found in the same way as a traditional profit and loss is measured — revenues minus costs. Simply take your revenues from the put (column 2) and subtract your costs (column 3).

1	2	3	4
Stock Price	$50 put will be worth	Cost	Profit/Loss (col. 2 - col. 3)
40			
45			
50			
55			
60			

For a stock price of $40, what will the $50 put be worth at expiration? Write that number down in the first blank space under column 2. Now work your way down the column and answer the same question for the various stock prices.

We are assuming the cost of the put is $2. Since the cost never changes, write $2 in every blank space under column 3.

Column 4 is taking the profit from the put in column 2 (if there is any) and subtracting out the cost. Write in these answers for each blank space under column 4.

If you filled out the table correctly, you should have the following numbers:

1	2	3	4
Stock Price	$50 put will be worth	Cost	Profit/Loss (col. 2 - col. 3)
40	$10	$2	$8
45	$5	$2	$3
50	$0	$2	-$2
55	$0	$2	-$2
60	$0	$2	-$2

Next we want to take the profit and loss in column 4 and plot it against the stock prices. For a stock price of $40, the profit is $8. We place a dot on a graph (below) that lines up with a stock price of $40 and a profit of $8. Continue this same process and you should end up with the following chart:

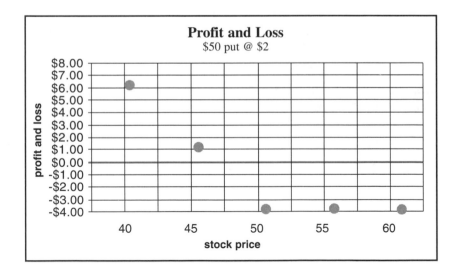

Now just connect the dots, and you have the profit and loss diagram for a long $50 put purchased for $2:

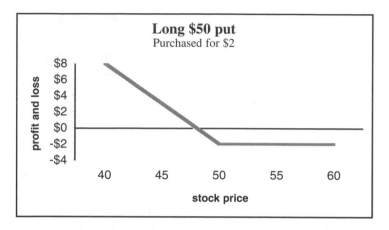

The long put is profitable if the stock falls below $48, which is the breakeven point and loses a maximum of $2 for any stock price above $50 at expiration.

Any profit and loss diagram can be constructed using similar reasoning. Simply list the stock and/or options in the trade and their values at expiration. Subtract out the costs and plot the profits and losses against the various stock prices. It may be a little tough at first, but mastering this skill separates those who understand option strategies from those who do not.

Chapter 7: What Gives an Option Value?

We know that options are contracts between two people to buy and sell shares of stock for a fixed price over a given time period. As the underlying shares of stock become more or less valuable, so, too, should the calls and puts.

If a stock is trading for $40, there is not much perceived value in owning an out-of-the-money $50 call that expires in one month. After all, if you want the stock, you can buy it right now for $40. Why should you pay a fee to give you the right to purchase the stock for a price higher than it is currently trading? The answer, of course, is that the market may be willing to pay for the $50 call if they think there is a reasonable chance that the stock will move higher. If the stock is very volatile — exhibiting large swings either up or down — the $50 call may actually become quite expensive.

This out-of-the-money value — its time value — is strictly caused by market perceptions. The value of the option rests on nothing more than a belief that it might become valuable. This is why out-of-the-money options are a speculative purchase. Say you pay $3 for this $50 call. The very next day, the company could announce some news that makes the market believe the stock will not be above $50 at expiration. The underlying stock does not even need to react negatively; it is possible that it may still trade for $40 or maybe only slightly less, yet the $50 call may immediately trade for 1/4-point (25 cents), leaving your $3 option virtually worthless. The value of options comprised entirely of time premium exists in the minds of investors. There is nothing there to give it any certain value. *It is purely a subjective value and therefore subject to large changes without changes in the stock price.*

But let's say the stock is currently trading for $60. Now the $50 call has some real value to it. Investors would certainly prefer to pay $50 for the stock rather than $60. In fact, investors will compete in the open markets for this contract and bid the contract higher.

Say an investor bids $5 for this contract in the open market. If they buy it for $5, they will effectively be able to purchase the $60 stock for $55. This is because they own the $50 call but had to pay $5 for it. So for a $55 cash outlay, they immediately own a $60 stock, which gives them a "free" $5, because they could immediately sell the stock for $60. Other investors realize this and continue to bid up the price of the $50 call option. When the $50 call is finally trading for at least $10 — the intrinsic value — the bidding pressure may or may not stop. If there is not much time remaining on the option, it will likely stop. But if there is substantial time remaining or the stock is very volatile, the market may still bid the $50 call to a value higher than $10, thereby giving it time value in addition to the intrinsic value.

The important point to know is this: *An option must trade for at least its intrinsic value.* If the stock is trading for $60, the $50 call must be worth *at least* $10; similarly, a $70 put must also trade for at least $10, because that is the amount of intrinsic value. Options with intrinsic value have that value because of market forces. The intrinsic value is forced to exist and is not based on perceptions. The intrinsic value of an option is an objective measure.

If you look at the option quotes on Microsoft (Chapter 2, page 28) you will see that all strikes below $44 (the price of Microsoft at that time) trade for at least intrinsic value. We will be talking about basic option pricing in Chapter 10 and explaining how the markets ensure that options will trade for intrinsic value.

Does an Option Need Intrinsic Value to Be Profitable?

Option traders do not necessarily have to have an option move in-the-money to gain a profit. If the previously mentioned $50 call is purchased for $3 and the stock quickly moves from $40 to $45, the trader may be able to sell the option for $4, giving the trader a simple return of 33%. Notice that the option never had any intrinsic value. However, keep in mind that this option could quickly become worth nothing; its value is not guaranteed. Therefore, long options with premiums existing solely of time premium need the stock to move quickly. If the stock just sits there, the option's value will eventually become zero.

Notice how this is different for the $50 call with the stock at $60. If this option is trading for $12, there is $10 intrinsic and $2 time value. If investors suddenly feel this stock is not going to move any more, the option's price will become slightly more than $10, effectively removing all of the time value of the option (of course, this is assuming the stock does not fall). This in-the-money option has a minimum value to it, which is the intrinsic value.

Just because an option moves in-the-money does not guarantee a profit either. Say you paid $3 for the $50 call with the stock at $40. At expiration, the stock is trading for $52, which is a substantial 30% move in a month. However, your $50 call is trading for $2, which is exactly the intrinsic amount. This leaves you with a $1, or 33%, loss!

Options have two types of value: one is perceived (time value), and the other is a real or immediate value (intrinsic value). This is why it is important to be able to break an option's price into these two components. If you do not understand where your option's value is coming from, you may end up with unwanted surprises at expiration.

How Much Time Premium Do Options Have?

Generally there will always be some time premium on an option, even if only a small amount. With all else constant, the longer the maturity of the option or the more volatile the option, the more you will pay in time premium. The reason is that, with all else constant, investors prefer to buy longer-term options because there is more time to gain intrinsic value. Likewise, investors prefer more volatile options because they have a greater chance of making bigger moves, thereby giving the option more intrinsic value.

Also, the farther in-the-money you look (the lower the strike for calls; higher for puts), the more time premium will decrease. If the stock is $100, the $95 call will have less time premium than $100 call, and the $90 call will have less time premium than the $95. This will continue to hold true on down the line.

If the option is deep enough in the money, the time premium will equal the risk-free rate. Why? If the stock is at $100 and the $80 call is sufficiently in-the-money, investors can buy the stock and sell the $80 call (covered-call position), thereby "guaranteeing" them $80 at expiration. As with any guaranteed trade, the interest rate will be the risk-free rate. A covered call is never truly guaranteed, because it is always possible for the stock to fall below the strike price of the short call. However, if it is sufficiently deep-in-the-money where the markets *perceive* it to be guaranteed, then the market will reward you only the risk-free rate for that trade. The important point to understand is that as you move to lower and lower strikes for calls (higher strikes for puts), they become increasingly more likely to have intrinsic value and will therefore have correspondingly lower amounts of time premium.

How Do I Use This Information to Trade?

We stated earlier that it is important to learn about time value and intrinsic value to understand what you are getting into with a particular option. Any option that has high time premium relative to the cost of the option is riskier. In trading terms, it will have a high gamma value, which we will talk about in Chapter 9. The reason it is risky is because the underlying stock must move sufficiently *and* in the proper direction enough to make up for the time premium. If it does not, you will end up with a losing trade.

For example, if you buy a $100 call option for $10 with the stock at $100, the stock must get to $110 (stock price plus time premium) to break even. If the stock moves to $108 at expiration, the $100 call will be worth $8, yet you paid $10 for a $2 loss.

Now compare this to the trader who may have purchased the $80 call, which may have been trading for $21 ($20 intrinsic + $1 time premium.) With the stock at $110 at expiration, the $80 call will be worth $30. This trader paid $21 and sold for $30 — a profit of $9, which is certainly different from the $2 loss taken with the $100 call.

Relative Time Premiums Determine Risk

Note that the $10 time premium for the $100 call is 100% of the total cost of the option. It is important to make this relative comparison to judge the risk level of an option. For instance, it may be possible to find another $100 stock that has a $95 call trading for $15 ($10 time and $5 intrinsic). It may be tempting to assume that both options are equally risky, because they both carry a $10 time premium. In this second case, however, the time premium is $10/$15 = 66% of the total value of the option as compared to 100% for the $100 call. You cannot compare one $10 time premium to another $10 time premium and declare both options equally risky; it is the time premium relative to the total cost of the option that determines the risk, which means the at-the-money options are considered the riskiest.

If you are looking for very quick moves in the underlying, you can afford to buy options with higher time premium. However, if you are interested in only speculating on the direction of the underlying stock, you should consider deeper-in-the-money options to avoid the high risk associated with high time premium options.

But avoiding the speed game (the need for the underlying stock to move) is not free. If you buy a deep-in-the-money option, you will pay more in total dollars (more intrinsic value and less time value). By doing so, you now have more money at risk if the stock should move against you. In addition, if the stock should fall, the deep-in-the-money option will fall nearly point-for-point through a certain range of stock prices before slowing. It is a delicate balancing act to find the appropriate option that suits your needs.

Option Trading Mistakes

One of the biggest mistakes new option traders make is to buy an option just because it is "cheap." The inexperienced trader will usually look to out-of-the-money options, because they can buy more contracts for a fixed-dollar investment or, similarly, pay less money for a given number of contracts. For example, if a stock is trading at $50, a new trader who is bullish on the stock will usually look at a $55 or higher strike. They often wonder why they should buy an in-the-money option because the stock has already exceeded the strike price. They feel they are "wasting" money by paying for the intrinsic value.

Usually cheap options are composed entirely of time premium and are often far-out-of-the-money (strike price is a lot higher than the stock price for calls, or strike price is well below stock price for puts.) Another way to judge the quality of your option pick is to check to see if it matches your sentiment on the underlying stock in terms of breakeven.

For example, if the stock is $100 and you want to buy the $115 option for $2, that stock will have to move to $117 by expiration to break even on the trade. Again, this is because the $115 option will be worth $2 with the stock at $117 at expiration. If you sell your call at this point, you will have exactly recovered your costs. If you do not think it is likely for the underlying stock to be at least $117 by expiration, you should probably consider another option. A deeper-in-the-money option will be more costly but have less time premium; it will not need the stock to move as far to break even. A $90 call may be trading for $10.50 ($10 intrinsic and $0.50 time premium). This $90 call needs to have the stock move to only $100.50 before it breaks even. With the stock at $100, that is only a 1/2-point move needed to recoup your costs, which is certainly more likely to happen than the 17-point move needed by the $115 call.

If you look at any set of option quotes, you will always see that the highest strike call has the highest breakeven (the opposite is true for puts). This may lead you to conclude that the highest strikes are the riskiest because the underlying stock needs to move further to break even. Remember though, that the higher call strikes will become increasingly cheaper to purchase, therefore putting less money at risk. The riskiest options are the at-the-money options.

Many strategies rely on the behavior of time premium. If you plan to increase your trading knowledge of options, you need to have a solid understanding of time and intrinsic values.

Volatility

Earlier, we mentioned volatility: the price swings of a stock. Volatility is actually a fairly complicated statistical measure, but all you really need to know is that the higher the volatility, the more likely the stock will move. Volatility is a nondirectional indicator, which means that a high volatility stock is as likely to move down as it is to move up. We will see in a later section that volatility is really the key factor that gives an option its value.

Higher volatility stocks will therefore bring a higher price in the option marketplace. Say a stock is trading for $49 and has zero chance of moving higher. How much would you pay for a $50 call? Obviously, you would not pay a thing for it. The $50 call has no perceived value. Now imagine that the stock has a high volatility and is swinging three to five points a day either up or down. You now think this stock could easily be worth $70 or higher at expiration. If so, the $50 call could be worth as much as $20 or more. Now investors will certainly give more value to the call option. This is why you will see "high-flyer" stocks commanding much higher prices for the options.

For example, at the time of this publication, Nvidia (NVDA) is trading for $75.40 and has easily been moving $2 to $6 per day. The 1-month $75 calls (at-the-money) are trading for $7.80. Now let's compare that to a lower volatility stock such as McDonald's (MCD), which is currently trading for $27.58 and moves just fractions per day. Its one-month $27.50 call (at-the-money) is only $1.05. If you look up other option quotes online or in the newspaper and compare at-the-money calls of high and low volatility stocks, you will quickly see that volatility is the key factor in determining an option's price.

There is probably one misconception about options that should be clarified here. Many investors believe that, because high-volatility stocks are more likely to move, they should only buy options on high-volatility stocks. This is not true. The market will price all options according to risk. Although you may be able to make more on the high-flyers, they will also cost you more. So do not think you should play only high-volatility options; the market should price them all so that they are equal on a risk-reward basis. As we will find out in Chapter 9, to trade options profitably, you need to determine the direction and speed of the option; the volatility is priced into it.

Chapter 8: Why Do Options Exist?

Now that we have covered the basics of options, terminology, trading terms, and profit and loss diagrams, we are in a better position to understand why options exist and what is actually happening with an option transaction. If you understand why they were devised and how they carry out the goal, this will provide you with insights into how to use them as well as basic option pricing properties. Once you understand this process, you will have a clearer understanding of option strategies. So while this chapter may seem mystifying, it is actually one of the most important to understand.

Options, as stated at the beginning of this book, have received negative publicity from the start, with no signs of slowing. This is partly because of the nature of the media wanting to report the negative news, which is what sells. The negative publicity is also caused by writers and investors who do not understand the true reasons why options were created.

You are about to take a tour through the fascinating world of investors, speculators, and market makers to learn what options are really all about. If you have a negative opinion about options, this tour will dispel any myths and present only the facts.

Limiting Risk

It all starts with an investor who wants to limit risk. That doesn't sound like such a bad thing, does it? It is certainly different from the legalized gambling theory presented by the financial press.

Options were created as a way for investors to buy and sell risk and, while this concept may seem unusual, it actually occurs in many ways in our everyday lives. For example, driving a car involves the risk of wrecks, injury, and theft. You do not want this risk but, for a fee, your auto insurance company does. You have, in fact, transferred the risk to them.

Notice that with this example, you want to limit your downside risk — the risk of a crash. The insurance company, on the other hand, is *speculating* that it will not happen. They are taking the fee, hoping that the policy expires without a claim against it. Options simply allow investors to transfer — or accept — unwanted risk. This concept is the next logical step in any well-developed financial market. So let's take a look at how options accomplish this with a simple trade — a long call option.

What Happens When I Buy a Call?

Assume for a moment that you are bullish on a particular stock that has been moving up rapidly. It is trading for $50 per share and you are, rightfully so, concerned that the stock may collapse. However, if you do not buy it, you run the risk of missing any of the potential upside.

Prior to options, you had one choice: Buy the stock and hope for the best. You stand to make point-for-point profit for all stock prices above $50, but you do so at the expense of $50 maximum risk. With options, you can alter your risk-reward profile and create a profit and loss diagram that is more suitable to your tastes.

Because you are willing to buy the stock at $50 but are afraid to do so, you could, instead, buy a $50 call and defer that stock purchase. This way, if the stock is trading for much higher, say $65, and you still want to own the stock, you can use your call to purchase it for $50 (or just sell the call to close in the open market for the $15 intrinsic value). But if the stock falls apart, you can let your call expire worthless and lose only the premium. In effect you have altered the profit and loss profile to one that is more acceptable to you. Somebody else in the marketplace accepted this risk for you — but who is this other person? You will soon see that this is one of the benefits of a market maker; they will find the hedger or speculator for you.

To see how options work, let's assume you buy ten $50 call options at market, which expire in one year. Remember, buying at market means you are guaranteed to be filled at the best prevailing price at the time your order hits the floor.

As discussed, you do not want the profit and loss profile of long stock, because that is much too risky in this case. You could theoretically lose the entire $50 you paid. The long call, as we have demonstrated, is much more appealing in this case. As a refresher, the long call profit and loss diagram looks like the chart below. For now, it is not important as to the strike or the cost; just focus on the *shape* (looks like a hockey stick) of the profit and loss diagram.

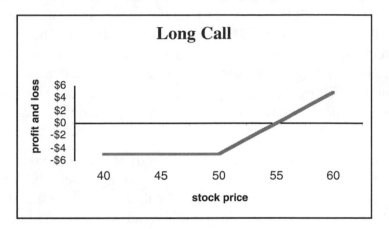

Let's take a look at the individual players in the market and see how your order is handled and how the risks are transferred.

When you place this trade with your broker, it will be sent to the floor of the exchange — perhaps the CBOE — and presented to a market maker in that option. Market makers are people who provide liquidity in the market and stand by willing to buy or sell if nobody else wants to. Market makers risk their own capital — or possibly a firm's — and fill orders to make a profit.

When market makers receive the order, they will "build" the risk profile that you want and sell it to you for a profit. This is really no different from any other kind of business; business owners take money and use it to build products or services and then sell them at a profit. Of course, the fierce competition of other market makers will keep them from price gouging. Even though your order is a market order, competitive forces keep market makers from charging you anything they wish.

The market maker realizes that because you want to buy a $50 call option, you are willing to buy the underlying stock if it is *above* $50 at expiration. To hedge this risk, the market maker will find another investor who is willing to buy the stock if it is *below* $50 at expiration. Once this is done, the market maker will have a guaranteed buyer at expiration — the market maker will sell to you if the stock is above $50 or to the other party if it is below $50.

Because the market maker knows he has a guaranteed sale at expiration, he will buy the stock today — something you were unwilling to do — and hold it for you until expiration. The market maker is now not at risk; he has a guaranteed buyer if the stock is above or below $50. Who would be willing to buy if the stock is below $50? Think about what you have learned so far with the basic option positions. What kind of position will assume the obligation to *buy* if it is below a certain price?

You have probably realized that it is a short put position. Somewhere in the market is a person who was willing to sell a $50 put. This person could be a speculator and willing to gamble that the stock price will stay above $50. Or this could be a hedger, someone who is looking to buy stock for long-term if it should fall and who is willing to assume the risk. Either way, market makers are always pairing up speculators and hedgers. Let's assume the market maker pays $5 for this put option.

At this point, the market maker is long stock for $50 and long a $50 put for $5; he must be long the $50 put so that he can fill the other investor on the short $50 put. The market maker's two positions — long stock and a long $50 put — look like the following chart:

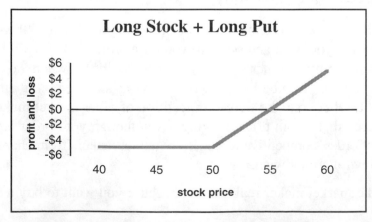

Why does the market maker's profit and loss diagram look like this? The market maker is long stock but has a long $50 put — an insurance policy — to sell it back to the short put if the stock is below $50 at expiration. The market maker is guaranteed to receive $50 less his cost for buying the put.

Now it is evident why the profit and loss line flattens out at a $50 stock price for a $5 loss. The put cost $5, so that is the most the market maker can lose. No matter how far down the stock is trading, the market maker can always sell his or her shares for $50. Below a stock price of $50, the market maker no longer takes additional losses; he or she is limited to the $5 loss from the cost of the put.

Notice something interesting here. The market maker's profit and loss in the previous chart is *exactly* the same one that *you* are trying to create by purchasing a long call, which was shown in the earlier chart. In effect, the market maker has gone out to the marketplace and "built" a product containing the properties you want. He has built a long call option. How much will he charge?

We know he paid $5 to the put seller. That is part of the market maker's cost in building this position for you. Assuming 5% interest rates, there is also an implied interest cost of $50 * 5% = $2.50. Why is there an interest expense? The market maker could have left the $50 per share in the money market and earned 5% for the next year. However, he has had to use it to buy stock and hold it for you, so will not receive his interest. That is another expense to the market maker. If the market maker will lose $2.50 in one year, he should be willing to accept the *present value* of this debt or $2.50/1.05 = $2.38 today.

What does "present value" mean?

The present value of money is simply the value of a future cash flow today — the present value. It is really very simple. Say you have $100 in a bank at 5% interest. In one year, you would have $105. That is called the future value of money — it is a sum of money today ($100) valued in the future ($105). Present value works backward. If you are owed $105 in one year, how much is it worth today? Simple; just undo the above calculation — $105/ 1.05 = $100. We would say the present value of $105 due in one year is $100 today if interest rates are 5% and the investment is risk-free. In other words, an investor should be indifferent between $100 today or $105 due in one year.

If the $105 is due in two years, you must divide by 1.05 twice, which mathematically is the same as 1.05 squared. So an investor who is due $105 in two years should be willing to accept $105/ 1.052 = $95.24 today if risk-free interest rates are 5%.

Finally, the market maker will want a profit. Let's assume, for simplicity, it is $0.12 per share. The market maker's total costs to build this profit and loss profile for you are: $5 + $2.38 + $0.12 = $7.50, and that is the price your long call position will be filled!

We said the market maker has built your risk profile by buying stock and buying a put. These are not things he wants; he was building them for you. So how does the market maker transfer this long stock and long put position to you? All he has to do is fill your order. The market maker will sell this to you by *shorting a call*, which allows you to be long the call — exactly what you wanted. By simply filling your order, the market maker has effectively transferred the long stock plus long put position to you.

You may think the market maker is at risk with the short call. But keep in mind his long stock + long put positions look like a long call and are called a *synthetic equivalent* of a long call. Synthetic options are positions that behave exactly like another position from a profit and loss standpoint (discussed further in Chapter 15).

Effectively, the market maker is long a call (his long stock and long put position) and short a call (the one he sold you) and so has no risk, which is what we said earlier. No matter what happens to the stock price at expiration, the market maker has a guaranteed buyer for $50 and has neutralized his risk with the short call position.

Notice what has happened. The market maker found a speculator or hedger in the market who was willing to buy if the stock fell. This is something you were unable to do but were willing to pay for. The market maker finds this person, fills your order, and passes those costs on to you in the process.

Conversions and Reversals

Another way to understand how option prices are determined on the floor of the exchange is through conversions and reversals. Conversions are simply a three-sided position consisting of long stock, short calls, and long puts. A reversal is just the opposite — it is a three-sided position of short stock, long calls, and short puts. Any trader holding a conversion will be effectively matched with another trader holding a reversal. Market makers love to use these positions because they are in a risk-free position through expiration.

We can view the above trade in another light — through conversions and reversals — and see how the long call option would be priced. Using the same assumptions, the trader has placed a market order to buy ten 1-year $50 strike calls at market with the stock trading at $50.

The market maker knows he will be short a call to fill the long call order. If so, his risk is that the stock rises. To cover that risk, he will buy 1,000 shares of stock today so that shares can be delivered regardless of how high they may be trading. Once he buys the stock, the risk is that it falls. To hedge this downside risk, he will buy a $50 put and again, we will assume that $5 per contract, or $5,000, is paid.

The market maker is in a guaranteed position to receive $50,000 in one year. If the stock is below $50, he will exercise the ten $50 puts and receive $50,000. If the stock is above $50 in one year, he will be assigned on the short calls and be forced to sell the stock for $50,000. On the off chance the stock is exactly $50, the short call and long put expire worthless, and he will be holding 1,000 shares worth $50. Whether the stock is up, down, or unchanged, the market maker's three-sided position is guaranteed to be worth $50,000 in one year.

The market maker is guaranteed to receive $50,000 in one year regardless of the stock price. How much is this worth today? The present value of $50,000 in one year is $50,000 / (1.05) = $47,619 today. The market maker should pay $47,619 today for these three assets — the stock, long put, and short call positions. If he pays $47,619 and receives $50,000 in one year, the return on investment will be 5%, which is exactly the interest rate he should receive for a risk-free investment.

The market maker will spend $50,000 for the 1,000 shares of stock trading at $50. He will also spend an additional $5,000 for the put for a total cash outlay of $55,000. We already figured that the fair price for this package of the three assets should be worth $47,619, yet he is paying $55,000 for it.

The market maker has overpaid by $55,000 - $47,619 = $7,381, so he will need to bring in a credit for this amount. How can the market maker receive a credit of $7, 381? He will fill your order on the ten $50 calls for roughly $7.38. In doing so, he will receive the necessary credit to make his -$55,000 cash outlay equal to -$47,619. Once the market maker tacks on his 0.12 profit we assumed in the previous example, the order will be filled at $7.50, which is exactly what we calculated before.

To summarize, the market maker's initial position looks like this:

Buy 1,000 shares at $50   = -$50,000
Buy 10 $50 puts at $5   = -$5,000
Sells 10 $50 calls at $7.38 = +$7,380
Equals -$47,620 cash outlay by market maker

This is guaranteed to grow to a value of about $50,000 in one year ($47,620 * 1.05 = $50,000) because of the full hedge provided by the three-sided position.

Again, this three-sided position (long stock + long put + short call) established by the market maker is called a conversion. If he had done the reverse (i.e. short stock + short puts + long calls) then it would be called a reversal, or reverse conversion. These two positions are very important to understand for options trading. Although they are generally not good trading strategies for retail investors because of bid-ask spreads and three commissions, market makers use them constantly. If you understand the basics of these positions, it will help you to better understand option pricing, enabling you to usually receive a better fill on a buy-write, which is a strategy we will talk about later.

Are Options a Zero-Sum Game?

We stated earlier that options are often reported to be a zero-sum game, which means money simply changes from the losers to the winners, and no new value is created.

Let's assume the stock closed at $70 at expiration and see how the market participants fared. The 20-point gain in the stock is distributed as follows:

You bought a $50 call for $8 and it is worth $20, giving you a total profit of $12.

The short put seller sold a put for $5, which expired worthless, so he keeps the $5 profit. So far, there are total profits of $17 gained by the market.

The market maker bought stock for $50 and sold for $70 for a gain of $20. His long put position expired worthless, so he lost $5. He keeps the $8 from the short call but must buy back the call for $20, giving him a net loss of $12 on the call. The market maker's gain is: +$20 - $5 - $12 = $3. The market maker will make $3 regardless of what happens to the stock. Again, this is because he has a riskless position.

You and the other investor gained $17, and the market maker made $3 for a total of $20, which is exactly the amount of gain in the stock. Had you purchased the stock yourself, you would have kept the entire $20. But because you were not comfortable doing so, you effectively paid $5 to the other investor to assume the downside risk and $3 to the market maker for carrying the stock and finding the other investor (the put seller). That is a total of $8 paid out of your $20 potential gain in the stock — and that's why you were left with exactly $12.

This also shows a misperception of options. Many times the press argues that options should not exist because they are a zero-sum game, meaning that no new capital is formed but that money just changes hands from losers to the winners. But after looking at the above scenario, we see that is not entirely true. All investors made money: You made $12, the put seller made $5, and the market maker made $3. In fact, the market maker had to purchase the stock from someone. But that person may have paid $40 for the stock, so no certain losses exist there either.

The options *themselves* are a zero-sum game though. Your long call gained $12 and the market makers lost $12. The short put made $5 and the market maker's long put lost $5. But when you look at how the options were placed together so that hedgers could meet speculators, nobody lost. Everybody just paid or received a fee to take specific risks and avoid others.

Hopefully this gives you a better understanding of what happens in an options transaction. Obviously, there are countless other strategies, but the concept is always the same. The options trader is either buying or selling risk through a market maker, who has the ability to find people who will take the other side of the trade and match their orders. Remember, this is a little simplified. You and the other person are really paired with the OCC to mitigate the risk of default by the other person. Conceptually though, the market maker has just paired you with another investor.

This should also help you to understand how option quotes are formed. In the above example, the market maker could make money by purchasing the put for $5. For example, he may therefore bid $5 and ask $5.50. He also made money by selling the call for $8, so he may bid $7.50 and ask $8. The market makers simply straddle the "fair values" of calls and puts and either buy them a little cheaper or sell them for a little more than their theoretical values. It does not matter what type of order comes to the market maker, because they can always hedge away the risk for a profit.

Now you should see another advantage of the options markets. If you want to speculate, how much will it cost you? If you want to hedge, how much will you receive? All you have to do is look at the option quotes, and you will see the highest bidders and lowest offers. It does not matter who this person is or where they are located; all you need to know is the price at which they are willing to buy or sell. You can effectively alter your risk reward profiles for better investing. Options were created as a way to buy and sell risk. Understanding how this is accomplished will help you understand options and strategies in a more meaningful way.

Chapter 9: The Black-Scholes Factors

As you trade options, you will at some time hear about the Black-Scholes Model. It is important to understand what it is and how the factors in the model affect the prices of calls and puts.

The Black-Scholes Option Pricing Model (named after its creators Fisher Black and Myron Scholes) is an option-pricing calculator, much like a financial calculator that tells you what your car payment should be if you give it the loan amount, interest rate, and time of the loan. In the same sense, the Black-Scholes Option Pricing Model will tell you the "fair price" of a call option if you give it five inputs. The model is highly complex and is considered by many to be one of the most important contributions to modern financial theory; in fact, Myron Scholes was awarded the Nobel Prize in 1997 for its creation.

The reason it is so significant is because prior to this creation, there was no way to fairly determine the price of an option. If any market is uncertain about value, buyers bid very low and sellers offer high. This leads to little liquidity and the market never gets off the ground.

This financial breakthrough led to the creation of the CBOE. Previously, options were traded through the over-the-counter (OTC) market on an unregulated basis and did not have to adhere to the principle of "fair and orderly markets." Today, largely due to Black and Scholes, the CBOE trades tens of millions of contracts per month.

According to the Black-Scholes Option Pricing Model, five main factors affect an option's price. Technically, dividends are a sixth factor but are not of much concern, because they are generally factored into the price of the option (and because all market participants know the amount of the dividend and when it will be paid). However, if it is a surprise dividend, dividend increase or cut, then it becomes a much more relevant factor.

The five main factors according to the Black-Scholes Model are:

1) Stock price
2) Exercise or strike price
3) Interest rates (risk-free rate)
4) Volatility of the underlying stock
5) Time to expiration

We will look at each of these in turn, including dividends, and see exactly the effects they have on call and put prices. Some will be fairly intuitive and others will not, but all are important if you want to understand options and how their prices will be affected by changes in the factors.

Stock Price

The stock price is probably the most obvious of all the factors that affect an option's price. This is because options are derivatives, which means their price is derived from the underlying stock

As the stock price increases, the price of a call will increase and the price of the put will decrease with all other factors constant.

This is a theoretical statement, so do not be alarmed if your call option is not up with the underlying stock trading higher. In fact, anybody who has traded options for any length of time has experienced this. There are sound reasons why this happens, so let's see if we can make sense of it.

First of all, there are many strikes for any given option. In fact, new strikes will be added if the stock is moving up or down significantly. If a stock is trading at $120 up $2, a $100 strike will likely be up a significant portion of that $2 — maybe up $1.50 or so — depending on the volatility and time remaining on the option.

What about a $130 strike? Here it is difficult to say. We know it is worth more *theoretically*, but it is up to the market to determine just how much. As an analogy, say you are betting on a runner to complete a 26-mile marathon, and the runner has just taken the first step across the start line. Do you adjust your bet upward?

Probably not, even though the runner is already closer to the finish line than he was one step earlier. So theoretically, you should be a *little* more confident in your bet that he will complete it. It does not mean you will adjust your bet.

This holds for the options, too. An option can be thought of as a bet that the stock will cross the finish line — the strike —by expiration. So, as the stock moves higher, all calls become worth more theoretically. Whether or not the market reflects added value remains to be seen. However, as we have stated earlier, once the stock has crossed the strike price and the option has intrinsic value, then the option must reflect all intrinsic value.

This same reasoning is true for puts but in the opposite direction. Because a put option confers the right to sell stock, it should be worth more as the stock moves lower. As the stock falls, theoretically all puts become worth more.

Strike Price (Exercise Price)

The effects of the strike price are closely related to the stock price. In fact, whether the stock price or exercise price is changed, it is really just looking at the same thing in two different ways. When we were considering the stock price in the previous example, we assumed the strike price remained constant. Now, if we hold the stock price constant but lower the strike, effectively we are doing the same thing; that is, in either case we are creating a narrower distance between the stock price and the exercise price.

As the exercise price (strike price) is decreased, calls become worth more and puts become worth less with all other factors constant.

By the same reasoning, as the exercise price is raised, puts become worth more and calls will be worth less.

Another way to understand this is by thinking of what a call does. It gives you the right to purchase stock. Would you rather buy stock for $100 per share or $120 per share? Of course, you would rather pay $100 and so would everybody else in the market. Market participants correspondingly bid the $100 strike higher, which is just a reflection of the higher demand.

Similarly, a put option gives you the right to sell your stock. Because everybody would rather get $120 per share as opposed to $100, investors bid the $120 put higher than the $100 strike.

Risk-Free Interest Rate

It is a little more difficult to understand how interest rates affect calls and puts. It may be helpful to remember that calls are a form of *borrowing* money. We saw this in Chapter 8 when the market maker created a call option for the buyer. To do so, the market maker had to buy stock today and pass along the cost of carry to the buyer. So although you pay for the call option, in effect you are borrowing funds. Because interest rates affect the cost of carry to the seller:

An increase in interest rates will increase the price of a call option and decrease the price of a put option with all other factors constant.

Although this is fairly easy to show mathematically, it is easier to remember if you understand it conceptually. So let's look at another line of reasoning.

Say interest rates are very high — 20%. You have $100,000 in a money market that you would like to invest in stocks. You can either buy the stocks today or, for a fee, buy a call option that gives you control of the stock but allows you to defer payment. The choice should be clear: Buy the call option so you can hang on to your money and continue to earn interest. The markets follow this same line of reasoning and bid the calls higher when interest rates increase.

What about the puts if interest rates are high? Puts give you the right to sell your stock, which represents a cash flow into the account. Cash is desirable if interest rates are really high. So, do you elect to buy puts to defer the sale? No, in fact, you may even *sell* the puts to generate cash into the account so it can earn the high rate of interest. Because few of the market participants are willing to buy puts relative to those wanting to sell them, put prices will fall.

As interest rates fall, there is more money to be made in stocks relative to the money market. Investors will then seek returns through the stock market and not buy calls; in fact, they will be induced to sell calls to generate returns. So as interest rates fall, so too will call prices.

For puts, as interest rates fall, investors will seek returns through the stock market as there is now relatively less to give up from the money market. Investors will even buy puts to protect the downside and hope for upside returns in the stocks.

A decrease in interest rates will decease the price of a call option and increase the price of a put option with all other factors constant.

There is one thing to be careful with whenever discussing topics that hold "all other factors constant" as we have done here.

In the real world, it is never the case that only one factor changes and all else stays the same. If interest rates rise suddenly, do not be surprised if your call options <u>decrease in price</u> and not increase as we have said so far. This is usually because <u>stock prices will fall</u> with increases in interest rates. We know that falling stock prices correspond with falling call prices. But it should be evident that all factors did not stay the same in this example — we assumed interest rates rose <u>and</u> stock prices fell.

This does not mean that holding other factors constant is useless. If you do not hold all other factors constant, then it is impossible to determine what will happen, which leaves you with no insights at all. Just understand that there are serious shortcomings to applying these principles in the real world and that you need to be very careful when analyzing the effects of option prices.

Volatility

Without a doubt, volatility is the single most important factor of the Black-Scholes Model. In fact, it is the only true unknown in the equation. For example, if you ask ten different people what the stock price is, they would all give you exactly the same answer.

Likewise, they would quote the same strike price, risk-free rates of interest, and time remaining on the option. But what should they tell you the correct volatility measure is for the stock? The 10-day average? The 20-day? The 50-day? Or should they quote the projected expected future volatility? It should be easy to see why this is the most important factor in the model — it is the only one that nobody knows for sure.

If volatility increases, both call and put prices will increase with all other factors the same.

You may be thinking if volatility increases, the stock becomes riskier. Why would somebody pay more for a riskier asset? After all, junk bonds trade for lower prices than government bonds because of the increased risk.

The reason for the apparent contradiction is that options have a limited downside; the owner can lose only what he or she puts into it.

Look at the following diagram. Assume one investor buys stock at $50 and another purchases a $50 call for $5:

	30	35	40	45	50	55	60	65	70	75
Profit/loss of stock purchased at $50	-20	-15	-10	-5	0	5	10	15	20	25
Value of $50 call purchased at $5	-5	-5	-5	-5	-5	5	10	15	20	25

If you purchased stock at $50 and the stock closes at $30, you are down $20. However, the call owner is down only $5. In fact, that is the most the call owner can lose; however, they can match the stock purchaser on profit for all stock prices above $50 (not counting the cost of the option). More volatility means a higher expected return for the option buyer — whether calls or puts — so investors will bid up the prices of options that are tied to risky stocks.

Time to Expiration

This factor is fairly straightforward. We said earlier that an option could be viewed as a bet that the stock will be above the strike price (for calls) or below the strike price (for puts) by expiration. In other words, you are in effect betting that the option will have intrinsic value. Because of this, the more time available, the more likely the stock will have intrinsic value.

The more time to expiration, the more valuable calls and puts are.

From a trading standpoint, the more time you buy, the better with all else being the same. This is because calls and puts become increasingly cheaper (on a per month basis) the more time you buy. For example, if a 1-month option were trading for $5, you would have to look at roughly a four-month option to double the price to $10. Many people think that a two-month option would double the price but it does not — in the real world, it takes between three and four times the amount of time to double the price. So the implication is that it becomes a better and better deal for the option buyer to buy time. Likewise, it becomes a worse and worse deal for the option sellers to sell longer-term options.

Please do not confuse this to mean that it is wrong to sell longer-term options or that it is wrong to buy little time because that is not necessarily true. It depends on many factors with the particular strategy at hand. With everything else constant, option buyers should buy lots of time and option sellers should sell short amounts of time.

Exception:

There is one small exception. It is possible for a deep-in-the-money European put option to become more valuable with the passage of time. This is because the European option holder must wait to receive the cash from the put. So a deep-in-the-money European put will be worth the present value of the future cash flow and will increase in price with the passage of time. However, options on the equity market (stocks) are always American-style, so this caveat

---

does not hold true for most of our discussions on equity-trading strategies. Just be aware that there is one exception to this rule, which you may witness if you trade some of the popular European-style indices such as the S&P 500 index.

Dividends

Last, we will consider the effect of dividends on calls and puts. This factor is fairly straightforward, too.

If a stock pays a dividend, the price of the stock is reduced by the amount of the dividend (rounded to the nearest 1/8-point) in the next trading session. The reason the price is reduced is because the company has paid out cash — one of its assets — so it is now worth less than before it paid the dividend. For example, say a $100 stock will pay a $1 dividend tomorrow. On the opening, the stock will be trading for $99 unchanged. (This is considered to be unchanged since the fall is not due to supply and demand factors.)

Think about it for a moment. If the stock price is down and all other factors stay the same, what will happen to the call? The call price will fall.

Dividend increases cause call prices to fall and put prices to rise with all other factors the same.

Why will put prices rise? Because the long put can force the short put to purchase the stock for the strike price. With the stock trading for even less after the dividend, the put option becomes more valuable.

The following table will help as a recap. The table shows the effect on call and put prices with the six factors being up. Of course, the reverse will be true if the factors are down.

	If this factor is **UP**:	**Call Price**	**Put Price**
1	Stock Price	▲	▼
2	Exercise Price	▼	▲
3	Risk-Free Rates	▲	▼
4	Volatility	▲	▲
5	Time to Expiration	▲	▲
6	Dividends	▼	▲

Most strategies are some form of a play on the five main factors that affect option prices.

Traders who know how the various factors affect option prices can better match their outlooks with strategies. In addition, new strategies may be formed. For example, assume you think interest rates will rise sharply over the next few months and the stock price will rise as well. How can you better take advantage of this outlook? Purchase longer-term calls, so their price will be more responsive to the changes in interest rates.

Understanding the five Black-Scholes factors and how they affect option prices is essential if you want to become a better options trader.

Chapter 10: Basic Option Pricing

In the last chapter we learned how the Black-Scholes Option Pricing Model could be used to determine fair prices, or theoretical values, of call options with only five inputs into the model.

Investors are often skeptical of a model that tells what the fair value of an option should be. They often argue that an option is worth only what someone else will pay for it. These same people often believe that option market makers can therefore post any price they want and can take unfair advantage of the market. Comments such as these are not only false, but their belief in them will limit your trading knowledge, trading opportunities, and potential profits.

It is therefore a good idea to have a basic understanding of how option prices can be determined without the use of a formalized model. Option prices follow a logical balance of many forms of economic and financial theory and are bound by strict rules within these fields. Market makers simply post prices within these boundaries; they cannot quote anything they please. Understanding how options are priced in the absence of a model will greatly enhance your ability to understand option pricing and strategies.

Trading Without Theoretical Values

The Black-Scholes Model is an invaluable tool for floor traders and retail investors alike. However, there are certain principal relationships that must remain within the options markets, with or without the Black-Scholes Model, otherwise arbitrage opportunities will be available.

Arbitrage is simply a process where speculators can make "free" money, also called a riskless profit. Many incorrectly feel that this should be illegal as if these speculators, called arbitrageurs, are cheating the markets. However, arbitrageurs are performing an important economic function by ensuring that prices are, in fact, fair for everybody. We will show you how this is done and why it is good for the markets to have arbitrageurs.

We're going to look at five basic option pricing relationships, which were popularized by Robert W. Kolb. To start, let's look at a basic relationship that you may already know to be true but are probably unsure why. Not understanding why will cause confusion when we talk about more advanced strategies, such as spreads.

Pricing Relationship #1: The lower the strike, the higher the call price and the lower the put price.

If you have two call options, say a $50 and $55 strike with all other factors alike (i.e., same underlying stock and time), the $50 strike will always be more expensive than the $55. Why?

There are a number of ways to show this. Whichever way is easiest to remember is fine — just as long as you understand it.

First, we can look at it from a basic probability standpoint:

←   **No Value**   →←   **Value**   →

$0 -- --- -- --- -------- $50 ---------------------$100

Looking at the diagram above, say a stock can trade between only $0 and $100 and you have the $50 strike call. You have, in effect, a 50%-50% chance of having intrinsic value at expiration. If the stock is above $50, your option will have some value; if it is below $50, it will be worth nothing. So how do we increase our chances of having intrinsic value at expiration? Simple. We buy a call with a lower strike price.

← **No Value** → ←   **Value**   →

$0 -- --- -- --- ---$25 ---$100

For example, buying the $25 strike gives us far more room to the right of the strike price (intrinsic value) as compared to the $50 strike. Thus, our chances are better of having some value at expiration. The markets figure this out and will bid the $25 strike higher than the $50.

The second method to show this relationship is simply from a financial cash-flow standpoint. Because an option gives you the right to purchase the stock, would you rather have an option that allows you to pay $50 per share or one that allows you to buy it for $25 per share? Obviously, with all else being the same, you would prefer to pay $25 rather than $50. Everybody in the market figures this out, which increases the demand of the $25 strike relative to the $50 strike, which makes the $25 call price higher than the $50.

This may sound good in theory, but how do we know that it will actually happen in the real world? What prevents a market maker from posting an unfair quote and asking more for the $50 call than the $25 call? Say we quote two options one day using the following prices:

> $50 call priced at $5
> $55 call priced at $6

Assume the same underlying stock and time to expiration. What will happen? We found out above that the markets *should* bid the $50 strike higher but, for some reason, it is lower. If this were to happen in the real world, the arbitrageurs would come to the rescue.

Arbitrageurs will execute the following trades simultaneously:

> Buy the $50 call: -$5
> Sell the $55 call: <u>+$6</u>
> Net Credit: +$1

They will receive a credit of $1 into their account. If the stock collapses, both options expire worthless and the arbitrageur will keep the $1. If the stock is trading higher, say $70, then the $50 call

---

What exactly is arbitrage?

We said earlier that arbitrageurs make "free money," which many people mistake to mean a guaranteed profit. A guaranteed profit is only half correct; the guaranteed profit must come from no cash outlay by the arbitrageur. If this second condition were not met, the purchase of a government bond would qualify as arbitrage because a profit is guaranteed. However, the government bond requires a cash outlay for a specific period of timebefore the profit is realized.

This does not mean that arbitrage profits must occur immediately either. You will see in the third pricing relationship presented that the arbitrageur must wait for the profit; however, you will also see that no money was spent.

will be worth $20 and the $55 will be worth -$15 (Remember, this call was sold. It will be worth $15 to the person who bought it.) for a net credit of $6 ($5 for the difference in calls plus the $1 credit from the initial trade).

This credit of $6 will be the result for any stock price at $55 or higher. What if the stock is between $50 and $55? If the stock closes at $52, the $50 call is worth $2, and the $55 expires worthless leaving the trader a credit of $3. So the worst that can happen is the arbitrageur makes $1, and the best is that he makes $6. Because there is a guaranteed profit with no cash outlay, it is an arbitrage. So don't worry; arbitrageurs will guarantee that the lower strike calls will always be worth more than the higher strikes. This is what prevents market makers from posting lower strike calls at a higher price.

For puts, the opposite relationship will occur for exactly the opposite reasons listed above. Put options will always be worth more with higher strikes with all other factors the same.

As a practice, you may want to pull up option quotes on your favorite stock and see if lower strike calls are always worth more than the higher strikes and the opposite for puts.

Insights into option pricing: Why can't I enter a buy-write for a net credit?

This leads to some interesting insights about option pricing. Theoretically, the optimal strike to own would be a $0 strike price (these do not exist, but let's pretend they do). What should it be worth? Well, the price of a call can <u>never</u> exceed the price of the stock, otherwise — you guessed it — arbitrage is possible. Say a $0 strike is trading for $51 with the stock at $50. Arbitrageurs will buy the stock for $50 and sell the $0 strike for $51, thus guaranteeing them a $1 profit.

We will be looking at a strategy later called a buy-write. These are basically covered call positions (where the investor buys the stock and simultaneously writes, or sells, the call) and must always be entered for a net debit. Now you know why. The call option can never be worth more than the stock. By the way, stock is, in fact, a $0 strike call with an unlimited time to expiration!

Pricing Relationship #2: At expiration, a call will be worth the difference between the stock price and the exercise price if it is in-the-money. If it is out-of-the-money, it will be worth zero.

All this says is that if a call expires with intrinsic value, then it must be worth the intrinsic value (the difference between the stock price and strike). If there is no intrinsic value, its price will be zero at expiration.

If the stock is trading at $57 at expiration, the $50 call must be worth exactly $7. (Actually, in the real world, bid-ask spreads will make it worth slightly less.) Why must an option always be worth the intrinsic value?

If it is not, an arbitrage opportunity is available. Say the following quotes exist:

> Stock trading at $57
> $50 call trading at $5

The arbitrageurs will realize the call is mispriced and perform the following trades simultaneously:

> Short the stock: $57
> Buy the call: -$5
> Net credit: $52

The arbitrageur will short the stock and buy the call. Now all he has to do is cover the short. How will he do this? Simple. He will use the option, which gives him the right to buy at $50, and exercise it immediately. After exercising, he will have received +$57 credit and spent $55 for a net gain of $2 — exactly the amount the call was mispriced. Because this is a guaranteed transaction with no cash outlay, it is an arbitrage.

Notice how the arbitrage process makes the prices fair for everybody else. The arbitrageurs will continue to sell the stock and buy the call until the arbitrage profits disappear. This process causes the stock price to fall (selling pressure) and the call price to rise (buying pressure). Once the arbitrage profits disappear, the assets will be fairly priced in relation to each other.

Pricing Relationship #3: **Prior to expiration, a call option must be worth <u>at least</u> the difference between the stock price and the present value of the exercise price.**

This one is a little complicated but still important for many strategies. This means that for any call option, the minimum price it must trade for is the cost of carry.

Why? Think about this. Say a stock is trading for $100 and your best friend comes to you and says, "I'm getting a huge bonus in one year, but I really want to buy 1,000 shares of this stock now. Would you be willing to buy it for me, and I will pay you the $100,000 in one year?"

If you see your friend as risk-free, you should charge them a minimum of $5,000 for your forgone interest. That is all this relationship is stating. Of course, if there is an element of risk, you should charge more than $5 per contract.

If your friend owes you $5 in one year, how much is it worth today? In other words, how much would you take today to settle the loan? To answer that, we need to take the present value of $5 owed in one year at the current risk-free interest rate, which we will assume is 5%.

Because your friend is borrowing $5 for one year, that amount is worth $5/1.05 = $4.76 today. Because your principal, the $100, is being returned in one year, the only thing you will be missing in one year is the $5 interest. So the call option should sell for *at least* $4.76. It could certainly trade for a higher amount if the market views the stock as risky — or if you see your friend's loan as a risk. The riskier the stock, the higher the price the call option will trade.

Assume now that your friend wants to buy the stock from you in a year but wants to pay only $80 even though it is currently trading for $100. Now, at the end of the year you will be out $5 in interest plus $20 in principal for a total of $25 loss in one year. How much is that worth today? Take the present value: $25/1.05 = $23.81 and that is how much the $80 call must <u>at least</u> trade for. Any price lower than this leads to arbitrage.

Mathematically, the formula for this relationship can also be written as:

Minimum call price = Stock price - Present value of the strike price.

Examples:

Let's use the above formula to calculate the minimum price of a call instead of the intuitive method used earlier. If the stock is trading at $100 and interest rates are 5%, how much should the one-year, $100 strike call trade for?

Stock price - present value of the strike price =
$100 - ($100/1.05) = $4.76

For the $80 strike call:
$100 - ($80/1.05) = $23.81

Why does this formula work? Remember, we said the call should trade for at least the cost of carry. If the stock is trading for $100 today, we can rewrite this relationship as:

$100 stock price today = $100 exercise price/1.05 + **$5 interest/1.05**

To isolate the interest amount or cost of carry (shown in bold), we can rewrite the formula as $100 stock price - $100 exercise price/1.05 = cost of carry, which is exactly the original formula above.

If the call option does not trade for this minimum amount, what will happen? This one is tricky to see, but an arbitrage opportunity does exist. Here is how the arbitrageurs will do it.

Say we see the following quotes:

Stock: $100
$100 call: $3
Time: 1-year option
Interest rate: 5%

We have already determined that this call option should be worth $4.76, yet we see it trading for $3.

Arbitrageurs will do the following trades simultaneously:

Short 1,000 shares of stock: +$100,000
Buy the call: -$3,000
Net credit: $97,000

Now, the arbitrageurs will owe 1,000 shares of stock at some time to close out the short stock position. By purchasing the call, they have guaranteed a maximum price for which they will be able to buy back the stock. They will leave the $97,000 in a money market (or T-bills) and receive $101,850 ($97,000 credit $*$ 1.05) in one year.

The arbitrageur now has two choices depending on where the stock is trading at the end of the year. If the stock is above $100, they will use the call option, pay $100, and keep the $1,850 (difference between the $101,850 received in interest and the $100,000 that must be paid to cover the short position). However, if the stock is trading below the strike price, traders will let the option expire worthless and buy the stock in the open market, thus increasing the profits further.

Insights into the Black-Scholes Option Pricing Model:

The Black-Scholes Option Pricing Model, in a simplified form, can be written as:

Stock price $*$ (Risk Factor) - (present value of the exercise price) $*$ (Risk Factor)

Without the "risk factors," you will see that the Black-Scholes formula is exactly the same as our formula above. Black and Scholes are simply saying that a call must be worth at least the cost of carry plus an additional amount if risk is present. The calculations of these risk factors won the Nobel Prize.

It is this third pricing relationship that is the foundation for the Black-Scholes Model and determines the true minimum price for which a call option must trade.

Pricing Relationship #4: The more time to expiration, the greater the price of calls and puts.

This relationship should be fairly obvious. The more time you have, the better your chances for the option going in-the-money and the more you should be willing to pay for it. The markets, knowing this, will bid the longer-term options higher. This is true for calls and puts.

Can we be assured this will happen in the real world?

Say we see the following quotes one day:

Three-month $50 strike call = $5
Six-month $50 strike call = $4
With all other factors being the same

Arbitrageurs will buy the six-month and sell the three-month for a net credit of $1. If the stock falls below $50, the arbitrageur will keep $1. What if the stock is higher than $50 when the three-month expires?

If the stock is trading at, say, $70 after three months, the person who owns the three-month call will exercise it and buy the stock from us for $50. That is acceptable, because we will exercise our call and buy the stock for $50. The reason we can exercise our call option early is because equity options are American-style, which means they can be exercised at any time. We still keep our $1 and have not lost a thing.

Here is a tricky question: What if these are European-style calls? European-style options can be exercised only at expiration, not before as with American-style calls.

If this is the case, and we are assigned on the three-month call, we would have to buy stock in the open market at $70 and sell it for $50. That is a loss of $20 to us although we still have our original $1 credit from the original transaction. It may appear as though we are faced with a $19 loss because we cannot exercise our call option.

So what happens now? Are we stuck? The answer is no, and here is why:

All we have to do is sell our call to close in the open market. Remember, under Pricing Relationship #2, the call must be worth at least the difference between the stock price and exercise price; therefore, our call will be trading for at least $20 ($20 intrinsic value + time premium). So by selling our call in the open market, we complete the arbitrage.

Pricing Relationship #5: For any two call options (or any two puts) on the same stock with the same expiration, the difference in their prices cannot exceed the difference in their strikes.

This relationship says that, for any two call options, the difference in their prices cannot be greater than the difference in their strikes. This is assuming that both options cover the same stock and have the same time to expiration. Say we see the following quotes one day:

> $50 Call = $10
> $55 Call = $4
> With all other factors constant

We know from the first pricing relationship that the $50 call should be worth more than the $55, and we see that it is. However, Relationship #5 says that there cannot be this much of a difference, because the difference in strikes is $5 yet the difference in price is $6. So the difference in prices has exceeded the difference in strikes.

How will the markets correct for this?

Arbitrageurs will buy the $55 call and sell the $50 for a net credit of $6.

> Buy $55   -$4
> Sell $50   +$10
> Net credit   +$6

If the stock collapses, the arbitrageur will keep $6. This will be true for any stock price below $50. If the stock closes between $50 and $55, say $52, the trader will lose $2 on the short $50 call but still keep the initial $6 for a net gain of $4.

The worst that can happen is for the stock to close at $55 or above $55, since the trader will be assigned on the $50 strike. We must then buy stock at $50 and sell for market price. Of course, we can always exercise our $55 call to buy the stock. No matter how high the stock moves, the worst we can be hurt is by the amount of the spread, in this case, $5. Because we made $6 initially, we will end up with a credit of $1.

The arbitrageur will make a minimum of $1 (for stock prices of $55 or higher) and a maximum of $6 (for stock prices of $50 or lower).

An easier way to understand Pricing Relationship #5 is to view the two option contracts as if they were money. Imagine you are bidding on a foreign currency and can buy any denomination of bills. If you bid $1 for 100 Yen, for example, you would never bid more than $2 for 200 Yen.

Likewise, options must obey a similar principle. If you think about it, there really is no difference in owning a $50 call versus a $55 call in terms of financial liability other than the fact that the person with the $50 strike can pay $50 for the stock, while the person with the $55 strike can pay $55. So the market will never give you more than the difference in strikes; this is true for calls and puts.

Insights into Option Prices:

Look at the following actual quotes on Microsoft call options.

Microsoft stock: $65.59

August Calls (20 days to expiration)

Strike	Price	Strike	Price
$30	$35.90	$65	$2.90
$35	$30.90	$70	$0.80
$40	$25.90	$75	$0.15
$45	$20.90	$80	$0.05
$50	$16.00	$85	$0.05
$55	$11.10	$90	$0.05
$60	$6.60	$95	$0.05

Look at the deep in-the-money calls such as the $30 through $45 strikes. What is the difference in prices? You can see they are exactly $5. If they ever exceeded $5, arbitrageurs would correct for it.

Now look closer to at-the-money such as the $60 through $70 strikes. The difference in option prices is less than the difference in strikes. This is because there is risk; compared to the deep-in-the-money options, these are not as certain to expire with intrinsic value, so the markets will not pay the full difference in strikes.

Finally, look for the far out-of-the-money quotes, such as the $80 through $95 strikes. There is no difference in the asking prices; the spreads between them have collapsed to zero.

Now you should have a basic understanding of why this relationship is true for any option quotes. If the option is deep enough in-the-money, the markets will view them as guaranteed to expire with intrinsic value, in which case the difference in strikes will equal the difference in price. Once risk is introduced, the spread will be reduced to something less than the difference in strikes.

Options clearly follow a set of rules governing their prices and are not arbitrarily posted by market makers. These are not rules set by exchanges or any person. Rather, they are economic and financial principles at work that ensure option prices are fair. Even without theoretical models, we can be reasonably certain about boundaries where options must fall. The Black-Scholes Model fine-tunes these boundaries.

Questions:

1) Is there an arbitrage opportunity in the following quotes? How would you perform it? (Hint: Determine which one, using the above principles, is underpriced. Buy the under priced option, sell the overpriced one, and then check to see if it guarantees a profit for all stock prices.)

    $60 put = $12
    $70 put = $10

2) The underlying stock is trading for $100 with the $110 put trading for $9. Is there an arbitrage opportunity? How would you perform it?

3) Which option should be worth more, the January $50 call or the June $50 call? Why?

4) Which option should be worth more, the June $75 call or the June $80 call? Why?

5) One day you see the following quotes: May $40 call for $7 and a May $45 call for $1.50. Is there an arbitrage opportunity? How would you perform it?

Chapter 11: Deltas and Gammas

Everything we have covered up to this point has been centered around option basics: from basic terminology, to placing trades, and even basic option pricing relationships. These sections were all necessary to understand the ultimate goal of learning option strategies. In this chapter, we will look at two very important terms related to option pricing: **delta** and **gamma**. A basic understanding of these terms will greatly help in your understanding of strategies, which options to buy or sell, and even help to explain why so many people lose money with options.

In Chapter 9, we learned about the five factors in the Black-Scholes Model: stock price, exercise price, risk-free interest rate, volatility, and time to expiration. There we also showed how each of these factors affects an option's price in a relative sense — either up or down. However, to understand option strategies better, it would certainly be nice to know *exactly* how an option's price will change, rather than just knowing if it will increase or decrease. In other words, how sensitive is an option's price to these factors?

To answer this question, option sensitivities have been developed, which are all represented by a Greek letter and are, consequently, known as option "Greeks." How an option's price will change from a small move in the underlying stock is represented by the Greek letter *delta* (Δ). In a similar concept, a change in interest rates will change an option's price by *rho* (P). Changes in volatility are represented by vega (also represented by *kappa* (K) because vega is not a Greek letter). And an option's sensitivity to time is represented by *theta* (θ). These factors show how an option's price will respond to small changes in the corresponding factors. There is one more Greek, *gamma* (Γ), but it does not measure the change in an option's price; rather, it measures the sensitivity of delta and is consequently sometimes called the "delta of the delta."

Although all of the Greeks are important to know, it is the understanding of delta and gamma that is probably the most important and, at the same time, the least understood. We will be focusing on these two very important option terms in the next two chapters. Investors with a working knowledge of delta and gamma will have a great advantage over those who do not.

If you have a basic understanding of options but still continue to lose money, this is most likely the area that is causing it.

To demonstrate why so many people lose with options, consider the following example: You are bullish on a stock and want to use options. What do you do? If you are like the vast majority of option investors, you would buy calls. After all, calls are bullish and puts are bearish, so if you are bullish, you certainly want to use calls. Although this sounds logical, it is a trap. It's the trap that causes more option losses than any other error.

We never even got to the point of *which* option to buy, and we have already made a critical mistake. There was no discussion as to whether we should buy a 1-month, 3-month, 6-month, or even a LEAPS option. There was no discussion as to which strike. We just invested a lot of money and sent a wounded horse to the starting gate.

Two Components to an Option's Price

The most common error in option trading comes from not understanding that options have two components to their value: direction and speed.

Stocks, compared with options, are much easier to trade. All you have to do is decide whether the stock is going up or down. You need to determine only the direction. Of course, anyone who has ever invested in stocks knows that this, in itself, can be incredibly difficult.

When trading options, you not only need to guess the correct direction as with stocks, but you also need to guess the speed at which it will move. It is this second component, speed, that makes investing with options so tricky. Delta measures direction and gamma measures speed. Although there are specific numerical measures of delta and gamma, we are going to consider them in a much simpler, conceptual format now, and then go into more detail further on.

Delta, as mentioned, measures direction. A <u>long call</u> position has positive delta; in other words, the value of the call will go up (positive) as the price of the underlying stock rises. Put options have negative delta; their value will go down (negative) as the price of the stock rises. Of course, the opposite is also true. If the underlying stock goes down, calls will lose and puts will gain in value.

Of course, a short position will have the opposite effects. A short call will have negative delta, meaning our position will lose value as the stock rises. Similarly, a put will have positive delta, meaning that the position will gain in value as the stock rises.

It should be easy to see now that there are <u>two ways</u> to obtain positive deltas: long calls and short puts. If you are bullish on a stock, long calls or short puts can accomplish the same objective.

KEY CONCEPT: If you are bullish on a stock, you want positive delta for your option position. If you're bearish, you want negative delta.

The Gamma of an Option

Gamma measures the speed component of an option. In a conceptual sense, gamma can be measured, as can any object with speed, with time. So time premium is a way to determine gamma. The higher the <u>time premium</u> of an option, the higher the gamma. Because the time premium is the portion of the option's price that erodes with the passage of time, it is this portion that is exposed to slow or no movement in the underlying stock.

Example: XYZ stock is trading for $50
XYZ $50 call is trading for $5
XYZ $30 call is trading for $21

Here, the $50 call is all time premium. Therefore, it will have a higher gamma. The $30 call has only $1 time premium so, compared to the $50 call, its gamma component will be much lower. Gamma can also be thought of as a risk measure. We can say the $50 call is riskier in terms of speed than the $30 call, because if the stock sits still, the $30 call can lose only $1 (3.23% of value), but the $50 call can lose the entire $5 (100% of value).

Another way to look at the risk factor is in terms of breakeven points. The $30 call will need the stock to trade at $51 by expiration to break even. Why? If the stock is $51, the call will be worth exactly $21, the price paid for the option. However, the $50 call must have the stock trading at $55 to break even. So again the $30 call, with respect to speed, is less risky. In other words, the $30 call does not need as much movement in the stock to break even as compared to the $50 call.

Although it may seem counterintuitive, <u>long</u> calls and <u>long</u> puts both have positive gamma. This is because you need speed in the underlying stock if you have a long option position; the underlying stock must move to make up for the time premium you paid.

KEY CONCEPT: If you expect a quick movement in the underlying stock, your option position should have positive gamma. If you expect the stock to move slowly or sit flat, your option position should have zero gamma or even negative gamma.

Example: A trader is bullish on XYZ trading at $100 with the following quotes available:

1-month $105 call is trading at $7
1-month $95 put is trading at $5

We said at the beginning of this chapter that most investors would be inclined to buy calls because they are bullish. Let's see what happens when we assume this trader is like most others and buys the call.

The trader is long the $100 call at $7. At expiration, assume the stock is trading for $110. The question is, was the trader correct in the bullish assumption? There is no doubt that the trader was correct. The stock is up a whopping 10% in a month (that may not seem like a lot but that is an annualized rate of over 200% — at that rate, you would more than triple your money in a year). Correct forecasts such as these are what traders dream about. So just how much of a killing did this trader make on the call?

The $105 call will be trading for $5 at expiration, exactly the intrinsic amount. The trader paid $7 and sold for $5, yet he was correct in the bullish assumption. That is a 28% loss on the investment, when he was actually correct about the direction! Does this sound familiar?

Now that we know about deltas and gammas, let's see if we can correct the mistake. This trader just made the classic mistake of trading options on only delta — the direction of the stock. Let's polish up the trade a bit by including gamma.

We know that the trader is bullish, so he should have positive delta — either long calls or short puts. But now let's say that we ask the trader, "How quickly do you think the stock will move?" He replies, "I think it will move up but very slowly."

Now we are in position to set up a winning trade, assuming the trader's assumptions are correct.

We now know he wants positive delta (because he is bullish), but he also needs negative gamma (because he believes it will move slowly). The following chart should help us determine what we should do:

	Delta	**Gamma**
Long Calls	+	+
Long Puts	−	+

How can we get positive delta and negative gamma? It may appear that we are stuck, since a positive delta appears to be matched with a positive gamma. Remember though, that these are long positions; short positions will give the opposite answers.

We can short the puts, which will give us the opposite signs as listed in the table above. Long puts have negative delta and positive gamma, so a short position will have positive delta and negative gamma — exactly what the trader needs!

If he had shorted the $95 puts instead of buying the $105 call, he would receive $5 and keep the entire $5 instead of losing $2 as he did with the calls. What if the trader does not want the risk associated with a short put or does not have the option approval level to be short? We could enter a credit spread that would lessen the risk, which we will discuss once we get into strategies. Another alternative is to understand that the trader desires negative gamma, but a gamma close to zero would also work. Remember, time premium is synonymous with gamma, so to get a gamma of zero (or close to it) we could also look at deep-in-the-money calls, because they have very little time premium associated with them.

With XYZ at $100, the $80 call may be trading in the neighborhood of $20.50 ($20 intrinsic + a small amount of time premium). If he buys the $80 call he will spend $20.50, and with the stock closing at $110 at expiration, he will be able to sell the option for $30, which is a profit of $9.50 or 46%. This is certainly better than the 28% loss taken when he traded on only direction alone.

Of course, this does not come for free. The $80 call stands to lose more money if the trader is wrong about the direction. Again, good option trading is not about finding the best trade; rather, it is about finding the proper balance of risk and reward. However, if you do not understand delta and gamma, it is difficult to properly determine the risk and reward.

Investors who do not understand gamma often make a second and more fatal mistake. They may be somewhat successful in guessing the direction of the stock, but after many losing trades caused by not considering gamma, they often try to reduce their risk by spending less money. This means they buy options further out-of-the-money — exactly the opposite of what they should be doing.

There are two components you need to determine when dealing in options: direction and speed. To make a profitable trade, a position with positive gamma <u>must move up</u>; a position with negative gamma does not have to move up, but it <u>cannot move down</u>. These are two very different situations. If you do not consider both, you will almost certainly set yourself up for a losing trade.

Now that we have covered the basics of delta and gamma, we are going to explore how delta is determined, other uses for delta, and how changes in other variables such as stock price, time, and volatility will change delta.

Delta and Gamma in Detail

The concepts of delta and gamma are of utmost importance for the options trader. In the previous chapter we learned that delta measures direction, and gamma measures speed of the option. But we explained the concepts without the use of numbers.

In this section, we will broaden the concept of delta and zero-in on an exact definition you can use and understand.

Delta is a mathematical relationship between the option and the underlying stock. It expresses the dollar amount the option will increase for a very small move in the underlying stock. How much is a small move? Technically we mean very small (as in infinitesimal), but it will probably be easier to understand if you think of a $1 move in the underlying stock.

For example, say an option is trading for $5 and has a delta of 1/2. If the stock were to move up $1 to $51 rather quickly, we would expect the price of the option to move up $0.50 from $5 to $5.50. In other words, the stock gained one point, but the option gained only $0.50. If that same option had a delta of 1/4 instead, then the price of the option would have moved to $5.25 — only 1/4 the move of the stock.

Delta will always be a number between 0 and 1 for calls (0 and -1 for puts). There are some exceptions to this, but they are usually minor and not too important for trading purposes. Delta constantly changes primarily from moves in stock price, time or volatility.

We now want to find out why the option does not move point-for-point with the stock. This may sound trivial, but it will change the way you see and understand options and strategies.

It will take some basic math, but we will make it as easy as possible. We will start first with a simple analogy to explain why deltas exist.

Why Does Delta Exist?

This often confuses new options traders. Often they will purchase an out-of-the-money call option that sits relatively flat in price — even though the underlying stock is moving up. They wonder how that can be, because call options are supposed to go up in value as the stock moves up. If you understand the following analogy, you will understand why the market will not price your option point-for-point with the underlying stock unless the option is very deep-in-the-money or in-the-money with little time remaining.

Analogy: Promotional Cell Phone Coupon

Assume you are holding a promotional coupon that allows you to purchase a particular cell phone for $100. The phone actually sells for $120. Also assume that this coupon is marketable; that is, it can be bought and sold freely by any number of buyers and sellers.

Notice that this is similar to a call option, because it gives the buyer the right to buy the asset for a fixed price.

If these assumptions are true, the coupon should be trading for $20. This is because someone could buy the coupon for $20 and use it to buy the phone for $100. The total purchase price would be $120, which is the market price of the phone. In this case, there is no net advantage to owning the coupon. The markets will always make sure there is no net advantage to owning one asset over another, otherwise arbitrageurs will correct for it.

Let's look at two different scenarios and see how the coupon will react:

Scenario I

It is announced to the market that the price of the phone <u>will increase</u> to $130. What will happen to the price of the coupon? For the same reasons as above, it will immediately move to $30. A consumer could buy the coupon for $30 and use it to pay $100 for the phone, thus paying the $130 market price.

Notice that the phone jumped by $10 (from $120 to $130) and so did the coupon (from $20 to $30). We could say the delta of the coupon is one. In other words, the coupon appreciates dollar-for-dollar with moves in the underlying asset, in this case, the phone. This will be true for any price appreciation or depreciation in the phone (assuming the phone price does not drop below $100, because the coupon cannot have negative value).

Scenario II

Instead of automatically increasing the price of the phone, let's say the phone company executives are meeting today to decide if the phone price should be raised from $120 to $130. After the meeting, these executives are in a deadlock and have decided to break the tie by flipping a coin: If it's heads they raise the price; tails, they do not. It is announced to the market that the price of the phone may increase to $130 with a 50%-50% chance; otherwise, the price will stay the same.

Now comes the tricky part. What happens to the price of the coupon?

Think about this: The price of the coupon will either move to $30 or stay at $20 with a 50-50 chance. If the market does not bid up the price of the coupon, there is an inherent advantage for speculators; they will bid up the coupon price hoping the decision is to raise the price of the phone. The speculators reason that if faced with this same situation multiple times, half of the time they would make $10 (when phone is raised to $130 and coupon jumps from $20 to $30) and half the time they will not make anything (when phone price stays the same and coupon stays priced at $20). So on average, if given this opportunity multiple times, investors will make $5; they make $10 half the time and make nothing half the time.

Mathematically, this can be shown as follows:

$$(1/2) * (+10) = \$5$$
$$(1/2) * (\ 0\ )\ = \underline{\$0}$$
$$\text{Net gain:}\qquad +\$5$$

Mathematically, this is called the expected value and is key to understanding delta. The expected value is nothing more than the sum of the probabilities multiplied by the outcomes.

So what should speculators do? Speculators will buy the coupon and bid up its price. They will stop bidding when the price hits $25 — the point at which there is no net advantage. For any price less than $25, speculators will continue to bid for the coupon, thus driving up its price. For example, if the market bids the coupon price to only $24, speculators now have a $1 net advantage.

The expected value is:

$$(1/2) * (+6) = +\$3$$
$$(1/2) * (-4) = \underline{-\$2}$$
Net gain: +$1

With the coupon priced at $24, speculators are putting $4 at risk to make $10. In other words, they pay $24 for the coupon and will make $30 ($6 gain) with a 50-50 chance. If the executives decide to not raise the phone price, the coupon will drop from $24 to $20, creating the $4 loss to the speculator. If this scenario were presented numerous times, half of the time speculators will win for a net gain of $6, and half the time they lose for a net loss of $4.

If they were allowed to do this many times, they would expect to win, on average, $1 per time. They continue to bid the price of the coupon to $25, so there is not net advantage.

When priced at $25, the expected value of the coupon is:

$$(1/2) * (+5) = +\$2.5$$
$$(1/2) * (-\$5) = \underline{-\$2.5}$$
Net gain: $0

When the price rises to $25, the buying pressure stops.

What happens if the markets immediately price the coupon to $30 as they did in Scenario I? For similar reasons, if the market prices the coupon at $30, again there is an inherent advantage for speculators; they will sell it, because it is theoretically overpriced.

The expected value will be:
$$(1/2) * (+10) = +\$5$$
$$(1/2) * (0) \quad = \quad \underline{\$0}$$
$$\text{Net gain:} \qquad +\$5$$

Half the time speculators will make $10 by selling the coupon at $30 and buying it back for $20 when the phone price is not raised; otherwise, they make nothing (sell the coupon for $30 and buy it back for $30). Again, there is a net advantage to being short, so speculators will compete for this money. For the same reasons as above, they will continue selling the coupon until the price is $25.

When the price falls to $25, the selling pressure stops.

Understanding Delta

A simple definition of delta should help you to understand why the markets will not price your option with dollar-for-dollar moves in the underlying stock: *Delta is the probability that the option will have intrinsic value at expiration.*

In the above example, the executives were faced with a 50-50 chance of raising the price of the phone. In other words, there is a 1/2 probability that the phone price would increase $10. Because of this, the markets increased the price of the coupon by only $1/2 * \$10 = \$5$.

If an option has a delta of 1/2, then the markets will compensate you for only 1/2 of the move in the underlying — otherwise there will be a net advantage for speculators to buy or sell.

Once the option is deep-in-the-money or in-the-money with little time remaining, the market will increase the price of your option dollar-for-dollar with moves in the underlying. This is because the market is effectively saying that the option will expire with intrinsic value. This is exactly what happened in scenario I with the cell phone coupon. There it was announced that the price would be increased; in other words, it was 100% guaranteed to happen. When the market heard this news, they priced the coupon dollar-for-dollar.

New Uses for Delta

You may hear that delta is of little concern for the average investor and is used only as a theoretical hedging value for floor traders. Although it is true that it can be used in this sense, there are also numerous insights that are practical, if not necessary, for retail investors.

First, because we know delta is the probability that the option will have intrinsic value at expiration, it will shed some light on your option picks. Often, new traders are attracted to short-term, out-of-the-money options because they are cheap. If it has a long way to get to the strike and little time to do it, what kind of probability do you think the markets are assigning to it?

The delta on short-term, out-of-the-money options are usually in the neighborhood of 0 to 20%. Now you know why they do not appreciate dollar-for-dollar with moves in the underlying. Usually, these options are lucky to see a few cents appreciation in them, which are often eaten away by bid-ask spreads.

If you are not having much success with your option trades despite getting the direction of the stock right, try using those with higher deltas.

What Are the Chances My Stock Will Be Called Away?

Here is a very practical use for delta. Many times investors are in a covered call position (long stock and short call) and want to know what the chances are that they will have their stock called away. Most brokers will tell you there is no way. This is completely false; the answer is the delta. If you are long stock and short a call with a delta of 0.70, at this time, the markets are telling you there is a 70% chance you will lose your stock.

Keep in mind that we said "at this time," there is a 70% chance. Obviously as information changes, so will the delta.

The Delta of a Put Option

Once you understand that delta is simply the probability that an option will expire with intrinsic value, the delta of a put option is easier to figure out. This is because for any pair of same-strike call and put, one must expire with intrinsic value. Because the area under a normal bell curve is equal to one, the call and put deltas must sum to one. If a $100 call has a delta of 0.72, the $100 put must have a delta of 0.28. If there is a 72% chance the call will finish with intrinsic value, there is a 28% chance that it will not. In this case, the put will have intrinsic value. Technically, the put delta would be -0.28 to show that the put will rise with a fall in the underlying stock and vice versa. However, it is impossible to have a negative probability. So for this reason, the minus sign on the put can be ignored, and the call and put delta will total one.

Why Deltas Change

To understand option strategies, it is necessary to not only understand the concept of delta, but also how delta will change when other factors change. Understanding how this works will enable you to specifically tailor risk-reward profiles based on your expectations.

Any of the five factors in the Black-Scholes Model will affect delta if they are changed. However, three are primarily of concern: stock price, time, and volatility in the underlying stock. Let's find out how these factors affect delta and why.

We could present this by using a lot of math, but the important concepts can be grasped easily by a simple example.

Sports and Deltas

The concept of delta can easily be shown in any sport where a time clock is used. We are going to use the game of basketball as an analogy for understanding delta in the options markets. It will probably be easy to follow the reasoning in this example. Once you do, the same reasoning can be applied to the options markets.

Let's assume you are an odds maker for an upcoming basketball game: the Miami Heat versus the Orlando Magic. You do your analysis and decide that the Heat has a 60% chance of winning before the game has even started.

The game is winding down, there are 10 minutes remaining, and the score is Miami: 70, Orlando: 72. As the odds maker, should you change your odds at this point? Probably not, because the score is too close and there is too much time remaining to be sure.

Example 1: Let's say that, instead, the score is Miami: 80, Orlando: 70, with five minutes remaining. Now, because your team is a bit further ahead, although not unbeatable, you will probably decide to increase your odds, right? You may, for example, think Miami has a 70% chance of winning. Whether you think it should be raised 70% or 90% is insignificant for our purposes. As long as you recognize that the probability increased, you have the idea.

Your job as the odds maker is to decide which team will win. Well, that is exactly what the market does with options. The market tries to determine which options will win — which ones will have intrinsic value at expiration. So as your option goes deeper-in-the-money, the odds of it expiring with intrinsic value will increase, which means the deltas will increase.

As the underlying stock rises, call deltas increase and put deltas decrease.

Now back to the basketball game.

Example 2: Let's assume that the score is Miami: 88, Orlando: 80. If we still had five minutes on the clock, this would be a close one to call. But instead, let's drop the time to only 30 seconds remaining. Now you would almost certainly boost your odds to nearly 100%, because it is almost a sure thing the Heat will win.

Notice the difference with the above examples. In the first example, a ten-point difference in scores boosted the odds from 60% to 70%. However, in the second example, an 8-point difference with little time boosted us to nearly 100%. Remember, you are trying to determine which team will win. In this case, you (the odds maker) see no possibility for the Magic to win at this point, so you boost the odds for the Heat to nearly 100%.

The markets will do the same for options. *As time decreases, options with intrinsic value will have delta increase. Out-of-the-money options will have delta decrease.*

In other words, the options that are "winners" (have intrinsic value) are becoming more likely to stay that way as time decreases. If your team is winning, then less and less time on the clock means you are increasingly more certain of winning and will raise your odds.

Example 3: Let's assume that the score is Miami: 88, Orlando: 80 with 30 seconds on the clock as in the second example. But this time, some key players for the Heat suddenly get removed from the game. Because of this, the Heat's scoring ability has now been reduced. So as the odds maker, instead of increasing the Heat from 70% to 100%, you would either not increase your percentages as much or possibly even decrease them.

A losing team is helped when key players enter the game (or when key players are removed from the winning team). Note that we can get the same effect by changing time on the clock. If your team is winning and the clock is reduced because of a penalty, you would increase your odds (delta will increase). Likewise, if your team is winning and time is added to the clock, you may reduce your odds.

This is exactly what happens when volatility or time is increased in the underlying stock. A losing option (out-of-the-money) is helped by increased volatility or time; it now has more "scoring ability." Because it has a better chance to become a winning option, the deltas will increase. Similarly, increasing volatility or time hurts an in-the-money option; it now is more likely to end up out-of-the-money.

As volatility increases, out-of-the-money options will increase deltas, and in-the-money options will lose deltas. An easy way to remember time and volatility concepts is that they are synonymous.

As time or volatility increases, all options become more at-the-money.

To be a good trader, it is not necessary to know the actual number for delta as much as it is to know the relationships between delta, stock price, time, and volatility.

Examples: Let's work through some examples to be sure you understand it. Remember that we are assuming all other factors are staying the same.

1) **The stock is at $50. Which option has a higher delta: a 1-month $60 call or a 6-month $60 call? Why?**

Remember, the market is trying to assign odds as to which option will be a winner or in-the-money. Because both are out-of-the-money, you would have to assign a higher probability to the 6-month call. It is much more likely to be a winner relative to the 1-month call. The 6-month call will have the higher delta. If the underlying stock moves up $1, the 6-month call will appreciate more relative to the 1-month call.

2) **The stock is at $100. Which has a higher delta: a one-month $90 call or a three-month $90 call? Why?**

Both of these options are currently winners because they are in-the-money. But the three-month option is more likely to become a loser relative to the one-month option, so the one-month option will have a higher delta. Remember, once you are winning, you want the time clock to go to zero! If the underlying stock moves up $1, the one-month option will appreciate more than the three-month option.

3) **The stock is $50, and a one-month $55 call has a delta of 0.45. Suddenly, there is increased volatility in the stock. Does delta increase or decrease?**

The option is currently "losing" because it is out-of-the-money. But with the added volatility, it is much more likely to become a winner. Delta will increase.

4) A stock is trading at $75. What is the delta of a $75 strike call?

Because this option is at-the-money, it is riding the fence between being in-the-money or out-of-the-money. In other words, you are about 50% sure that it will have intrinsic value and the delta will be very close to 1/2. Technically, the delta will be a little higher than 1/2 for calls because of the continuous compounding assumption in the Black-Scholes Option Pricing Model. But for most trading purposes, an at-the-money option has a delta of 1/2.

5) You want to use a call option as a substitute for stock. Would you look at short- or long-term? In-the-money or out-of-the-money?

If you really want the option to behave virtually like stock, you should look at short-term, deep-in-the-money calls. Because these are in-the-money with little time, there is close to a 100% chance they will expire with intrinsic value. The market will have to increase the option dollar-for-dollar with moves in the underlying stock. Because the markets will price short-term, deep-in-the-money options point-for-point with the underlying stock, these options make great substitutes for stock.

If you continue to work with the concept of delta, it will help you greatly with your option trades, whether you're a beginner or an advanced options trader. It will shed new light on the risks involved with short-term out-of-the-money options. It will explain why longer-term options are more desirable than shorter-term if you are looking at out-of-the-money options. You will start to understand strategies in new ways and more closely match your positions to your opinion on the market. You will become a more informed and accomplished options trader, which can only mean better trades.

Questions:

1) Which option will have a higher delta: a shorter-term at-the-money or a longer-term at-the-money? Why?

2) The stock is $108 and a $100 call has a delta of 0.75. Volatility in the underlying stock is increasing. Do you expect delta to rise or fall?

3) A $75 call has a delta of 0.30. What would you estimate to be the delta of the $75 put? Why?

4) You are holding an in-the-money $100 call with a delta of 0.60 and one month remaining. 20 days later, the stock is the same price. Do you expect your delta to have increased or decreased? Why?

5) A stock is trading for $80. Which do you expect to have a higher delta: the one-month $80 call or the three-month $80 call? Why?

6) What is the approximate delta of an at-the-money option? Why?

7) You think a stock will fall slowly over the next month, and you want to create an option position to take advantage of your outlook. You should have _____ (positive, negative) delta and _____ (positive, negative) gamma.

8) You are holding a $75 put option with a delta of 0.70 and gamma of 0.05. If the stock immediately falls one point, what do you expect the new delta to be (assuming all else remains the same)?

Chapter 12: Early Exercise with Options

We discussed the differences in American and European options in Chapter 2. There we found that American-style options allow the buyer to exercise early, and the European counterpart requires the buyer to wait until option expiration before exercising the option. On the surface, it certainly seems like there is a distinct advantage in owning an American-style option rather than a European-style option.

The question is this: Is it ever advantageous to exercise an American-style call option early, that is, prior to expiration?

The answer will be very obvious to you once we go through some examples but, surprisingly, this is one of the most common sources of option errors.

If you trade options, be sure you understand this chapter, because it will keep you from making one of the most costly and common mistakes in option trading.

Exercising Early

Let's start with the answer and then we will explain why it is true:

It is never optimal to exercise a call option early except to capture a dividend.

There are many ways to show that this is true. Unfortunately, most of the methods involve fairly complicated comparisons between two different portfolios of stocks and options, and then further comparing them after early exercise to see if one portfolio has an advantage over the other. These methods are not particularly useful for most investors, because the math and logic can be quite complicated. Nonetheless, we will show you one of these methods anyway just to provide further proof that you should almost never exercise early. Here's a simple story to better explain why you should-n't ever exercise a call option early (except to capture a dividend).

This is a true story and actually happened while I was working at the trade support desk of a large brokerage firm. The trade support desk handles customer trade disputes. If a customer thinks they received a bad fill price, the wrong number of shares, the wrong stock, or any number of possible mistakes that happen on trading floors, the trade support desk reviews it and makes a decision to side with either the customer or the firm. On this particular dispute, the customer claimed that the wrong symbol had been entered, and he was now the owner of a stock he had never heard of. We listened to the recorded phone call to hear what was said during the con-versation with the broker and, sure enough, the customer was right — the broker transposed two letters, which coincidentally happened to be another stock's trading symbol.

We called the customer later that day to inform him of the news. We said we would fix the trade and put the correct shares in the account at the original price (if it was more favorable). As for the unwanted stock, it was trading up about a half point or so from his purchase price of $75, so he could keep the stock and sell it for a slight profit. If so, we would waive the commissions for the buy and the sell. If he did not like that choice, we could remove the stock from the account as if the trade had never happened.

The customer then asked, "What exactly does this company do? Do you mind if I research it for five days and get back to you?"

It should be apparent that the answer is no. If you are not sure why, think about this. If the stock rises, the customer will call back and say he definitely wants to keep it. However, if it falls, he will call back to have the trade backed out. This puts him in a risk-free situation because he can potentially make a lot of money and has no money at stake.

But let's add a little twist to the story. Assume we told the cus-tomer he could have five days to research the stock and get back to us. Let's say after one day of research he thinks this stock will be bigger than Microsoft and Intel combined and realizes he must have the shares. The question is: Should the customer call back the next day to buy the shares? Or should he wait until the end of the fifth day when his time limit is up?

Hopefully you realize the answer — he should wait until the end of the fifth day. There are two reasons. First, the brokerage firm is holding the stock, so they are the ones at risk. If the stock falls, the customer can always back out of the trade. If the stock continues higher, the customer is locked into the $75 price, so there is nothing to gain by purchasing the shares early. In fact, the shares could be purchased after the first day, and they could collapse sometime later. It is clearly better for the customer to let the brokerage firm assume the risk for as long as possible.

The second reason the customer should wait concerns the time value of money. Because the customer is locked in to the purchase price, he pays the same amount whether he pays today or in five days. As with any payment, you should pay as late as possible to hold on to the money and earn interest.

The answer is clear; you wait as long as possible and call your broker on the fifth day to purchase the stock.

The situation we just described is a call option — for no money. Think about your rights with a call option. You have the right, but not the obligation, to buy over a fixed period of time, and that is exactly what the customer was asking for. However, he was not paying for the privilege, which is exactly why we said no.

Assuming the customer was given five days to decide, his answer is still the same; he waits as long as possible before committing to the purchase. Any fee paid for this right should only emphasize the need for waiting as long as possible.

This answer to that example may seem blatantly obvious. But don't laugh; this was a real situation, and many advanced option traders make this same mistake every single day. The situation we just described above is a call option and many mistaken traders elect to call the shares away early.

Insights into Option Pricing:

If your broker did decide to take a fee for the arrangement, is there a price he must accept? Yes, and that price is $75. At $75, you have effectively removed all risk to the brokerage firm, so they would have no reason to not accept this bid. In fact, you saw in Chapter 10 that the highest price a call can trade is the price of the stock, and now you know why. This is also why buy-writes (buying stock and selling calls simultaneously) must be entered as a net debit — because the price of the option can never exceed the price of the stock.

Why Traders Feel They Must Exercise Early

Traders who exercise early make the mistake of not realizing exactly what is happening in a call option agreement. Often, this is how they view the situation. Say the trader purchases a $100 call option for $15. The stock is now $130 with more than a month left. The option is trading for $32. The trader often feels he does not want to "lose" the value of the call option. So before the market gets the best of him, he decides to exercise it and walk away the winner. This is wrong for the same reasons as the customer at the trade support desk! Remember that the trader is <u>locked in to the price</u> of $100. The stock can be trading for $200 and have split twice by expiration, and the stock price is still $100 to the owner of the call option. If he exercises early, however, the stock could completely collapse, so he would have been better off not exercising. Also, by not exercising early, the $100 stays in the money market longer to earn more interest.

So what should you do if you feel your option is really high in value and you want to get out before it falls? Sell the call to close. In this example, the trader exercised early and received stock worth $130 but paid only $100 for a gain of $30. After subtracting the $15 cost of the call, his net gain is $15. But if he sold the call to close in the market, he would receive $32 for a net gain of $17 after subtracting out the $15 cost. In other words, if you exercise your call option, you will receive only the stock in exchange for the strike price; you receive only the intrinsic amount. If you sell the call to close, you will collect the <u>intrinsic</u> amount <u>plus the time premium</u>. You will always be better off selling the call to close if you do not want to continue holding the call option.

The last thing you want to hold is the stock; that is the reason you buy the call option in the first place. We found another way to think about this in Chapter 7. There it was found that the owner of a call option has implicitly purchased a put option from another investor. The cost of the put is passed on to the owner of the call and, in exchange, the long call profit and loss diagram flattens out at the strike price; there is no additional risk below this point. Once you exercise your call, you have just released your put option and have increased your risk by the amount of the strike price.

Trading Example:

One day a trader called to complain after he viewed his balances on the computer that morning. His net worth on the account was $120,000 and had been $124,000 the day before yet all of his stocks were trading at about the same price or a little higher.

After searching through the transactions, it was discovered that he exercised 10 calls the day before. The option was 20 points in-the-money, but the call was selling for $24 the previous day. When he exercised, the four points of time premium were lost, and that is what happened to his $4,000. If he had sold the contracts to close the previous day, his balance would have still been $124,000. If the investor had just said "sell" instead of "exercise" he would have saved $4,000.

Now you might think that had this trader not exercised his call, he would not be holding the stock, which offers certain benefits. If for some reason the investor wanted to own the stock, he still should have sold the calls to close and then purchased the stock in the open market. This would put the shares in the account, just as the early exercise did, but he would also have an additional $4,000. No matter how you look at it, you are better off selling the call to close if there is time premium to be captured.

Remember, when you exercise a call, you receive only the difference between the stock price and the exercise price; if you sell the call to close, you receive that same amount <u>plus</u> some time premium.

Market Penalty

One way to reason that exercising early is not optimal is that the market will "charge" you a penalty for doing so. Say the stock is $50, and the $45 call is trading for $6 ($5 intrinsic + $1 time). If you exercise early to get the stock, you effectively pay $51 for a stock trading for $50. This is because you give up the call option worth $6 in exchange for purchasing the stock for $45. This $1 "penalty" is the time premium you gave up on the option. Remember, you either exercise an option or you sell it — not both. The markets will never reward you for exercising early.

Covered Calls Cannot Get Around It

If you are still not sure why you should not exercise a call option early, think about this scenario. Say a trader has a covered call position and bought stock at $100 per share and sold a 1-year $100 call for $25. If they get assigned, they will lose the stock but make a 33% profit (effectively buying the stock for $75 and selling it for $100 a year later.) An investor who enters this trade considers the 33% profit a good deal, based on the risk of the stock, for one year's time.

What is the best thing that could happen to this trader? He should check his account the next day and see the stock called away. Now he has received 33% in a day instead of a year, which is a much better return (too big to print!). Well, if it is a better deal for the short call position to be called early, it must be an equally bad deal for the long call. This is because options are a zero-sum game, and one trader's gains are exactly the other trader's losses.

If you like to write covered calls, do not expect to be assigned early. Because the long call has control, that investor will do what is best for him — he will wait until the very end of the year to exercise the call and receive the stock.

Mathematical Models

It was mentioned at the beginning that we would look at a mathematical model in addition to the simplistic proofs covered so far. Here, we will look at one of many mathematical proofs that show it is never optimal to exercise a call option early on a non-dividend-paying stock.

Consider two portfolios: A and B.

Portfolio A: Present value of exercise price in cash + call option

Portfolio B: Stock

At expiration, the cash in Portfolio A will grow to be worth E, the exercise price. Portfolio A will use this cash to secure the exercise price. If the stock is <u>above</u> the strike price and Portfolio A exercises the call, the investor will receive the value of the stock price minus the exercise price (S - E) plus E from the cash, which can be written: S - E + E = S. So if Portfolio A exercises <u>at expiration,</u> Portfolio A is worth the stock price — exactly as Portfolio B, which contains only the stock.

However, if the stock price falls <u>below</u> the exercise price, E, at expiration, then Portfolio A will lose the value of the call and be worth only E, the cash. Portfolio B will be worth less than Portfolio A because the stock price is below the exercise price.

Therefore, Portfolio A is always worth <u>at least</u> as much as Portfolio B.

But if Portfolio A exercises *early*, the portfolio is worth S minus E (from the exercise) minus the present value of E, which must be less than S. Why? Recall that the present value of E must be less than E. If you start with S and subtract E and then add back a number smaller than E (because it is the present value), you must end up with a number smaller than S. This is the only time Portfolio B can dominate Portfolio A, so A should not exercise early.

I mentioned before that I do not like these proofs, and now you can probably see why. They make sense for those who understand the principles, but these are usually not the people who need to be convinced. Whichever method works for you, just make sure you leave this chapter understanding that it is *never* optimal to exercise a call option early on a non-dividend-paying stock. This knowledge alone will save you money and headaches as an options trader.

Capturing a Dividend

We have shown that it is never optimal to exercise a call early, but what about the exception? Why would an investor want to capture a dividend? The main reason is to reduce a loss in the option caused by the dividend being paid on the stock. If the dividend is large enough, you may find it beneficial to exercise the call early to be the owner of the actual stock and therefore receive the dividend. If this is the case, the investor should still wait as long as possible before exercising the call; it should be exercised the day before ex-dividend date.

For example, say a stock is trading for $100 and will pay a $1 dollar dividend tomorrow. A trader is holding a $95 call trading for $5 that will expire in a relatively short time.

The stock will be trading ex-dividend for $99 tomorrow morning, because the price of the stock is reduced to reflect the dividend payment from the company. What will happen to the call? It will trade for $4 because the stock is down $1, so the trader may elect to exercise the call early to reduce the loss. By exercising early, the trader will effectively pay $100 for the stock, because they are paying $95 with the call but discarding the $5 value in the option. The trader now has the $100 stock, which will be worth $99 tomorrow, but he will also gain the $1 dividend to bring the account back up to the $100 value. If he held the call option, he could effectively buy stock for $99 that is worth $99 but would be missing the $1 dividend. Exercising a call early to capture a dividend is therefore more of a loss-reducing strategy as opposed to a profit-seeking strategy.

One Condition for Exercising Early

Before you exercise a call option early to gain a dividend, make sure the call has no time premium (trading at parity) or a very small amount remaining. If there is significant time premium on the call, you will be better off selling the call to close and then purchasing the stock in the open market. For example, say a $100 call is trading for $11 with the stock at $110. This option is $10 in-the-money and therefore has $1 time premium. If you exercise early, you lose the $11 from the call but gain a $110 stock — effectively paying $111 for it. This is the market "penalty" we talked about earlier. If the stock pays a $1 dividend tomorrow, your stock position will be worth $109, plus the $1 dividend will make your total position worth $110. Because you paid $111, you will lose $1.

However, if you sold the call to close, you lose the $11 call but gain $11 cash. If you buy the stock in the open market, you lose $110 cash but receive $110 worth of stock. On a net basis, these transactions are a wash and your account value stays the same. On ex-date, your $110 stock is worth $109 but you also gained the $1 dividend, so your total account value is unchanged.

If you decide to exercise early to capture a dividend, there should not be a significant amount of time premium remaining on the option. What is significant? That really requires taking into account the total dollars lost, including commissions, by exercising early versus selling the option to close. For instance, 1/4-point time premium may seem insignificant. However, if you have 30 contracts, it will make a huge difference to sell the call to close and capture the remaining time premium. Likewise, 1/2-point time premium may sound rather significant. But if you have one contract, you may be better off exercising the call early. The reason is that you will pay only one commission to exercise the call, which is usually the same commission you would be charged to purchase the stock. However, if you sell the call and then purchase the stock, you will be charged two separate commissions. The net effect of these transactions is what determines the time premium's significance.

Even though capturing a dividend is a valid reason for exercising a call early, it is still rarely done. This is because most dividends are relatively small, and most investors find the protective value of the call worth missing the dividend. Just because a stock is paying a dividend does not mean that it is necessarily a good idea to exercise early. You have to weigh the tradeoffs. Is the dividend sizeable? Do you mind holding the stock, even if only for a day, and accepting all of the downside risks? If you are not comfortable holding the stock in exchange for the dividend, you should probably give up the dividend.

One Exception for Margin Traders

Here is a great tip you will not see in any books or hear from brokers. It is one exception to the rule about never exercising a call option early on a non-dividend paying stock. Say you trade on margin (borrowed funds) and are holding a very deep-in-the-money call, maybe a $30 call with the stock trading for $100. Assume there is some time left on the option; it could be a few days or even months.

If you exercise early, you will meet the Fed call for the stock just by exercising! This is because the call is so deep-in-the-money. Because you are receiving stock so highly valued relative to the strike, your margin cash available and buying power can explode to the upside. So if you are in a situation where you need to generate margin cash or buying power to take advantage of a certain stock or perhaps to meet a margin call, exercising a deep-in-the-money call option early may be your answer.

The reason you never see this in the textbooks is because, by itself, exercising early gains you nothing in the asset. It is only in other market mechanics of margin trading where you may benefit. Keep that in mind if you ever are lucky enough to have a call option go very deep-in-the-money and need to trade on margin. You should definitely check with your broker for specific details and calculations.

Early Exercise with Puts

Early exercise with puts, unlike calls, may be advantageous to the long put holder. This is because put options represent a cash *inflow* to your account. If the put option is sufficiently deep-in-the-money (technically where delta is equal to one), the put should be exercised. As an example, assume you are holding stock and a $100 put option with three months remaining. The stock is trading at $40 and you see no hope of it coming back above $100 by expiration. If you wait until expiration, you will receive $100 for your stock. If you exercise now, you will receive $100 for your stock.

Which do you prefer? As with any cash inflow, it is preferred to have it paid earlier as opposed to later. So we exercise the put and take our $100 now.

Although options trading can be used as a tool to buy or sell stock, most options contracts, somewhere in the neighborhood of 95%, are never exercised. This is because most option traders use them as a hedge. For example, say an investor has 100 shares of stock at $50 and also has a $50 put. The stock is trading at $40 on expiration day. Rather than using the put to sell the stock, the option trader will close out the put for a $10 gain and use that to offset the $10 loss in the long position. Because of this fact, most option traders are not very familiar with exercising options.

Make sure you become very aware with the mechanics of exercising, as well as when and why to do it. It has been emphasized that exercising a call option early is never optimal, with the possible exception of capturing a dividend, yet everyday option traders make this costly mistake.

One day in early March 2000, I spoke to a client who had early exercised 10 contracts of Cisco Systems (CSCO), 10 contracts of Dell Computer (DELL), and 20 contracts of Intel (INTC). I politely mentioned to him that, for future reference, he might want to reconsider before exercising early. When he asked why, I started to tell him that, by exercising early, he gave up his time premium on the option and paid for the stock earlier than required, which meant he was missing out on the interest that could have been earned. In addition, he was giving up the protective value of the call options. He did not understand what I meant by the protective value, so I started to explain. I continued, "For example, you exercised 20 CSCO $60 calls with the stock trading at $70. In the worst case, if the stock falls to zero..." At that point he immediately interrupted and said, "See, this is why I do not like to talk to finance people because they are not business-minded. These are all great companies and stocks I've wanted to own for the long-term. I am absolutely certain they will not fall to zero, so your argument is invalid." If that was not bad enough, he hung up the phone.

The customer had exercised the contracts early when Cisco was trading for $70, Dell was around $51, and Intel was at $60 . Today, roughly a year and a half later, those stocks are trading for $19.25, $27.75, and $29.50 respectively. What is even worse is that he exercised options early with over one year remaining! When people talk about a zero stock price in option strategies, it just makes the math easier to follow and makes the insurance aspect of calls easier to understand. Whether it is a realistic argument or not, the important point to understand is that calls do provide downside protection, and you give that up by exercising early. I am sure this long-term investor now wishes he had not exercised the calls early even though the stock price is not zero.

If you learn from this investor's mistake, you have a big advantage in trading options.

Questions:

1) You are holding a $100 strike call option trading for $12 with the stock at $111. The stock is paying a dividend tomorrow, which will reduce the value of your call. Should you exercise early to get the dividend? Why? What is a better strategy to capture the dividend in this case?

2) You have a $60 call trading for $6. The stock is currently $65. If you exercise the call, what is your cost basis on the stock? What would be a more efficient way to own the stock?

3) What is the one condition that should exist if you are going to exercise a call option early?

4) Is it ever optimal to exercise a put option early? When?

Chapter 13: Selling Options on Expiration Day

If you are an avid options trader, you may have noticed that in-the-money calls and puts will often trade for less than the intrinsic amount (the difference between the stock price and the strike) on, or near, expiration day. This is especially true for deep-in-the-money options. For example, on February 16, 2001 (option expiration day), Juniper Networks (JNPR) was trading for $83.63. It has been stated throughout this book that an option cannot trade below its intrinsic value, so you would certainly think the Feb $70 call would be trading at parity — exactly intrinsic — and be quoted at $13.63.

However, it is currently quoted at $12.38 on the bid. Many investors accept this as normal functioning of the market and will sell their options to close below its intrinsic value. For example, say you hold 10 of the above JNPR Feb $70 calls and want to sell them. You could sell at the bid and receive $12.38 * 10 * 100 = $12,380.

But there is a better way to handle this apparent inconsistency.

In Chapter 10 (Basic Option Pricing), you may recall that, in theory, an option cannot trade for less than the intrinsic amount. The theory says that if an option does trade below the intrinsic value, arbitrageurs will sell the stock and buy the call for a guaranteed profit. This buying and selling pressure will continue until intrinsic value is restored.

So how do you trade your in-the-money option that is trading below parity? The same way the arbitrageurs would.

Instead of selling your call at the bid, simply place an order to sell the stock, and then immediately exercise the call option.

The stock is currently $83.69 on the bid. So, you place an order to sell 1,000 shares at $83.69. It does not matter if you even own the stock or not. Why? Once the sell order is executed, you simply submit exercise instructions to your broker and buy 1,000 shares at $70. Now you received $83.69 but paid $70 to deliver the shares. Your proceeds are $13.69 * 10 * 100 = $13,690 for an additional $1,310 of profit compared to the trader who sold the call at the bid price! Your broker will charge you an extra commission to sell the stock, but I think you realize it can be well worth it.

There is one important note to make here. There are people, brokers included, who will tell you to "short" the stock, instead of using a regular sell order, and then exercise the call. However, shorting the stock subjects you to unnecessary risk and can be more costly. If you short the stock, you must have an uptick, and there is never a guarantee of this. So it is possible you may never get the stock sold. In addition, if you short the stock, you will be subjected to a 50% Reg T charge and may not earn interest on that amount while waiting for settlement of the exercise.

The regulations always allow you to sell shares (without it being a "short sale") that are not held in your account. Many investors keep shares in safe deposit boxes and deliver the shares within the three-day settlement period. This is perfectly acceptable. Now, it is possible your firm does not allow shares to be sold that are not in the account. Sometimes the deep-discount brokers have restrictions like this because they spend too much time chasing down people to deliver the shares they promised to deliver and do not generate the revenues to make it worth their while. Further, it costs the firm money to file extensions in the event the shares are not delivered. However, even if your firm requires the shares to be in the account to be sold, let your broker know that you are immediately submitting exercise instructions to purchase the shares. There is no reason they should not allow it; the OCC guarantees delivery of the shares at settlement.

Once you <u>sell</u> the stock, immediately submit exercise instructions. It is very important to submit your exercise instructions on the <u>same day</u>, otherwise the sale of stock and purchase from the option exercise will not have matching settlement dates. Although this is not a major problem (it won't cause you to lose the sale), it is something your broker does not want to become a habit. I won't go into the details, but as long as you submit your exercise instructions on the same day you sell the stock, you will be fine.

What about put options? Assume the JNPR Feb $100 puts are trading for $15.88 on the bid. If you sell 10 contracts, you will receive $15,880. But, with the stock trading at $83.75 on the ask, we see they are below intrinsic and "should be" priced for $100 - $83.75 = $16.25.

If your put options are trading below intrinsic value, simply buy the stock and then exercise your put.

You would pay $83.75 to buy the stock and receive $100 from the exercise of the put, leaving you with the intrinsic amount of $16.25 or $16,250 — a difference of $370 when compared to the trader who just sold the puts at the bid price of $15.88. Again, the extra commission can be well worth it.

In fact, years ago, there used to be an order called "exercise and cover," meaning that the broker would sell the stock and cover the sale by exercising the call (or buy the stock and exercise the put). With increased liquidity in the options markets, this order has disappeared, although there are certainly times it could still be used.

Why will options trade below intrinsic? There are numerous reasons, but the main reason is that the market makers are having a difficult time spreading off the risk with the current liquidity.

For example, as discussed earlier, the Feb $70 calls are trading for $12.38 but "should be" trading for $13.63. This is strictly a result of having more sellers than buyers. Everybody wants to sell their calls, and nobody wants to buy; the new equilibrium price is $12.38, which is below the theoretical value.

You may be wondering why nobody is buying the calls and selling the stock to restore the equilibrium. They are. Market makers are buying at $12.38, then selling the stock. However, there is just not enough volume or interest to bring it to equilibrium. In the meantime, the stock continues to fall, so by the time they short the stock they may be in for a loss (even though market makers are immune to the "uptick" rule). With a bid at $12.38, they feel that is worth the risk while awaiting executions.

What about retail investors? Why do they not join in and buy the call and sell the stock? They can; however, they must purchase the call on the ask at $13.63 and sell the stock at the bid of $83.63, leaving zero room for error! If you sell stock at $83.63 and buy the $70 call, you will have a net credit of $13.63, which is exactly what it will cost you to buy the call.

Now you may think to compete with the market makers and try to notch up the bid price a bit. In other words, if you bid $12.63, you will now be the highest bidder and the quote will move to $12.63 on the bid and $13.63on the ask. If you purchase the call for $12.63, you could certainly sell the stock and make money. But, here is the catch: If you bid at $12.63, the market makers will bid $12.73, giving them a call option for $0.10! How? Market makers would love to buy the call option below the "fair value" and hold an asset that will behave just like the underlying stock. But, if the stock falls, the market maker will sell it back to you at $12.63 and be out 10 cents. In other words, they will use your buy order as a guaranteed stop order. If they buy it for $12.73 and it does not work out, they know they have a buyer at $12.63 — you! This is called "leaning on the book" and is a common practice among market makers.

Just because the market is offering you a price below the fair value, that does not mean you must accept it. Learn to correct for it and improve your option trading results.

Questions:

1) You have ten $100 call options near expiration. The stock is $110 and the bid on your option is $9.50. If you want to close out the option, what is the best method? How much more money do you make with this method as compared to a straight sell?

2) Why would a market maker bid below intrinsic value near expiration?

3) You have five $50 puts bidding $9.20 near expiration. The stock is $40. If you want to close out your options, what is the best method? How much more money will you make when compared to a straight sell?

PART II
Option Strategies

We have covered just about everything you need to know about options to fully understand basic strategies. In Part II, we'll be discussing basic option strategies in depth, and you will see how all of the earlier information will come into play.

What Is the Best Option Strategy?

You have probably heard many opinions about which option strategies are the best. Covered calls are best because they reduce the risk but still allow for a profit. Naked puts are the best because you are getting paid to buy stock. Straddles are the best because they allow you to make money whether the market is going up or down.

If you've been trading options for a while, you no doubt have heard many others. But when you hear comments like these, all you hear are opinions of one trader's preference for a certain risk-reward profile. To really understand option trading, you need to understand that all option strategies come with their own sets of risks and rewards, and the market will price them accordingly. Be careful of anyone who tells you that a particular strategy is superior to another; they either do not fully understand options or they're trying to sell you something!

Traders who tout superior option strategies focus on one aspect of the strategy — either the risk or reward side — and completely neglect the counterpart. They will make comments such as, "Calls are superior to stock because the return on investment is much higher." It is easy to make them consider the risk side by replying, "Sure, but lottery tickets are superior to calls because the return on investment is even higher."

The best option strategy is one that directly matches *your* set of risk and reward tolerances for a given outlook on the underlying. This is the level of option trading you want to achieve. Learn to dissect a position into its component parts, and see if you're willing to accept the associated risks. Learn the various strategies and learn how to further tailor them to match your needs better. Don't spend your time looking for the superior option strategy. It doesn't exist.

Understanding Risk and Reward

To fully understand the relationships between risk and reward with options, we need to look at profit and loss diagrams. If you compare the profit and loss diagrams of <u>any</u> two strategies, there will <u>always</u> be a part of the diagram where each strategy dominates. This is because options offer different sets of tradeoffs. For every strategy, there are good points and bad points. It is up to you as a trader to decide which tradeoffs are good and which are bad. Once you understand all the risks and rewards associated with particular strategies, you will be able to make educated choices and be much happier with your decisions.

For example, let's revisit the earlier comment. Are call options superior to stock? Assume one investor buys stock for $50 and another buys the $50 call for $5.

We can plot the profit and loss, at expiration, for each position, and we will get the following diagram:

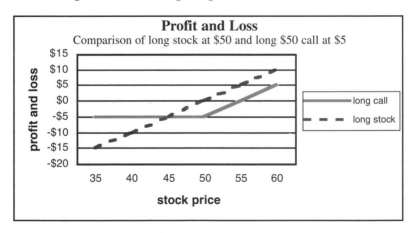

For example, the trader who buys stock at $50 will make $5 profit if the stock is trading for $55. If you look at the above chart, you can see that the profit and loss line (broken line) crosses the $5 profit line for a stock price of $55. Likewise, if the stock is trading for $45, the stock trader will incur a $5 loss.

The diagram also shows that the long $50 call buyer (solid line) will lose $5 if the stock is $50 or below and will break even if the stock is $55. At a stock price of $60, the $50 call buyer will make $5 profit (the call option will be worth $10, but the trader paid $5).

Notice the profit and loss diagram for stock (broken line). It is superior (lies above) the profit and loss line for the long call (solid line) for all stock prices above $45. This is because the call option buyer is effectively paying $55 for the stock ($50 strike for a cost of $5.) If the stock stays above $45, the long stock position is the better strategy (the broken line is above the solid line.) But if the stock falls below $45, the call option becomes the better strategy (the solid line is above the broken line), because the most the long call will lose is the premium. One strategy is not better than the other; it depends on your outlook of the stock and the amount of risk you are willing to accept.

An investor who believes the stock will stay above $50 is better off buying stock. Of course, there is a tradeoff of accepting a potential $50 maximum loss. Conversely, an investor who believes the stock is heading higher but does not want the exposure to the downside is better off buying the call. The tradeoff is that he will pay $55 for the stock instead of $50, but in return he'll be subjected to only a $5 maximum loss.

If traders are more concerned with the downside risk, they will bid up the price of the call. If they believe the price of the call is too high relative to the stock, they will sell the call (either naked or covered). These actions will price the call fairly with respect to investors' opinions, and neither strategy will be superior to the other.

What about naked puts? They must be better than stock, because you are actually getting paid to buy the stock, right?

Let's look at the profit and loss diagram between stock purchased for $50 and a naked $50 put sold for $5:

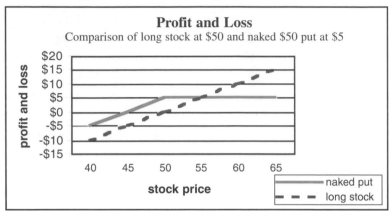

Again, in some areas of the chart the long stock position dominates, and in other areas it does not. The long stock position is better for stock prices above $55. With the stock above $55 the long stock investor will realize unlimited profits, while the naked put will profit only by the premium received from the sale of the put.

However, if the stock is below $55, the naked put is the better strategy. Below a $50 stock price both investors lose, but the naked put seller is ahead by the premium.

Is a long call better than a naked put? Some may reason that the long call position makes more money than the short put if the stock rises, and loses less if it falls, so it is a better strategy. Let's assume a long $50 call and short $50 put are each traded for $5:

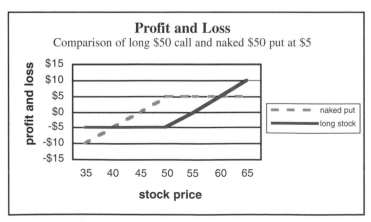

Looking at the next chart we see that the long call position (solid line) does dominate for all stock prices above $60 and below $40. But if the stock stays between these prices, the naked put is clearly the better choice. Your outlook on the stock and tolerance for risk will determine which strategy is best for you.

Pick any two strategies and look at their profit and loss diagrams. Each strategy will dominate over a given range of stock prices. Try switching one position from long to short. Try changing strike prices. You will soon see that it does not matter; one strategy cannot dominate another for *all* stock prices.

Strategies come in all shapes and sizes. Now you should more clearly understand why. Different strategies alter the risk-reward relationships, and it's up to you, the trader, to decide which is best. Don't be afraid to alter the strategy to meet your taste — that is what option trading is all about. If you accept somebody's strategy as the "best," you are, by default, accepting his or her risk tolerances, too. If those tolerances are not in line with yours, you will eventually learn, the expensive way, that no strategy is superior to another.

Better to Buy or Sell Options?

Many investors adamantly believe that you are better off selling options as opposed to buying. They reason that since most buyers lose money, it must be better to be a seller. This may make sense on the surface, but it completely neglects other factors of option trading. With a little effort, we will show you that neither the buyer nor the seller has a long-term advantage.

This is not to say that, under certain conditions, a buyer or seller cannot have a theoretical edge on the trade. That happens all the time. We are talking about making an unconditional statement that one side has an advantage over the other.

Efficient Market Theory

The reason that no option strategy is superior to another or that selling is better than buying is explained in a concept called the *efficient market theory*. The three forms of the theory are the weak, the semi-strong, and the strong. We won't go into the details of the various forms, though the basic concept is the same; that is, you cannot beat the market by using current news or looking at charts of past prices. The theory assumes that for any actively traded market, all information will be priced immediately — efficiently — into the asset. Notice it assumes an actively traded market; the theory will not necessarily hold true for real estate, art, coins, antiques, or other inactively traded markets where information cannot be immediately reflected in the price. Further, for any of these inactive markets, there will always be minor differences in the assets that can account for differences in price. In other words, two identical coins or antiques are not truly identical. This is not so with stocks and options. One share of IBM stock is *exactly* the same as another share. When one asset is exactly the same as another, they are said to be *fungible*. It is this property that makes the efficient market theory so powerful when applied to the U.S. financial markets.

To understand stock and option trading better, it is imperative to have a basic understanding of this theory. Without knowledge of it, you can quickly make decisions that can lead to large losses. The theory can easily be explained by the following simple example:

Is it better to own a Porsche Boxster or a Ford Taurus?

Many people unfamiliar with the efficient market theory are tempted to answer that the Porsche is clearly the better choice. Efficient market theory holds for any actively traded product, not just stocks and options. We can use it to show that there is, surprisingly, no difference between the two cars.

To start, assume that the Ford Taurus and Porsche Boxster are both priced the same. With both cars priced the same, most would agree that you are better off with the Porsche. If so, people will buy the Porsche over the Taurus. This will put buying pressure on the Porsche and raise its price relative to the Taurus. Say the Porsche is now bid up to a price $3,000 above the Taurus. Most would agree that it is still a better deal and continue to buy it. This action will continue until the markets are not so sure that an additional $1 is worth jumping from the Taurus to the Boxster. If it were worth it, they would do it.

It may seem counterintuitive, but as long as there is no net bidding up or down of prices between the two cars, you are equally well off with either one. While the Porsche may be faster and have higher quality and resale value (not to mention it just looks cooler), it also comes with higher repair bills, insurance rates, and theft occurrences. The car market will reflect all pros and cons in the prices of the two cars.

Similarly, the financial markets will price all assets to reflect their risks. Quality assets are bid up and riskier assets are sold off. This is why a government T-bill yielding 5% is equal to a risky junk bond priced to yield 10%. The government bond is higher quality but also has a lower yield. The markets realize that, all else constant, you are better off with the T-bill and so they will continue to bid that price up. If the price gets too high, the risk of the junk bond will be attractive relative to its yield. The markets will start to buy the junk bond and sell the T-bond. Once both prices have stabilized, there is no net difference between the two bonds. If there were an advantage, the markets would continue taking action and reflect it in the price.

In more technical terms, the market's action in the above examples is a form of the *semi-strong efficient market theory*, which states that all publicly available information, news, and charts are priced into the asset. The markets will price all assets so that the risk-reward ratios are equal across the board.

So is it better to be a seller of options as opposed to a buyer? There is no difference between the two choices. The markets will reflect the risk in the prices.

If it were <u>always</u> true that sellers of call options were better off, the market would continue to sell calls and drive down their price. The price will stop falling when buyers purchase all that is for sale and there is no net selling. At that point, equilibrium is reached and the assets are priced fairly. Do not be lured into strategies that claim you are always better off as a buyer of this or a seller of that. Efficient market theory predicts that in an actively traded market, no strategy is superior to another and that sellers of options do not have a net advantage over buyers of options over the long haul.

Questions:

1) Your friend is new to options and exclaims that covered calls are the ultimate options strategy because you get paid for selling your stock. How do you comment?

2) When comparing any two option strategies, one will always dominate the other for all stock prices. True or false? Why?

3) Anybody who tells you that one option strategy is better than another is failing to recognize either the risk or reward aspects of the trade. True or false?

Chapter 14: Calls and Puts:
The Building Blocks of Option Strategies

Call and put options are the most basic of option strategies. But do not let that fool you into thinking they are not powerful. It is the understanding of calls and puts that allows you to combine them with other assets and create better risk profiles. In fact, calls are puts and puts are calls if combined with the underlying asset in the proper way. If you take the time to understand the basics of these assets and the various reasons for using them, the following strategies will become almost second nature.

Long Calls

The long call option is one of the most widely used strategies. This is because stocks, historically, have had an upward bias and the odds are tilted a little in the favor of a stock rise rather than a fall. Long call strategies are relatively easy to understand and are simple to monitor. With a quick quote on the option, the investor can see if he or she has a profit or a loss and can easily get out of the position with a simple sale.

But let's look a little deeper into the long call strategy and see the different reasons that motivate people to buy these assets. Remember, options are about changing risk-reward profiles compared to that of stock. We aren't looking for the "best" strategy; we're only trying to find different uses that are considered to be more beneficial under certain situations.

The first step in understanding the strategies behind call options is to understand that calls are a form of borrowing money. That's right, if you buy a call, you are implicitly borrowing money. In fact, earlier in the book we learned that finance charges are passed from the market maker to you when you purchase a call. Even though you are not specifically borrowing money, somebody else is borrowing on your behalf, and you must cover those interest charges.

Any time you borrow money, you are deferring a payment. If you borrow money to buy a house, you must pay interest to the bank; however, you do not owe the money today. You also have more money in your account to earn interest, because you didn't use money today to buy the house. These two ideas — borrowing money and deferring payments — give long call options their speculative and conservative powers.

Borrowing Money

The first conservative motivation for buying calls is to simply borrow money. Often investors want to purchase stocks, but they do not immediately have the money available. Maybe you want to buy 1,000 shares of a $50 stock, but you're waiting for a bonus check from your company, which is due in three months. If you wait to buy the stock, you may miss out on potential upward moves. Instead, you could purchase a three-month call option (or a little longer time) and defer the payment. If this is the case, you should consider purchasing deep-in-the-money calls, because they will have very little time premium associated with them and will therefore only increase your cost basis from the current stock price by this amount. For example, if you bought the stock today, you would pay $50. However, you may be able to purchase a $40 call for $10.50. If you buy this call, you can exercise it in three months with an effective cost basis of $50.50, which is only 50 cents higher — the time premium — over the current price of the stock.

Long Calls as Leverage

Because call options are a form of borrowing money, they are also a form of financial leverage. By leverage, we mean that any gains or losses in the stock are magnified. The financial field borrowed the term from physics, which demonstrates how a person, for example, can lift a car by applying very little force to a jack. In the same sense, a tiny amount of money can be magnified into large amounts through financial leverage. Any time money is borrowed, financial leverage is gained.

For example, say you buy 1,000 shares of stock at $50 and sell it for $60 for a gain of $10,000. You could also put $50,000 in a margin account with your broker and borrow $50,000. With this you could buy 2,000 shares of stock and make a $20,000 gain for the same $10 move in the stock. Because half of the funds were borrowed, the resulting leverage is 2:1, meaning that the gains and losses are magnified by a factor of two.

It is financial leverage that speculators seek, and that's why so many trade in margin accounts. With options, you control every price movement above the strike price but for a fraction of the cost of buying the stock. this allows you to create very leveraged positions.

This is the most popular use of calls and also the reason why so many traders lose at the options game. They buy calls to take "long shots" on a price run in the stock and potentially make a lot of money. If not, they lose only the amount paid. It is this lottery-style payoff that attracts speculators to options.

To use options in a speculative manner, speculators usually seek out-of-the-money options so they can buy a large number of contracts for relatively little money. For instance, you may see a $50 stock with a $55 call trading for $1. You can buy 20 contracts (2,000 share equivalent) for $2,000 as compared to the $100,000 it would cost to buy 2,000 shares of stock. Assume the stock moves to $60 at expiration. The $50 call would then be worth $10, and your 20 contracts would be worth $20,000. You have increased your investment by a factor of 10 and turned $2,000 into $20,000. If you had purchased the stock, you increased your investment by a factor of 1.2 and turned $100,000 into $120,000. You can certainly see the incentive for speculators to use options! Further, the speculator had only $2,000 at risk as compared to the stock trader's $100,000. This is because the long call position has the right, *but not the obligation*, to buy the stock. If the stock is below $50 at expiration, the trader will just walk away from the call and let it expire worthless.

The leverage works both ways. Even if the stock moves up, the option trader will lose $2,000 as long as the stock does not exceed $55 by expiration, whereas the long stockowner would make $10,000 if the stock closes at $55.

How much leverage can you get with options? A lot. I have seen, on more than one occasion, accounts with a total value in the neighborhood of $50,000 to $70,000 increase to more than $1 million *the next day* using options. Of course, these speculators had huge out-of-the-money positions with a large ensuing rally or buyout in the underlying stock. You will definitely hear other stories such as this as you trade options. Just remember that for every story like this you hear, there are hundreds of thousands of investors who lost. You should never bet more than you are willing to lose in hopes of being the next story.

It should be pointed out that while calls provide more leverage, their total return is usually less than that of stocks. For example, with the stock at $55, the stockowner makes a 20% return and a total of $20,000. The long call makes a 900% return and a total of $18,000. This is because $2 total was paid for the option and is gone for good. As long as there is a time premium on the option, the long call buyer will always under perform the long stockowner in terms of total dollars earned, even though they will outperform the stock-owner in terms of the percentage gains (return on investment). This really should not come as a surprise, as the long stockowner, as we stated, had more at risk and should make more in returns. It is the leverage that provides the higher percentage gains for the option owner and the option premium that prevents him from outperform-ing the long stock position in total dollar terms. This should further emphasize the point we have been making throughout that options are not necessarily a "better" strategy; they simply allow you to alter risk-reward profiles.

Long Calls as Insurance

We can also view call options as a form of insurance. In fact, the owner of a call option implicitly buys a put option from the market. Call options used in this manner are a more conservative approach. The investor is not necessarily looking for large gains on small investments and is probably more interested in purchasing the stock. In many cases, they do actually have the money to buy the stock today but are a little afraid for short-term reasons.

For example, you may want to buy a $100 stock but you're afraid it may fall. Instead, you could buy a $100 call and assume it is trading for $10. If the stock falls, the most you can lose is $10. The tradeoff for this privilege of using the call option is that you have a higher effective purchase price and a high probability of losing the $10. If you buy the call, you effectively will pay $110 for the stock even though it is currently trading for $100. Had you just purchased the stock initially, you would have paid only $100. That is why the breakeven point on the profit and loss chart is $110:

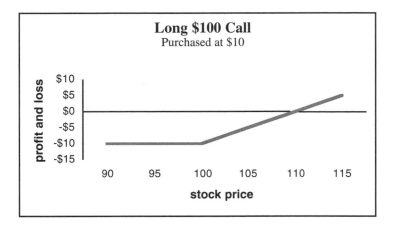

Also, according to the Black-Scholes Option Pricing Model, an at-the-money option will end up losing 100% of the investment nearly half the time. Recall that the delta of an at-the-money option is roughly 0.50, which means it has a probability of 0.50 that it will finish with intrinsic value. Also, an option that finishes with intrinsic value does not necessarily mean profits. As we see in the above profit and loss diagram, a stock price of $105 is $5 in-the-money, yet still produces a loss. So while many people speak about the protection that call options provide by limiting your cost, be aware that it comes with a high chance of 100% loss.

This shows you how and when to use calls as insurance. If you are concerned about the downside risk of a stock but are still interested in purchasing it, consider using long calls instead. They will provide you with limited downside protection and allow you to profit fully if your forecast on the stock is correct. Investors who use calls for their insurance value typically use at-the-money or out-of-the-money calls and sometimes slightly in-the-money. Their goal is to reduce the amount of money they have at risk. This can be a great strategy to use when upcoming news is expected. If you want to buy a stock today but know they are releasing earnings in a few weeks, expecting an FDA approval, or some other important announcement, long calls can be a great investment.

If your outlook on the stock is correct, you can take one of two actions at expiration: Either sell your call to close and capture the profit to offset your higher cost basis, or exercise the call. Either choice will effectively accomplish the same thing.

For example, say the stock is trading for $120 at expiration. You can purchase the stock in the open market for $120, which is $20 higher than when you were first looking at it trading for $100. However, your $100 call is worth exactly $20. You can sell the call, which offsets the $20 loss. Note that this does not regain your time premium (the original $10 spent) — that is gone for good. But this is not necessarily bad because the stock could have plummeted, in which case you would be happy you bought the call instead of the stock. That was the cost of the insurance. The net effect from buying the stock and selling the call in the open market is that you pay $110 for the stock.

The other alternative is to exercise the call. If you tell your broker you want to exercise your $100 call, the shares will be in your account three business days later. At the time the shares arrive, your account will be debited for $100 per share. Notice that you received an asset worth $120 and paid only $100 for it, which is a $20 gain. However, your call has been exercised and cannot be sold, which creates a $20 loss and exactly offsets the gain. The net effect from exercising the call is that you paid $110 for the stock by paying the $100 strike plus the $10 premium.

Riskless Investing?

You may hear of a strategy that is really a variation of the previous strategy. It is touted as a risk-free trade that has tremendous gains. It's definitely not riskless, but can help you understand the advantages of call options.

The strategy involves taking the present value of an amount of money and investing in zero-coupon bonds. Then take the remaining funds and buy long-term call options on stocks or, better yet, a broad-based index such as the S&P 500. If the market is bullish, you make money from the options; however, if it falls, at least you get your principal back at expiration of the bond.

For example, say you have $100,000 to invest in the market. You could buy a five-year, $100,000 face zero-coupon bond for about $78,350 (if interest rates are 5%), take the remaining $21,647 and buy the options. At the end of five years, hopefully the options will have provided a profit. In the worst case they all expire worthless, but your zero-coupon bond has matured to $100,000, which is your original principal.

There are many brokers who used this strategy years ago as a way to prospect for clients by telling them they know a way to invest in the stock market with no risk. Hopefully, you see there is a risk in that, had you not bought the options, your $100,000 today would be worth roughly $127,628 at the end of five years at 5% interest. *Effectively this strategy allows you to speculate today with future interest.* In other words, you are giving up $27,628 in future interest over the next five years in exchange for $27,628/1.05⁵ = $21,647 with which to speculate today.

So just because you get your principal back does not mean it came for free. Still, it is an interesting strategy and, in fact, is the essence of the Black-Scholes Model in valuing a call option.

Which Strike Do I Buy?

Again, there is no right or wrong answer. Different call strikes will provide you with different sets of risks and rewards. If you buy a higher strike call, you'll have less downside risk (the option will be cheaper) but a higher breakeven point (the stock will have to move further to get your money back). The proper balance is entirely up to you. Just be very aware of what you are gaining and what you are losing with each consideration. The further out-of-the-money you go, the more speculative the trade becomes and the bigger the move is needed in the underlying stock to gain a profit. At-the-money calls are the riskiest in terms of the total time premium at risk. The at-the-money options will have maximum time premium but will not have the highest breakeven point.

Once you match the proper considerations to your outlook on the stock, you will find the trade that is best for you.

In general for calls or puts, if you are speculating on a big move in the stock and willing to roll the dice a little, you can use out-of-the-money options. If you recall the content from Chapter 11 on deltas and gammas, out-of-the-money options require a fast move in the underlying stock and in the right direction. However, if you are interested in speculating on only direction but not how quickly the stock will get there, you should use in-the-money options. In-the-money options will allow you to make money on much smaller moves in the right direction. They do not rely on speed of movement like out-of-the-money options.

Which Month Should I Buy?

If you are using calls as a means to purchase stock but are trying to defer the payment, you should probably match your cash flows. For example, if you want to buy 500 shares of a $50 stock but need a bonus check that will be paid in three months to pay for it in full, you should probably buy a three-month option.

However, if you are using calls as in investment tool, you should buy as much time as possible with all else being equal. This is because options become increasingly cheaper (on a time basis) the more time you purchase. The total price of an option will increase with additional time; however, if you consider the *time premium per month* you are paying, they are becoming cheaper.

For example, IBM near August 2001 expiration was trading for $106 with the following option quotes:

Contract	Price	Time premium	Time premium per month
Sep $100	$8.80	$2.80	$2.80
Oct $100	$10.80	$4.80	$2.40
Jan '02 $100	$13.90	$7.90	$1.58
Jan '03 $100	$22.90	$16.90	$0.99
Jan '04 $100	$29.00	$23.00	$0.79

You will recall that option *prices* become more expensive with the addition of time. However, the time premium per month is decreasing. September options have about one month of time, so you would pay $2.80 in time premium for the one month. October options have $4.80 in time premium, but they are good for two months of time or $2.40 per month. You can see that Jan '04 options, while the most expensive in total cost, are actually the cheapest in terms of monthly time premium. The Jan '04 option will respond less if IBM were to immediately move one point up, whereas the Sep $100 would respond the most. This is because the $100 strikes are all in-the-money, but the September has less time remaining so its delta will be much higher than the Jan '04 option.

Also, the longer-term options will decay at a slower rate than shorter-term options. If IBM sits flat over the next month, the Sep $100 calls will lose the entire $2.80 in time premium and be worth $6, while the Jan '04 will lose almost nothing. Remember, even if you buy a very long-term option, you do not keep the option until expiration; you can always sell it in the open market. The graph on page 160 shows how an option will typically decay from the passage of time. Many think it would decline in a straight line but it doesn't. The closer you get to expiration, the faster the rate of decline, which is another reason short-term options can be so difficult for the buyer to make money.

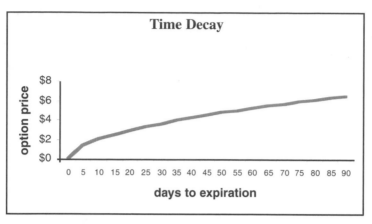

If you are trying to use calls to speculate, such as with day-trading or other shorter-term trading, you should probably use the current-month option and fairly deep-in-the-money. This will get the option's delta close to one and it will behave like the underlying stock. Even if you are looking for a stock substitute for longer periods of time, it may still be best to use current month options and then "roll" them at expiration. For example, if you have a January $50 call with the stock at $60 and expiration is approaching, you can simultaneously sell your January $50 to close and buy the February $50 to open. Using options that are deep-in-the-money with little time remaining makes them behave like the stock, and you can continually roll them for very little time premium. This strategy leaves you with less risk to the downside compared to the stockholder, yet you're not terribly disadvantaged with time premiums because the deep-in-the-money options carry very little time premium.

Options are all about tradeoffs, and it is definitely wrong to say that current-month options are the best because they are the cheapest. This is the same thought process that causes most people to lose with options. Remember, current at-the-money and out-of-the-money calls (the ones most often purchased) will have lower deltas and higher time decay than longer-term options. They are cheap for a reason. Different months have different uses, and it is up to you to find which one is best.

Diversify with Long Calls

Long calls can be used as a way to diversify your assets. Modern financial theory focuses on asset allocation. Although it is far too broad a subject to discuss in detail, the majority of returns from a portfolio deal with how assets are allocated rather than which stocks you buy or at which times. This is a conflict in the minds of most investors who usually buy two or three stocks and hope to buy near bottoms and sell near tops. At any rate, stock market timing accounts for about only 2% of total returns!

If you properly diversify, most of the company-specific risks (also called unsystematic risks) of stocks can be erased — diversified away — with as little as 18 to 20 stocks. Keep in mind this means 18 to 20 stocks that are properly allocated and not all sitting in one specific sector. How can call options allow you to diversify? Again, this has to do with paying a fraction of the stock price to buy the option.

Let's say you want to invest in the stock market, but you have only $50,000 to spend. It is highly unlikely that you could use this to effectively buy 20 different stocks. Instead, you could elect to purchase 3-year LEAPS and spread your risk through reduced costs.

Deep-in-the-Money-Calls

Probably one of the most underutilized strategies in options is that of long deep-in-the-money calls as a substitute for long stock. Recall that deep-in-the-money options carry very little time premium and have deltas close to one. The low time premium means your effective cost basis is very close to that of the investor using stock. The high delta means that the option will behave very close to the underlying stock, moving nearly point-for-point with the changes in the stock.

For example, MRVC is trading at $40 and the $40 strike is $9.50. However, this is all time premium because the stock is still below the strike price. There is substantial risk if the stock does not move quickly enough to recoup this time premium.

Let's say we have two traders with $40,000 to invest. The first trader buys 1,000 shares of MRVC at $40 for a total outlay of $40,000. The second trader buys a deep-in-the-money call such as the Jan $20 trading for $21 for a total price of $21,000, and leaves the remaining $19,000 in the money market.

The deep-in-the-money option investor is participating nearly point-for-point to the upside just like the long stock position that paid $40,000. But let's say the stock falls substantially — down to nearly $20. Now the long stock position is down $20 while the long call position is down less than this. Why? Because now the option is more at-the-money, and the time premium is <u>increasing</u>; it provides a crutch for the option holder. So long deep-in-the-money option holders enjoy the benefit of point-for-point upside movement and less than point-for-point downside. In the worst-case scenario the first investor is bankrupt, while the second investor still has $19,000 sitting safely in the money market.

Think about how powerful this strategy is, especially for those volatile tech stocks you may be trading. You participate in all of the gains to the upside but not to the downside. It is a tough strategy to beat whether you are using it for longer-term investing or speculative day trading.

For example, one client was an avid day trader with about $100,000 in the account. He usually traded in 1,000 to 3,000 share lots of one stock — using nearly all of his capital — and hoping for the best. Of course, his account balances would go through large swings from day to day. These cash balance swings alone can be the death of a day trader because they often take more and more risk trying to regain lost principal. I suggested using deep-in-the-money calls (or puts if he was bearish), but choosing several stocks instead of just one. Deep-in-the-money calls will behave closely to the underlying stock but cost a fraction. For example, Microsoft (MSFT) is currently $72.50. If this trader were going to day-trade it, he could buy about 1,375 shares after commissions. However, the $60 calls are trading for $12.70 (20 cents time premium). For about $18,000 he can control 1,400 shares that will behave almost point-for-point like the underlying stock. This frees up $82,000 to spend on several other deep-in-the-money options and spread the risk. How deep-in-the-money do you need to buy? That is actually easy to figure out. Simply find one with a small amount of time premium such as 1/2-point or less. This option will behave almost like the underlying stock but cost pennies on the dollar.

This strategy becomes even more appealing closer to option expiration because nearly all in-the-money options will quickly lose their time premium. Because of this, you will not need to buy a very deep-in-the-money option to get it to behave like stock. It will be even cheaper compared to finding one with a month of time remaining.

Volatility Traps

Before we move into other basic strategies, there is one last item that is important to understand. As you trade options, you will undoubtedly encounter *volatility traps*. This is one of the most puzzling problems that new, and even experienced, traders encounter.

We have been saying all along that call options are bullish and gain in value as the underlying stock rises. In fact, we stated in Chapter 9 that the Black-Scholes Model says that call options rise as the underlying stock rises. Recall though that the Black-Scholes Model assumes that all other factors are constant. If not, seemingly strange events can happen.

There will be many times when you are holding a call option that is trading down for the day, even though the underlying stock is up. Investors new to options initially think it may be a bad quote or that the market maker is manipulating the prices. However, what is happening is that you are caught in a *volatility trap*. If you understand the mechanics behind it, it will make sense to you then next time you see it (although you will not feel any better).

Here is the situation. A stock is trading for $100, and it is rumored that it will be purchased for $120 in the next few days. In fact, let's assume that this is almost a sure thing — as good as inside information. The $100 strike is trading for $5. You could make a lot of money spending $5 for the option and selling it for $20 in the next few days (which is the minimum at which it would trade if the stock is $120). So what would you do? Of course, you would buy it.

But so will everybody else, thereby bidding up its price.

Let's say that later in the day the option is trading for $10. New entrants with the information will think the same thing you did. They can buy for $10 and sell for $20, so they will continue to bid up its price.

This process continues until the price of the option is trading for at least $20 — the expected intrinsic amount — plus some time premium. In other words, one of the uses of options is to use them as a benchmark to gauge where the market thinks the stock will be in the future. Let's assume the $100 strike ends up trading for $23.

At this point, all participants are thinking, "I believe the option will be trading much higher, and I'm going to sell!" Keep in mind this example is highly simplified, and the actual time it takes for this option to be priced at $23 is measured in seconds. Actively traded markets will immediately reflect all information.

A novice investor also hears the news about the buyout and knows to buy calls if he is bullish. So he also buys the $100 strike for $23.

The next day, the new headlines flash the news they have all been waiting for: The company is purchased and the stock is trading for $120 in the pre-market.

This new trader cannot wait to capture his huge profits. After all, he purchased the option when the stock was around $100 and, in one day, will be trading for $120. That will certainly make the value of his call go up.

The markets open and — guess what — everybody *sells* their options. The stock is trading up 20 points and the option is trading at $21 down $2. The reason this happened is because everybody "knew" of the news and is selling once the news hits. It is this trading philosophy that created the Wall Street adage, "Buy the rumor, sell the news." Once again, the efficient market theory will not let a trader profit from trading on current news. The people who profited were those ahead of the news and taking risk.

Notice that the option was trading for $23 the day before the news. That was all time premium because the stock was trading around $100. If you were to value this option at that time according to the Black-Scholes Model, you would find that the "implied volatility" was incredibly high as compared to historic stock volatility. This makes sense when you consider that the market was pricing in the information and *expecting* the volatility to be greater. Once the news hits, the market is not expecting any more volatility. The time premium is therefore reduced, and so is the price of the option.

This is the classic "volatility trap" where a trader gets caught purchasing an option with high implied volatility and having it return to historical standards while holding it.

The next time you hear or read about some pending big news on a stock, be careful when you purchase options on rumors. There is a very good chance that information is priced into the asset, and you will be caught holding the high-implied volatility.

The above example is a little oversimplified because we assumed the buyout was a given. Even then, we see that not everybody will make a profit. Usually news is not that certain, which makes it even tougher. Think of how many times you read that ABC Company is expected to have a record quarter and are announcing earnings after the bell today. You buy call options only to see the option trading down even though the stock may be trading up. Again, this is because the market was expecting this positive news for several weeks, if not months. The information was already priced into the option, and everybody is selling on the news.

All strategies are subject to volatility traps; however, it is most apparent in the long call or long put strategies, which is why we included it under our first strategy of long calls.

It comes down to this: If you want to make really big money in the market, you have to take really big risks. The traders who get rewarded are the ones who "took the chance" weeks or months before the news was out. You cannot expect the market to compensate you for reading a news story the day of the event and capture "for sure" profits. If you try, the volatility trap may be your reward.

Short Calls

Remember that the long call has the right to exercise and buy stock; the short call has an obligation to sell the stock if assigned. There are basically two types of short call sellers — naked (also called uncovered) and covered. A covered call writer owns the stock and sells calls against it. If assigned, the investor will always be able to deliver the shares no matter how high they may be trading. We will be discussing this strategy later. Naked call sellers are speculative in nature; they are betting that the stock will either fall or sit still, and they will keep the premium. Their outlook on the stock, therefore, is neutral to bearish.

When selling naked (uncovered) calls, the investor takes in the premium and, in exchange, is willing to assume the upside risk of the stock.

Let's take a look at the profit and loss diagram assuming an investor shorts 10 MRVC Jan $40 calls at $9.50:

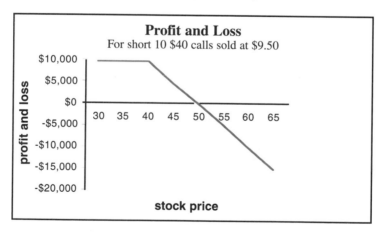

We see the maximum this investor can make is the $9.50, or $9,500 for 10 contracts. The investor is also exposed to unlimited upside exposure if the stock continues to climb above $49.50. The investor starts to lose profits for any stock price above $40 — the strike — at expiration. However, because $9.50 was received as an initial credit, the investor can afford to have the stock rise to $40 + $9.50 = $49.50 before losses are incurred. It is this relatively small and limited reward in exchange for unlimited upside risk that makes naked calls among the most dangerous of all option positions.

What happens if the naked call trader has the stock close at $60 at expiration? The trader will be assigned and be forced to sell stock (that he does not have) for a price of $40. He will have to purchase the shares in the market for $60 and receive $40 for them once they are delivered to the long call holder, which creates a $20 loss ($10.50 loss after accounting for the initial $9.50 credit). Of course, the trader could just go into the options market and buy the call to close, thus creating an offsetting position. This will relinquish him from any obligations to the long call holder. The $40 call will be trading for exactly $20, so either way the trader is stuck with a $10.50 loss.

Option Requirements

To sell naked calls or puts, your broker is going to require you to "set aside" some money to ensure they will not be stuck with large losses. This is largely because of OCC requirements to ensure contract performance. Assume you want to sell the 10 $40 calls for $9.50. As a rule of thumb, your broker will require you to set aside roughly 25% of the underlying stock's value. Because you are selling 10 contracts (1,000 shares worth), this requirement would be roughly $40 * 25% = $10,000. If the stock starts to move up, you will receive a call from your broker saying they need more money to insure the short position; this is called a *maintenance call*. Usually these must be met immediately through a cashier's check deposit or sale of securities. You should definitely check with your broker regarding specific calculations and mechanics of maintenance calls. The point is that you may be forced out of the short position just when the stock starts to move in your favor. Investors cannot sell naked calls or puts and hang on until expiration hoping for the stock to turn around in their favor.

Long Puts

A put option gives the buyer the right, but not the obligation, to *sell* stock for a fixed price over a given amount of time. It is the put buyer, (the long position), who has the right to sell stock.

The long put strategy is therefore bearish, because the value of the put rises with decreases in the underlying stock. When we say that the put will rise if the underlying stock falls, that is assuming all other factors remain the same. It is entirely possible for the put to fall in value even though the underlying is falling, but this is usually caused by changes in other factors such as time or volatility.

Long put options provide more leverage than short stock for speculators who are bearish. In other words, for a given dollar investment, the return on investment for the owner of a put option is much higher compared to the investor who shorts stock. However, as with call options, the leverage works both ways. The long put owner may lose 100% of his investment with just a small adverse move, whereas the short seller will lose only a small fraction.

Example:

You are bearish on Intel (INTC) currently trading for $31.75. Let's compare a short seller with a long put buyer.

With short sales, there is usually more leverage than with the purchase of stock. The reason is that most speculators will post only the required Reg T amount of 50%.

If a speculator wants to short 1,000 INTC, he would need to post a minimum of 50%, so the total credit would be $31.75 * 1.5 * 1,000 = $47,625. Remember, when you short stock, you receive a credit; you will purchase the stock later for a debit.

The accounting looks like this:

    Credit = $47,625
    MVS   = $31,750
    Equity = $15,875

Notice that your equity is $15,875, and when that is divided by the market value short (MVS) of $31,750 you get 50% equity, which is the Reg T amount.

Let's assume the stock falls to $25 per share. With the stock at $25, the market value short is now $25,000 and the account looks like this:

Credit = $47,625
MVS   = $25,000
Equity = $22,625

Notice that the credit balance does not change; it is simply cash sitting in the account. The MVS will change, which will change your equity. If the MVS falls, your equity will rise and vice versa.

The stock fell, in this example, about 21% from $31.75 to $25, giving the investor a 42% increase in equity from $15,875 to $22,625. The reason the investor doubled the move of the stock is because they posted only 50% of the requirement, creating 2:1 leverage.

Let's look at the puts now. A March $30 put is $1.25 and an investor could instead elect to purchase 10 contracts to control 1,000 shares and pay only $1.25 * 10 * 100 = $1,250. Later, with the stock at $25, the $30 put will be worth at least $5 (more if there is some time remaining on the option). Here the investor paid $1.25 but sells for $5 (and maybe more) for a minimum 300% increase.

Your return on the short stock is 42%, and the return on the option is 300%. This is what is meant by leverage. The investor who bought the put options, in this example, has a return on investment that is more than seven times higher as compared to the short stock trader.

What if the stock rises substantially? The short stock position has an unlimited amount of risk because a stock can continue rising without bounds. The long put holder, however, is at risk for only the $1.25 regardless of how high the stock moves. Therefore, the long put holder also has some peace of mind by holding the option; he knows the maximum loss up front.

As with call options, you must be careful in interpreting return on investment. In the above example, the option trader had a much higher return on investment (300% versus 42%). However, the short stock position makes more dollars. The short stock seller gained $6,750, while the option trader gained $3,875. This will almost always be the case, because the put buyer must pay some sort of time premium. The only time it will not hold true is if the option is trading at parity — exactly the intrinsic amount. However, as you continue to trade options, you will see that the parity condition rarely occurs at the asking price. The smaller the time premium, the more the total dollars will match that with the stock trader.

We can see the effect of the protection by the profit and loss diagram. Again, the most the option investor can lose is the $1,250 paid for the 10 put contracts. Yet, they participate in all of the downside moves below the $30 strike price.

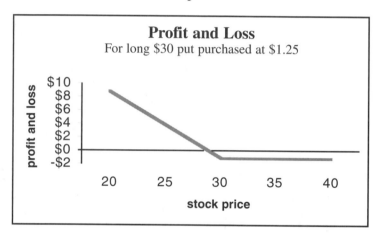

This added upside protection is not free. We can also see that the breakeven point is lowered from $30 to $28.75 for the put buyer. The long put position needs not only the stock to fall, but needs it to fall far enough to recoup the $1.25 cost.

Questions:

1) What is a benefit of owning a call option over the stock?

2) Your friend claims that the only way to truly have insuance is through put options. How would you comment?

3) How do call options provide leverage?

4) You are bullish on a stock that is trading for $100. You think it will rise a couple of points over the next few days and would like to make a short-term trade. With all else being

equal, which is the better strike to buy, the $90 or the $110? Why?

5) You are bearish on a stock and have sold it short. To protect you from upward price moves in the stock, your friend tells you to use a buy stop order to protect yourself from upside moves in the stock. How would you comment? What else could you do to protect yourself from upward stock moves? How does this differ from a buy stop order?

6) Deep-in-the-money call options will move nearly point-for-point up and down with the underlying stock. True or false? Why?

7) You bought a $100 call for $7 yesterday, and the stock is up 1 point today but the option is trading for $6.75. Is this possible? How would you explain it?

Long Puts as Insurance

A long put can also be used as an "insurance policy" when combined with long stock. Say you purchase 1,000 shares of stock trading for $30. Your total position is worth $30,000, but you fear it may fall in the short term. If you purchase 10 of the $30 strike puts for $1.25, you will raise the cost basis of your stock to $30 + $1.25 = $31.25 and be hedged for all prices below $30.

Assume the stock falls to $25 at expiration. Your stock is now worth $25,000, which is down $6,250 ($31,250 cost less $25,000). But your long $30 put is worth $5,000. You can elect to take one of two actions: (1) Hang on to your stock and sell the put for $5,000, which will help to offset the $6,250 loss. The missing $1,250 is the cost of the put, which is lost for good; or (2) Exercise your put and sell your shares for $30. If you do, you receive $30,000 for a position initially worth $31,250 and lose $1,250, which is the cost of the put. There is no financial difference between exercising the option and selling the put to close, although there certainly may be some tax considerations you may want to consider. If you exercise the put, you trigger a sale of stock. Exercising the put still leaves the stock long in the account.

Long puts can be especially useful if you trade stocks on margin and are close to a maintenance call. Sometimes it is worth a little bit of money to protect yourself from a forced sale of your stock.

If you did not want to spend $1.25 for the insurance, you may decide to buy a lower strike put such as the $25 strike. The $25 will be cheaper than the $30 because you are, in effect, assuming a $5 point deductible as compared to the $30 strike. In other words, protection with the $25 strike will not start until the stock is trading below $25. As with any insurance policy, the higher the deductible, the lower the premium. We also learned this in Chapter 9 when we said the Black-Scholes Model will assign a lower value to a lower strike put; we reinforced this in Chapter 10 where we saw how arbitrageurs will make sure this holds true.

For example, say you purchased the $25 put for $0.50. Purchasing this put raises your cost basis by $500, so your total position is now worth $30,500. If the stock closes at $20 at expiration, your total position is down from $30,500 to $20,000 for a $10,000 unrealized loss. But your $25 put is trading for $5,000. Again you can either sell the put in the open market, or exercise it and sell the shares. Either choice will make your position value worth $25,000. What happened to the missing $5,500? The majority of this amount, $5,000, was risk you assumed by purchasing the $25 put when the stock was trading for $30. By purchasing the $25, you are saying that you want protection only for stock prices below $25. The remaining $500 was the cost of the put, which is gone for good.

Which strike is better to buy in this example? There is no answer to this. It depends on your outlook on the stock and how well you deal with risk. If you are fairly confident in the stock, but you really want "disaster" insurance, then the $25 strike, or possibly lower, may be appropriate. If you absolutely cannot afford to have it fall below $30 (maybe close to a maintenance call), then there is no choice but to buy the $30 strike.

In some cases, it may be appropriate to purchase in-the-money put options, such as the $35 or $40 strike or possibly higher. The reason concerns whether or not you need protection *at expiration* or if you need it on a daily basis. For example, in the above example, we assumed you purchased the $30 put for $1.25. At expiration, you were guaranteed to have a minimum value of $30,000. But let's say you are close to a maintenance call and cannot afford to have the stock drop at all. The $30 put will have a delta of roughly 1/2, which means if the stock drops from $30 to $29, your position will lose $1,000, but your 10 puts will gain only $500. Only *at expiration* will the 10 contracts be worth $1,000. If you cannot afford to have your stock drop at all starting from the day you purchase the puts, you will need to have a delta very close to one.

There are many ways to do this. Probably the easiest is to buy deep-in-the-money puts, which will gain dollar-for-dollar for each dollar fall in the stock. Another method is to make sure the total deltas are equal to one. If you want to use the $30 puts, you would need to buy 20 contracts since each has a delta of 1/2. With delta at 1/2, the 20 contracts will behave like 10 deep-in-the-money contracts. The only problem with this method is that they will behave like 10 contracts for the next short downward move. If the stock continues to fall, they will start reacting more like 20 contracts, thus providing unnecessary insurance.

Long Calls in an IRA?

The combination of long stock and long puts can be a nice solution for speculative stocks in your IRA (Individual Retirement Account). We explained how call options provide protection when faced with speculative decisions. Put options can do the same thing. In fact, if you own stock and own a put, you effectively have a call option! These are called synthetic equivalents (discussed further in Chapter 15), and you may recall that is the combination the market maker used in Chapter 8 to create a long call.

If you want to buy a stock but are afraid of the downside risk, try using the combination of long stock and a long put in your IRA. Effectively it is a call option; however, your return on investment will not be as great as with a call because you are actually buying the stock and are not as leveraged. Also, both positions — the long stock and long put — can be executed simultaneously to avoid execution risk. Execution risk occurs when you are filled at unfavorable prices simply due to minor fluctuations in the market. For example, say you place an order to buy the stock when it is trading for $30 and the $30 put is trading for $1.25. While you are waiting for a confirmation, the stock starts to drop. Your confirmation comes back at $30 and you are now ready to place your put order. However, the put is now trading for $1.375. Had you placed both orders together, they would have been filled at the same time. If the stock rises during this time, you will pay more for it, but may pay less for the put. Likewise, if it falls, the stock will be cheaper, but the put may cost more. In either case, it is about a wash and you are usually not better or worse off. It is only when you place the orders separately, even if only by a few minutes, that execution risk becomes very real.

In fact, any time you execute simultaneous orders, you are likely to get a better price for the package. Market makers love these "package deals" because it is much easier to spread the risk, and they will probably give you a better price for it. We will look at a very common use of simultaneous order when we talk about *buy-writes* later.

The drawback to the combination of long stock plus long put is that you effectively raise the cost basis of your long stock position by the amount of the time premium for the put. But this is true with any insurance policy. You effectively raise the purchase price of your car every time you renew your auto policy, yet people do it every year. If you are more comfortable "insuring" your stock, there is nothing wrong in doing so. Just be aware of what you are giving up in return and that it doesn't come for free.

Continuous Insurance

Although the idea of insurance on a stock portfolio certainly has appeal, many investors are tricked into continually buying puts against the full value of their portfolio. Month after month, they buy new puts just in case their stocks nosedive. However, the historical return of U.S. stocks is about 12% annually, while put option premiums typically run 20% or more on an annualized basis. If you continually use puts to insure your portfolio, you will lose at an average rate of about 8% per year.

So do not use puts to insure a portfolio month after month, year after year, especially for the full value. Instead, use them only in times of high uncertainty and when the losses can be devastating. For example, if you have a large position on margin (borrowed funds), the use of puts prior to an earnings announcement may be wise. Remember, stop orders will not guarantee a price!

Put options combined with stock is a form of insurance and you should make the same considerations in purchasing puts as you should for any other form of insurance. Typically, you want insurance for events that are high severity and low probability. In other words, you want insurance for events that are unlikely to happen but can be devastating if they do. This is why you probably own hurricane insurance on your house (high severity, low probability) but do not have insurance to guard against a neighborhood kid throwing a baseball through a window (high probability, low severity). Treat put buying the same way. Ask yourself if you are really going to be devastated if your stock falls from $30 to $28, for example. If not, the $30 put is probably not the one you need. Purchasing the wrong kind of puts for insurance usually causes disappointment for many stock investors.

Risk-Free Portfolio

A strategy was peddled years ago by many unscrupulous (or unknowing) brokers. They claimed you could buy stocks and guarantee yourself the risk-free rate. Their strategy was to purchase the stock and then buy a put option with a strike price higher than the cost of the stock by the risk-free rate. For example, if interest rates are 5%, you may buy a $100 stock and buy a 1-year $105 put. They claimed that if the stock went up, you simply let your put expire worthless and keep the gains on the stock. If the stock falls, you sell your stock for a 5% gain by exercising your put option.

Hopefully you understand enough about options by now to see this hardly needs explaining, but you still may hear of it from time to time. The reason this does not work is that the put has intrinsic value plus *time premium* that must be paid for. Once you pay for the put, you have raised the cost basis of your stock and are no longer in a risk-free situation. For instance, if you pay $100 for the stock, a 1-year $105 put will guarantee you 5% at the end of the year — if there is no cost. Assume you pay $1 for the put. Now at the end of the year you are guaranteed $105 for a position that cost $101, which is not a 5% return. Even with a low volatility of 20%, this $105 put will cost about $8 and will be close to $13 with 35% volatility.

Nothing comes for free in the financial markets — not even with options. Be careful when you hear of any strategy that sounds similar!

Stop Order Alternative

The long stock plus long put strategy is a nice alternative to stop orders. Many traders elect to use stop orders when they believe the stock price may fall. As we learned in Chapter 4, the problem with stop orders is that they can be traded through if the stock gaps down at the opening. If so, you can be stuck with a much larger loss than you anticipated. Another equally discouraging situation is to have your stop order trigger and then watch the stock trade much higher a short time later. Put options can prevent both of these situations from happening.

If you use a put option, you have all the way until expiration to decide if you want to sell your stock. Stop orders are dependent on the movement of the stock while protective puts depend only on time. With puts, you have all the way to expiration to decide if you want to exercise it, which is a luxury you do not get with stop orders. The tradeoff between the strategies is that the put option costs money but gives you time, while the stop order cost nothing but depends on the stock price.

Short Puts

The strategy behind the <u>naked</u> (or uncovered) put is neutral to bullish. The investor is betting that the stock will either rise or sit still. The short put has the obligation to buy stock for the strike price if the long put decides to exercise. We made the analogy earlier that long puts are similar to insurance policies; in a similar sense, short put sellers are like the insurance companies. They are selling policies for a fee but may be forced to pay out if disaster strikes.

Short put sellers are either speculators or hedgers. Speculators will sell puts betting that the stock will either rise or sit still, which will net them the premium at expiration. Speculators usually have no interest in owning the stock. They are simply looking for short to intermediate trends to make money based on speculating

Hedgers, on the other hand, will use short puts as a way to purchase stock. Hedgers tend to be more investment-oriented and are either indifferent to owning the stock or are using puts as a means to purchase stock. The scope of the investment changes if you are selling puts on stock you want to purchase anyway. Selling puts against stock that you do not mind owning is similar to getting paid to place buy limit orders below the current market.

For example, using the earlier INTC price examples, say you want to purchase shares of Intel but think it may fall to $28 in the short term. Many investors would place a buy order with a limit of $28 and hope it hits. If it does not, they have completely missed any profitable opportunity. Compare this to the short put seller. The short put seller may want to purchase the stock but he is afraid it may fall to $28. This investor sells the $30 put for $1.25. If the stock rises, at least this investor receives $1.25. If the stock falls to $28 at expiration, the short put seller will be forced to buy a $28 stock for $30; however, they received $1.25 for it, which makes their cost basis $28.75. Granted, their cost basis is a little higher than the investor who used the limit order. But, the limit order will have zero profit if the stock rises; they'll miss out on all opportunities.

Using short puts as a way to purchase stock can be a tough strategy to beat. In fact, we will show other variations on this theme when we talk about systematic writing and spreads.

From a profit and loss standpoint, the short put looks like this:

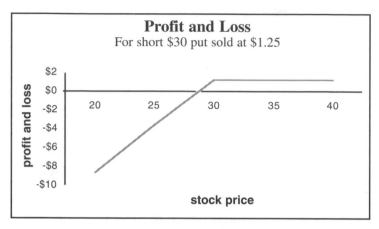

We see the maximum this investor can make is the $1.25 from the sale of the put. But if the stock falls, the investor starts heading into losses. If you are willing to purchase the stock regardless, then it is difficult to say these are truly losses — at least when compared to a speculator who sells puts with the intention of never buying the stock. The short put seller who intends to purchase the stock is, in fact, potentially deferring the purchase but getting paid if it rises. If the stock falls, he may be forced to buy stock, but he was going to purchase it anyway. The big tradeoff with short put selling for stock you want to buy is that the stock may take off to the upside, and you are left with only the premium from the put.

Combination Strategy

An alternative hedging strategy is to do the following: Buy half the amount of shares you are willing to purchase, and sell puts on half the shares. As an example, if you are willing to purchase 1,000 shares of stock trading for $50, buy 500 shares and sell five $50 puts. If the stock moves higher, you will profit on the 500 shares plus the premium from the puts. If it moves down, you were willing to assume this risk anyway, but now you have lowered your cost basis on the second lot of 500 shares by the time premium of the put. Other combinations work well, too. You can buy 800 shares and sell two puts, or buy 300 shares and sell seven puts, for example. Each unique combination creates a different profit and loss profile.

For example, assume the $50 put is selling for $3. You can see the effect of this strategy in the following profit and loss chart where one investor buys 1,000 shares and another buys 300 shares and sells seven $50 puts for $3:

The 1,000-share position makes more money if the stock rises but also loses more if the stock falls below $53.

Spreads as an Alternative to Naked Puts

Although we will be talking about spreads in detail later, we want to introduce you to them now. Spreads are simply option positions where you buy one option and sell another one. We want to cover them here because, with a little twist, they can be a powerful alternative to naked puts. It is one strategy highly overlooked, even by the most seasoned investor.

Assume you are willing to buy 1,000 shares of Intel currently trading around $42.50. Instead, you elect to sell a naked put and the Jan $40 put is trading for $3. If you sell 10 contracts at $3, you bring in a credit of $3,000 and keep this amount regardless of what happens to the stock. If the stock should fall below $40, the strike, you may be required to purchase it at $40 if the long position decides to exercise. From a profit and loss standpoint, your max gains and losses are as follows:

Maximum gain: $3,000
Maximum loss: $37,000

The most you can make is $3,000, but the risk is that you may be forced to buy stock at $40, which theoretically could be worthless. You offset this $40 loss with the initial $3,000 credit for a max loss of $37,000.

Let's now compare a trader who enters a spread order. He will sell the $40 put for $3, but simultaneously buy a far-out-of-the-money put, say a Jan $25, trading for $0.25. This trade results in a net credit of $2.75 (sold for $3 but paid $0.25). Because these are simultaneous orders, it is very likely to get a better fill between the two prices (but we will ignore that for now).

From a profit and loss standpoint:

Maximum gain: $2,750
Maximum loss: $12,250

This trader will take in a credit of $2,750 instead of the $3,000 the naked put trader received. This is because the spread trader will use $0.25 ($250) of his proceeds to buy the $25 strike put. In doing so, he now eliminates 25 points of risk to the downside. His maximum loss is only $12,250 versus $37,000 for the naked put.

The result is that the naked put trader increased his returns by only 1/4-point in return for accepting an additional $24,750 potential loss ($37,000 versus $12,250). That is a very expensive 1/4-point.

Naked puts are great strategies, especially if you are selling against stocks you would like to buy regardless. However, when things go bad, they can really go bad. This is the real risk of naked put writing. Using spreads can eliminate this risk cheaply.

Comparing the two profit and loss diagrams:

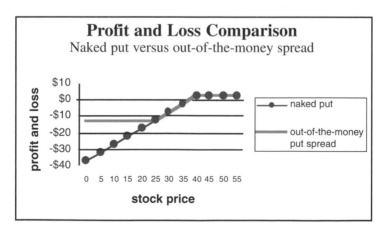

We see the two traders are virtually identical for all stock prices down to $25. In fact, they are separated only by 1/4-point, which was the difference in the initial proceeds. However, if INTC falls below $25, the spread trader will be very happy to have the long $25 put as insurance.

Which profit and loss diagram looks more appealing to you? Would you pay 1/4-point for it?

Additionally, most brokerage firms will charge you the lesser of the full spread requirement (difference in strikes less the credit) or the naked requirement. You will never be worse off (from an option requirement standpoint) with the spread order. Granted, it will cost you an extra commission, but in many cases this will be well worth it. In addition, if you are not approved for naked positions in your account but are approved for spreads, this is a way to nearly place naked puts in your account!

In this example, the spread trader bought "catastrophe" insurance. Take a look at the following charts to see just how big and fast a catastrophe can happen!

Headline: Lilly Shares Fall More Than 31% As Ruling Speeds Generic Prozac (8/09/00):

Headline: Apple Computer Falls More Than 52% On 4th-Quarter
Earnings Estimates (9/28/00):

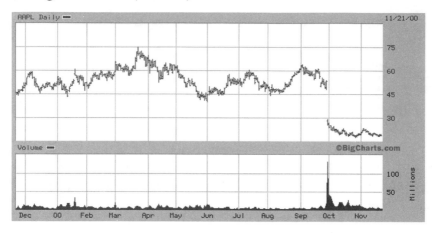

Here are some other headlines without charts:

- Priceline.com Down 42% On 3rd-Quarter Estimates(9/27/00)

- Xerox Down 26% As Sales Decline And 3rd-Quarter Loss
  Expected (10/03/00)

- Eastman Kodak Falls 25% On Profit Warning (9/26/00)

- Intel Falls 22% On 3rd Quarter Revenue Warning (9/22/00)

- Lucent Shares Fall 23% On 4th–Quarter Earnings (10/10/00)

I remember one client who had a $7 million account — before
he discovered naked put selling. The whole idea sounded too easy,
and he successfully wrote naked puts on Dell Computer for about
three months during a huge bull run between October and December
1999. During that time, Dell had run from about $25 to nearly $35,
and the put strategy paid off well. The stock continued to climb and
he continued to write. He decided to write LEAPS because there
was more time premium, and he could make even more money. He
kept writing as Dell continued to climb up to its peak of about $55, at
which point the investor was short over 2,800 puts! Then the stock
headed south quickly. It fell from $55 all the way down to the mid-
$30 range and required six-figure maintenance calls on a daily basis.
The customer was forced to sell other stocks and bring in other

money, which he confidently did because it was a good company. By March of 2000, he threw in the towel, closed all the naked put positions — and was left with an account balance of $3 million. Granted, this is still a lot of money; however, how long will it take to get the account back to $7 million? How much interest is he missing out on during that time? What about the compounding of returns? It should be apparent that this is a devastating loss, all from using a "conservative" strategy on a great company. The put spread we described would have prevented this type of loss at the expense of only very modest reductions in profits.

Hopefully you will see far-out-of-the-money put spreads as an enhanced alternative to naked put selling. Good companies do not always report good news as the above charts and headlines demonstrate. During these times the value of the far-out-of-the-money spread strategy will be realized.

Questions:

1) You recently purchased 300 shares of a stock at $40. It is now trading for $70 and the company is due to release earnings in a few days. You are concerned the stock may fall sharply if they release an unfavorable report. You do not want to sell your stock yet for tax reasons. How can you protect your position?

2) Is a short put a bullish or bearish position?

3) Assume the same scenario in question #1. You purchase three $65 puts for $2. What is the total cost not counting commissions? If the stock is trading for $60 at expiration, what is your stock worth? The put? How do you explain the discrepancy between the loss on the stock and gain in the option?

4) You just bought 100 shares of a $50 stock and a one-month $50 put for $2. What is your cost basis on the stock? Assume the stock is trading for $45 a few days later, and you're down $500 on your stock position. Why is the put not up $500 at this point to fully hedge your position?

5) You own shares of a stock currently trading for $75 but are looking to buy 300 more shares if it should fall below $70. You decide to sell three one-month $70 puts for $3.50. How much will you receive from the short put not including commissions?

You also notice a one-month $50 put trading for $0.25 and decide to buy it. What are your total proceeds from the sale and purchase now? How much have your reduced your downside risk? Compare the risk of the naked put versus the spread. Considering the total credits from both positions, which is more appealing to you?

Chapter 15: Combination Strategies

We just covered the basic option positions of calls and puts both long and short. Now that we have a better understanding of why an investor would use them, we can advance to strategies involving combinations of options. Options paired with other option positions can further tailor the risk-reward profiles to better meet your needs. We will be covering some basic, intermediate, and advanced combination strategies in the next several sections.

Straddles and Strangles

One of the most basic combination strategies is to combine a call and a put, which is called a straddle. Variations of these are known as strangles, strips, and straps. These strategies are discussed in the next several sections and are important to understand, whether or not you ever intend to use them. They will demonstrate how new and interesting profit and loss profiles can be formed that cannot be obtained with any other asset. Once you learn to combine options with stock or other options, their true potential will be realized.

The Long Straddle

The long straddle is a combination strategy where the trader buys a call and a put with the same strike and expiration. For instance, if you buy a $50 call and a $50 put, you are holding a long straddle. The straddle has a lot of intuitive appeal, because it starts to earn money whether the stock moves up or down. Notice the term "earn money" and not "earn profits." To be profitable, the straddle must make up for both the cost of the call and put. If you think trading calls and puts by themselves can be difficult, try straddles! Many new traders jump to trading straddles because they think they will make money regardless of what happens to the stock. In fact, you will probably hear about books and seminars boasting that they'll teach you how to "make money in any market." If so, this is probably the strategy they are talking about. If the stock moves up or down, technically you are making money on one of the legs — either the call or put — but being profitable is another story. Straddles cannot work as these people describe; if it did, it would be the only used option strategy, and everybody would make money.

This strategy is often suggested, even by professionals, to be used prior to a big announcement, such as an earnings report or FDA approval for a drug company. If the report is favorable, the stock may run rampant to the upside; if not, it may come crashing down. However, this is not really correct. Other market participants are thinking the same thing (remember the volatility trap?), so the put and call will be bid up to much higher prices, making it difficult to recoup your costs.

Probably a better use of straddles is to buy them if you expect *increases* in volatility. Increased volatility will increase the price of both calls and puts. So if you're faced with a big announcement, you should probably buy the straddle only if you think the market has underestimated the volatility. To use the straddle effectively, you really have to bet against the norm and expect a large move when others feel the stock will sit still.

Nonetheless, the strategy attempts to play both sides of the market, hoping that the move in the underlying stock, whether up or down, is sufficient to cover the cost of the losing option.

Example: A trader buys a March $50 call for $5 and a March $50 put for $3 for a total of $8.

The profit and loss diagram looks like this:

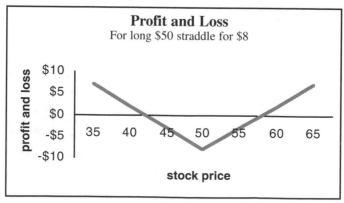

Profit and Loss
For long $50 straddle for $8

Notice that the maximum loss in the profit and loss chart occurs at the strike price of the call and put. If the stock closes at this point at expiration, both options expire worthless and the trader loses the $8 paid.

Because the trader buys both the call and put, the breakeven points will be raised significantly. In this case, the stock must rise above $58 (the strike price plus both premiums) or fall below $42 (the strike price minus both premiums). Because only one of the options — either the call or put — can expire in-the-money , the downside to this strategy is that you are effectively buying a very expensive call and a very expensive put. Only one of the options can have value at expiration; however, both premiums must be recovered before a profit can be made. If the stock closes at $58 at expiration, the long put will be worthless and the long call can be sold for $8, in which case the trader breaks even. Likewise, if the stock closes at $42 the long call will be worthless, and the long put can be sold for $8. In this example, the stock must move from $50 and either rise above $58 or fall below $42, a 16% move on either side, before profits are earned. Before entering a straddle, it is a good idea to calculate your breakeven points to determine if a move of this size fits your outlook.

The straddle can make a theoretically unlimited amount of money if the stock rises and can make a maximum of the strike price minus the net debit if the stock falls to zero. In this example, if the stock falls to zero, the trader will make $42 per contract ($50 strike - $8 debit).

The wide breakeven points do not necessarily make the straddle a bad strategy. But do not get lured into thinking it is a sure bet. The two premiums will almost always make the straddle a sure loser. (In trader's jargon, the high gamma and negative theta components usually will not allow it to be profitable.)

Ironically, straddles can also be discouraging even if they make money. Sometimes straddle holders regret using them because of the modest gain, despite the large move in the stock. Imagine that you paid $8,000 for 10 contracts in the above example. The stock closes at $59 at expiration, leaving you with $1,000 profit for an *18% move* in the stock — and risking $8,000 for it.

Use the straddle when you are, in fact, expecting a really BIG move in one direction or another and you believe the market has underpriced it (underestimated the volatility).

Bull and Bear Straddles

Usually, straddles are initiated at-the-money. If the stock is trading at $50, most traders buy the $50 call and $50 put. However, you can even adjust your straddle to reflect a slight bias toward one direction or another. While straddles are used when unsure of direction, most people have some opinion if they had to guess. If so, you may want to stack the odds a little in favor of that direction.

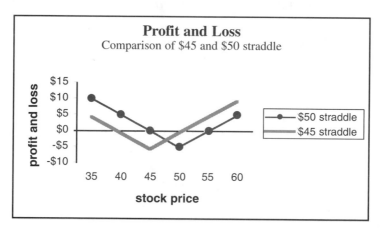

If the stock is trading for $50 and you are a little more bullish than bearish, you may want to use the $45 straddle, thus putting the call in-the-money. This makes the straddle a little more responsive to upside moves in the stock and is called a bull straddle. It is easy to see in the above profit and loss diagram that the $45 straddle will break even sooner to the upside than the $50 straddle. Of course, if you are wrong and the stock falls, it will take longer to make money with the $45 straddle.

Notice that the person holding the short $45 straddle would have a *bear straddle*; they think the stock will fall first from $50 to $45 and then sit still. Bull and bear strategies can be used to hedge your bet for any strategy, not just straddles.

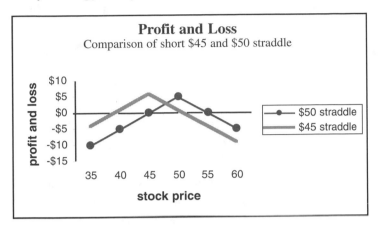

Trading Tip: Closing the Long Straddle

Many times traders closing out a straddle will close both the put and call near expiration. They enter the straddle realizing that one of the legs will be a loser, so when they cash in on the profitable call or put they often close out the losing leg at the same time. It is as if the straddle cannot be split apart. Using the same example, say a trader is holding the $50 straddle *near expiration* with the stock at $60. The $50 call will be trading for $10 plus a little time premium and the $50, but it will have a very small bid — possibly zero. Even if there is a small bid, you will net zero from it after commissions. Rather than close out the entire straddle, just sell the call to close and hang on to the put as a "wild card" — you never know! After all, you paid for the put, and it 's good all the way through expiration. If you aren't going to get anything for it, why give it up? Because it is a long position, there is no risk in holding it (this is not the case with the short straddle). Further, you will pay a commission to close out the put, but if it expires worthless, there is no commission to close it. It certainly makes sense to split the position and hang on to the losing leg.

Keep in mind this trading tip applies only to long positions *near expiration*. If the stock is trading at $60 with significant time remaining, this trader may sell the call for $11 and also get $1 for the put. In this case, it may make perfect sense to pay commission and close both legs out at the same time. When you get nothing for the losing leg (counting commissions), then you should split up the straddle when closing.

Trading Example:

A client had one of the best possible scenarios happen while I was working for a brokerage firm. In mid-March 2000, a client had purchased ten March $180 straddles on Microstrategy (MSTR). If you look at the circled area of the following chart, the stock was apparently starting to break down after a tremendous run from $18 to $180. The trader thought the stock was about to crash hard. But he also accepted that it could continue to run higher, so he initiated five $180 straddles. It did run higher (hitting a high of $333 on March 10) and the trader called to close out the entire straddle two days before when it broke $300. With just eight days left until expiration, the $180 puts had little time premium in them, and the trader was thrilled to cash in on the astonishing profits. I mentioned to him that he should hang on to the puts for the reasons already discussed. He agreed and, luckily, held on. The March options expired on the 17th and guess what — the stock unfolded for the next 19 days, hitting a low of $63 on March 21. On expiration day, the stock had still exhibited large swings and traded between $85 and $119. The trader closed the puts with the stock at $115 and captured far more profit on this "wild card" put than he did with the straddle.

Options are about creating profit and loss profiles that match your point of view. Learn to see opportunities by understanding that options can be paired — and split — to create opportunities, and possibly profits, you never imagined.

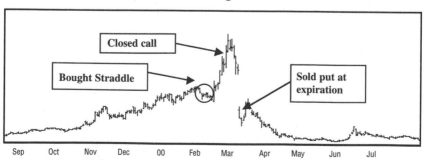

The Short Straddle

If the long straddle is almost a sure loser, then the short straddle must be the ultimate option strategy, right? Not so fast. Yes, it is true that over time the short straddle will win far more than it will lose; however, when straddles go against you, they can bite hard. We showed you how devastating naked puts can be. With straddles, you are naked the put and call, and exposing yourself to equally damaging results regardless of the direction of the stock. You need to be prepared to accept a large loss before entering into the short straddle.

From a profit and loss standpoint:

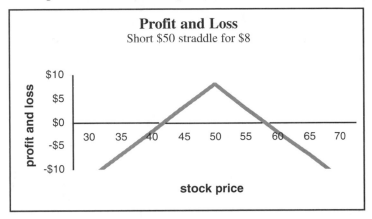

Here, the short trader will receive $8 in our example and have breakeven points of $42 and $58. Beyond these points, large losses can quickly develop.

Short straddle sellers are motivated by the relatively large premiums they receive, and consequently have large breakeven points before heading into losses. If you think a stock is going to sit flat for a while or that the market has overestimated its volatility, the short straddle can be a very rewarding trade.

If you are short a straddle, you are at risk if the stock makes a large enough move up or down. However, we showed earlier how naked puts could be viewed as a conservative option strategy if written against stock you are willing to purchase. If you are willing to buy the stock, then the downside risk of the straddle may not concern you as much as the upside. If this is the case, you may want to consider an interesting variation of the straddle, which we will talk about next.

Alternative Strategy: The Covered Straddle

A viable alternative for the short straddle is called a *covered straddle*. It is called a covered straddle, because the long shares cover the more dangerous of the two risks involved with short straddles — the risk of the stock moving higher. Here, the investor is long the stock and then sells the straddle. Assuming the number of call options does not exceed the equivalent number of long shares (e.g., buy 300 shares and sell three straddles), the investor is fully covered to the upside. The risk is that the stock falls. But if the investor is willing to buy more shares, this downside risk was willingly assumed and can make for a powerful investment strategy.

Example:

An investor is long 500 shares of stock purchased at $50. He then sells five contracts of the above straddle for $8 and receives 500 ∗ $8 = $4,000. If the stock is above $50 at expiration, the investor will be assigned on the short call and sell his shares — effectively for $58. But if the stock is below $50, the trader will be assigned on the short puts and be forced to buy stock at the lower price. You can see the benefits of this strategy if you are a longer-term investor. If you are willing to buy more and are not afraid to sell your shares, the covered straddle is a tough strategy to beat.

Assume the stock closes at $45 at expiration. The investor will be assigned on the five short puts and forced to buy an additional 500 shares at $50. After the assignment, the investor is long 1,000 shares, something he was willing to do from the beginning, for an effective cost basis of $46 per share.

Be careful when you calculate the breakeven points (cost basis) on the covered straddles; they are not the same as the breakeven points for the long straddle. While this may seem counterintuitive, it will make sense once you understand that the long stock position affects these points as well. For example, we said this investor has breakeven points of $42 and $58 on the earlier long straddle.

However, assume the investor buys 500 shares at $50 and sells five $50 straddles for $8, or $4,000 total. If the stock closes at $58 at expiration, the investor is assigned on the short call and the short put expires worthless. The investor sells 500 shares at $50 (500 * $50 = $25,000), and he gets to keep the $4,000 from the straddle sale for a total profit of $29,000. On average then, the investor received $29,000/500 shares = $58 per share. Notice the upper breakeven point is $58 as with the long straddle.

Now assume instead that the stock closes at $42 at expiration, which is the lower breakeven for the long straddle. The trader will be assigned on the short $50 put and forced to buy another 500 shares of stock for $50. The investor has now spent a total of $50,000 and received $4,000 for a total payment of $46,000, or an average price of $46 per share for the thousand shares. The investor has paid $46 per share for a stock worth $42 for a $4 loss. The reason this lower breakeven point is not the same for the covered straddle is that the investor bought shares <u>twice</u> but sold the straddle only <u>once</u>. This makes the credit from the short straddle half as effective for the downside. Notice that the investor did not need to purchase shares if assigned on the short call.

The most you will ever make from the short straddle is the initial credit, which is $4,000 in this example. The upper breakeven point on the covered straddle is therefore $4,000. Note that a stock price of $58 for 500 shares nets this profit. Likewise, a stock price of $46 at expiration is the result of the trader paying $50 per share but reducing this price by $4,000.

If formulas are easier for you, the upper breakeven point will be the strike price plus the credit from the straddle, and the lower breakeven will be the strike price minus half the credit from the straddle.

This is important to understand for trading purposes as well as for taxes. Many tax preparers are notorious for making this mistake with covered straddles.

Questions:

1) You buy a $50 call for $3 and a $50 put for $2. What is this position called? What are your breakeven points? Show why you would break even at those points.

2) Your friend tells you that straddles are the best strategy because they allow you to make money regardless of the direction of the stock. How would you comment?

3) You own a $100 call and a $100 put for a total cost of $8 for the two positions. What is your maximum gain if the stock rises or falls? What is your maximum loss?

4) You paid $6 total for a $50 straddle, which is five days away from expiration. The stock is now trading for $60 with the $50 call worth $10.25, and the $50 put has no bid. If you want to close out the straddle at this time, what is the best way to do it?

5) You own 500 shares of a stock trading for $50 and are willing to buy 500 more. If you sell five $50 calls and five $50 puts for $3 each, how much will you bring in from the sale not including commissions? What is the long stock and short straddle position called? Are you at risk if you are assigned on the short call at expiration with the stock trading at $60?

6) What is the risk of a short straddle? If you sell a $30 call and a $30 put for a total of $5, what is the most you can lose if the stock moves higher or to zero?

Strangles

There is a related strategy to straddles called a *strangle* — sometimes called a *combination* or "combo" for short.

The idea behind straddles and strangles is the same: The investor is looking for a large move in one direction or another. The strangle differs slightly because the strike prices are different.

The Long Strangle

Earlier, we assumed a trader with the stock at $50 bought the $50 call and $50 put, for a total of $8. Now let's say that same trader buys a strangle instead. They may buy the $55 call and the $45 put with the same expiration for a total of only $5. In trader's lingo, this is called a $45/$55 strangle. When you see a strangle written this way, it is always assumed that the put strike is lower than the call strike. We will see shortly that it makes a difference on the maximum amount you can lose.

Strangles are cheaper than straddles (assuming all else is the same) but the tradeoff is wider breakeven points for the strangle; this trader's breakeven points are $40 and $60 instead of the straddle trader's $42 and $58. The strangle's breakeven points are found in the same way as the straddle. You simply add the total cost of the strangle to the call strike and subtract it from the put strike.

The fact that strangles have wider breakeven points than straddles does not mean they are a poor strategy or that straddles should always be chosen over them. Options are about creating risk-reward profiles that suit your needs. Choosing which strategy is better — strangle or straddle — is up to you. Both should be considered when you're looking for large moves in the stock and uncertain about the direction. Many times you will find one to be better than the other.

As with straddles, be careful when choosing strangles. Make sure you understand what the underlying must do to make a profit. Use strangles when you expect really explosive moves in the underlying, or increases in volatility, and not because it is cheaper than the straddle.

From a profit and loss standpoint:

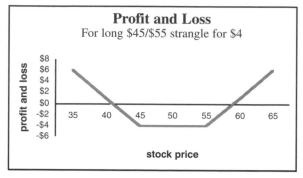

It is easy to see that the stock must make a really large move to be profitable. Also, there is no reason traders must limit themselves to a five-point difference in strikes as implied by many textbooks. One can use a ten-point difference, as we have done in this example, and you can even change the range of prices you want to cover. For instance, assume the stock is $50, and you are a little more bullish than bearish. You could choose a $45/$50 strangle or a $40/$50 strangle or any other combination, as long as they cover the same expiration months. Keep in mind that as you make the difference in strikes wider, your breakeven points become wider as well.

The Short Strangle

The short strangle is similar to the short straddle, although from a risk/reward standpoint, it may be a more attractive deal for most investors because the breakeven points are so widely stretched.

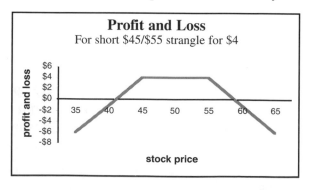

In-the-Money and Out-of-the-Money Strangles

One small point should be clarified here. In the prior example, we assumed the stock was at $50 and the trader bought a $45 put and $55 call to complete the strangle.

This is specifically known as an out-of-the-money strangle because both the call and put are out-of-the-money. There is another alternative position — sometimes called a *guts* by floor traders — where the trader will buy, say, the $45 call and the $55 put.

Be careful when discussing strangles with your broker. For example, say the $45 call is trading for $8 and the $55 put is trading at $6, for a total purchase price of $14. It is very easy to think that the maximum loss is $14. However, this position has a built-in box position (which we will talk about later) because one of the options must always be in-the-money. This particular strangle must be worth $10 at expiration (of course, the bid/ask spreads will make it worth slightly less). Why must it be worth at least $10? Work through some numbers, and you will see that it is impossible to have both the call and put expire worthless. In the original example, however, the call and put would expire worthless for any stock price between $45 and $55.

The maximum loss for this in-the-money-strangle is only $4 — not $14 as many traders think. In addition, you get the benefits of in-the-money calls and puts working for you, so your time decay diminishes significantly.

Just be aware that there is a difference. An out-of-the-money strangle has the *put with the lower strike and the call with the higher strike*. In this case, the maximum loss is the total cost of the two positions.

The in-the-money strangle has the *call with the lower strike and the put with the higher strike* — exactly the opposite of the out-of-the-money strangle. Here, the maximum that can be lost is the premium minus the difference in strikes. In our example, $14 - $10 = $4.

Straddles and strangles are popular strategies, especially in many beginning courses, because they are combination positions that are easy to understand. From a trading standpoint, the long straddle/ strangle is not very practical because of the wide breakeven points. Typically, the stock will bounce around between these two points, and you will watch your position erode from the time decay.

In fact, you can even combine these strategies to create others. We will show you later how to use straddles and strangles to create butterfly spreads. This is why it is so important to understand all of the basic strategies if you want to become proficient by using your knowledge of trading options. Many strategies are really combinations of other strategies in disguise. Once you learn to dissect the individual strategies, you will have a much better understanding of the risks and behaviors of various strategies.

Strips and Straps

We have just shown how options can be combined to form new risk profiles. Options can also be combined in varying amounts to increase or decrease the steepness of the profit and loss diagrams.

Although the terms are not used much anymore, strips and straps are two very basic combinations that demonstrate this ability.

Strips

A strip is a strategy where the trader buys one call and two puts with the same strike and expiration dates.

Because a strip is a combination of long calls and puts, it should be apparent that it is similar to a long straddle. However, because they are done in different proportions — *one* call and *two* puts — the steepness of the profit and loss lines will be altered, which is readily apparent in the following profit and loss diagram:

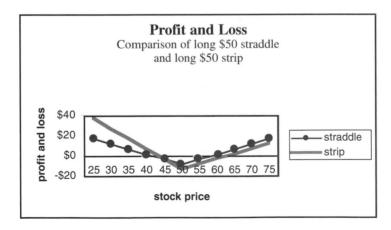

It is evident from the profit and loss diagram that the investor will profit more from a fall in the stock as compared to a rise. If you are uncertain about the direction but leaning a little toward the downside, strips may be a perfect solution. The tradeoff is that the strip costs more than the straddle (because you are buying an additional put for the strip). Because of this additional cost, a bigger rise in the stock will be necessary before breakeven is achieved to the upside with the strip as compared to the straddle. Conversely, the strip will show a profit quicker as compared to the straddle if the stock should fall. Both strategies hit maximum loss at the strike price, because all options will expire worthless here.

Straps

A strap is basically the opposite of the strip: The investor buys two calls but only one put. In this case, the investor is uncertain about the direction but is betting that there is a higher chance the stock will rise. Let's look at the profit and loss diagrams for the straddle and strap:

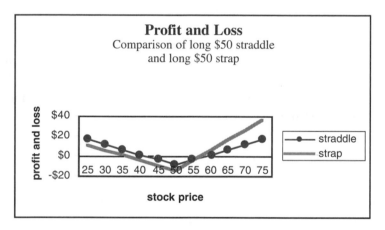

Again we see the trader's biases built in to the strategy. If the stock rises, he will profit at a much greater pace. However, if the stock falls he will still profit but will have a much lower breakeven point as compared to the straddle.

These simple strategies should suggest just how powerful options can be. Not only can you build your profit and loss lines in the direction you want, but you can also adjust the rates of profit and losses.

In addition, there is no reason to stop here. An investor could easily buy three puts for every one call or three calls for every put. You are undoubtedly starting to imagine the versatility and power of options that are not available through stock investing alone.

Questions:

1) You are uncertain about the direction of a stock and want to use a straddle. However, you are a little more bearish than bullish. Instead of a straddle, would you use a strip or strap?

2) If you buy a strip, why is the breakeven point higher for the upside compared to a straddle?

3) What is the difference between a strip and a strap? How does each differ from a straddle?

Covered Calls

For many investors, the covered call is their first encounter with options. It is a popular strategy, because it generates cash into the account and is relatively simple to understand. Unfortunately, there are a lot of misconceptions about this strategy, which can lead to devastating losses; and there are many professionals and academic journals that fail to recognize it. If you are interested in covered calls as an option strategy, make sure you understand this section.

What Is a Covered Call?

A covered call is a strategy where the investor buys stock and then sells a call against it. This is sometimes called a buy-write or covered-write strategy because you are buying the stock and writing (selling) the calls. By selling the call, you are giving somebody else the right to buy your stock at a fixed price.

The reason this strategy is called "covered" is because you are not at risk if the stock moves higher. This is different from the trader who sells calls "uncovered" or "naked," because that position continually loses money — theoretically an unlimited amount — as the stock moves higher. Because of this risk, naked call writing is among the most dangerous of all option strategies. But with covered writing, this upside risk is removed; you will always be able to deliver the shares regardless of how high the stock moves. The short call option is "covered" by the long stock.

For example, you may buy 200 shares of JDSU currently trading for $102, and you sell a one-month $115 strike call currently trading for $4.50. For the next month, you <u>may</u> have to sell your shares at a price of $115 if the long call decides to exercise, regardless of where the stock is trading. If the stock is trading at $200 at option expiration, you are virtually guaranteed to be forced to sell your shares for $115. For this right, the person buying the call paid you $900. On the surface, it does not seem to be a bad deal. It 's like getting paid to place a sell limit order at $115.

However, there is significant risk to the downside. With our JDSU trade above, we paid $102 for the stock and received $4.50 for the option. The stock could fall $4.50 to $97.50, and we would still be okay — that is our breakeven point. That's another small benefit of covered calls; they provide a little downside protection by reducing the cost basis of the long stock position. But if the stock continues downward from there, we get deeper into a losing situation. In fact, the maximum we could lose, theoretically, is the $102 we paid for the stock less the $4.50 we got for the option — a total of $97.50. In other words, we are at risk for everything below the breakeven point.

Trading Example:

I remember one investor who bought 7,000 shares of Egghead (EGGS) at $55 during the "dot-com" craze. (To make matters worse, it was on margin or borrowed funds.) He was laughing all the way to the bank when he discovered that a three-week option was bidding $8 for a $55 stock. "Wow, that is over 15-fold on your money" he exclaimed. "At that rate, it would take less than two and a half years to turn $1,000 into $1,000,000."

The trader bought the shares and wrote the calls waiting patiently for his windfall to arrive. At option expiration, the stock was trading at $4. Yes, he did get to keep the entire $8 premium for the calls. I will let you decide if it was worth it.

There was a reason the markets were bidding up the options so high. They wanted someone else to hold the risky stock. The risk is that the stock falls.

Many professionals and even academic journals will tell you that the risk of a covered call position is that you may lose the stock! Nothing could be further from the truth. Risk, for most people, is not defined as missing out on some reward. It is defined as loss of principle. This is not to suggest that losing the stock is not a type of risk — it is certainly a lost opportunity. However, every sale of stock faces this "risk." If you buy stock at $102 and sell it on your own at $115, you still face the "risk" that it could be trading for $200 at a later date. However, most investors recognize this possibility and openly accept it. For some reason though, when in the covered call position, they suddenly view it as a risk of the option. When analyzing option strategies, it is therefore important to understand which risks are dependent on the *option* and not other factors.

If a professional tells you the *risk* of a covered call is losing the stock through assignment of the short call, ask him or her why it is called a *covered* position? They will likely tell you, "That is because you are not at risk if the stock moves higher — you will always be able to deliver the shares." Think about it. The broker tells you the risk is that the stock moves higher, yet also tells you that you are not at risk if it moves higher. Which is correct?

If you are in a covered call position, you are the one holding the stock. The risk is that the stock goes down.

In fact, think of covered call writing as being similar to investing in bonds. If you buy a $10,000 face bond, you will receive interest payments every six months as your return. However, those interest payments constitute a good return only if you get your $10,000 face value back at maturity. Covered calls are very similar. You buy a stock and receive an "interest payment" of your call premium. Granted, this is not a recurring stream as with a bond, but the idea is the same. To yield your expected return, you must get back the "face value" of the stock. If not, the strategy can end up a loser.

Two Types of Covered Call Writers

The risk of a falling stock is independent of the option and should not be considered a risk of the option itself — *assuming you were willing to assume that risk*. Many people are not willing to assume it, yet they still enter into covered calls because of the apparent high rates of return. This brings us to the two types of covered call writers. It is crucial to differentiate between the two in order to use the strategy competently.

There are two basic categories of call writers: those who use it as an income-producing strategy against stock they would hold regardless, and those who are "premium seekers."

If you write calls against stock you are willing to hold, then the covered call strategy can be arguably one of the most powerful strategies for most investors. After all, you are getting a little downside hedge and getting paid to sell the stock at a price you see as favorable. If it is a stock you like, then you obviously are willing to assume all of the downside risk. You would hold the stock whether options were available or not. As stated earlier, this is no different from someone getting paid by the market to place a sell limit order on his stock.

However, some do not understand the downside risk side of covered calls. They are sometimes called the "premium seekers." These people look through the option quotes, find one that pays a high premium relative to the stock price, and then enter into a covered call. Usually they follow up this trade with a comment like, "By the way, what exactly does this company do?"

If you trade covered calls this way, stop! I have seen million-dollar accounts on two occasions fall below $10,000 doing nothing but covered calls using this method. This is where option trading can be very deceptive. It is easy to forget about the individual pieces (long stock and short call) and look at only the potential rates of return from the whole package. It is important to distinguish which asset — the stock or the option — is leading the decision. If the option is leading the decision, and you are not willing to assume the downside risk, the following example is a demonstration of what can happen.

Another Word of Caution

Many times you will hear people claim that the risk of the stock going down in a covered call position should not be of great concern. Their reasoning is that you can always write another call after the first call expires and eventually "write your way out of the stock." There is big danger in believing this. Covered calls realistically give you only <u>one</u> chance over the short term to write the calls. This is not to say that you will never be able to write a second call against your stock. It 's just that you may have to wait a long time to do it.

For example, say a stock is trading at $100, and you write a $105 call for $5. At expiration, the stock is now $75. At this point, you decide to write another call. You will be lucky if the $105 call, if it exists, is trading for pennies, which after commissions will net you zero. How about the $80 call? Yes, you will definitely get some money here — let's assume another $5. If you write this call and the stock goes up to $80 or higher at expiration, you just locked yourself into a loss! How? Your cost basis is $90 ($100 originally paid for the stock less two calls written for $5 each) and you just gave someone the right to buy your stock for $80, which locks in a $10 loss.

Sometimes you will hear people tell you to "roll down" or "roll up" if the stock is moving significantly. However, there are drawbacks with those strategies as well, so we will take a look at each. It is important to understand that covered calls do have a sizeable amount of risk and that you may not be able to realistically keep writing calls month after month.

Roll down

We just saw a situation where an investor bought stock for $100 and wrote the $105 call for $5 but would get locked into a loss if he wrote the $80 call at expiration. Many investors incorrectly think you can beat the market to the punch by rolling down your strike as the stock falls.

A roll down for covered calls is simply a strategy where an investor buys the short call to close and simultaneously sells a lower strike call to open. The new position is a covered call but at a lower strike; the investor has thus "rolled down" the strike price.

For example, say the stock is trading at $100 and the investor wants to roll down from the $105 call to the $100 call. He will receive a credit less than the $5 difference in strikes. The investor has given someone the right to purchase his stock for $5 less than originally anticipated, yet he received less than $5 to do so — a net loss.

Let's see what happens if he rolls down for a net credit of $3. Remember, the original trade was buying stock at $100 and selling the $105 call for $5, which gives a cost basis of $95. Once the roll down is executed, we are assuming the investor receives an additional $3, which gives a new cost basis of $92 for an $8 gain if the stock is called at $100 (paid $92 and sold for $100). The original trade, however, had a profit of $10 if called at $105 (paid $95 and sold for $105).

The reason the investor has reduced the profit margin by $2 (only an $8 gain rather than $10) is because that is the net loss on the roll down. Credits can be deceiving with options. A net loss develops because the investor gave somebody the right to purchase his stock for $5 less, yet he received only $3 for it.

If you roll down long enough, you will eventually lock in a loss. Be very careful when rolling down and keep track of your effective cost basis.

Roll up

The opposite of the roll down is the roll up. To enter a roll up with covered calls, buy the call to close and simultaneously sell a higher strike call to open.

Let's assume our investor is, instead, faced with the stock trading up to $110 now. If he rolls up, he may, for example, buy the $105 call to close and simultaneously sell the $110 call to open. Again, we will assume they pay less than the difference in strikes, which will always be true prior to expiration. If the investor rolls up to the $110 strike for a net debit of $3, he has paid $3 to gain $5.

On the surface, this does not appear to be a bad deal. However, with the original position, the investor is more likely to receive $105 from the exercise of the $105 call. Now they are short the $110 call, (the same price as the stock) which means there is inherently more risk with the roll up. This does not mean that investors should never roll up a covered call; rather, they should use it sparingly in situations where they are very confident that the stock's price will not fall too dramatically.

Another way to view the additional risk is that, with each roll up, you are raising the cost basis of your long stock position. If you chase a fast-rising stock with roll ups long enough, you will eventually end up holding a long stock position with a relatively high cost basis on a stock that may come crashing down.

Most people try to roll up to get themselves out of a "losing" situation – like the investor who wrote the $105 call. If the stock is suddenly trading for $120, most investors try to undo the "damage" by rolling up. However, you should always remember your reason for writing the call. If you purchase the stock for $100 and are willing to sell it at $105 for a $5 fee (the option premium), you should probably let the stock go. If you never intended to sell your stock, then you must question why you wrote the original call in the first place. Remember, a short call is an agreement to give someone else the right to purchase your stock. If that is not what you want to do, then writing calls is the wrong strategy.

Getting Out of a Covered Call

Many times investors write calls, and then regret it later when they see the stock trading for a much higher price. If you have a renewed confidence in the stock, you may want to consider closing out the short call.

Many investors, however, have trouble with this because they believe they are taking a huge loss. This is absolutely false and a simple example will explain why. Say an investor has $40,000 cash in his account with no other positions. If he buys 100 shares of stock for $100, he now has $10,000 worth of stock and $30,000 cash. Now assume he writes a $100 call for $3, which gives him $30,300 in cash for a <u>total account value of $40,300</u>.

Now assume the stock is $130 at expiration, which make the $100 call worth $30. If the investor buys the call to close to not lose the stock, he must pay $30. Because he received $3 initially, he has incurred a loss of $27. *But investors often fail to realize that the stock position is now worth more, too*. If he buys the call to close, he will pay $3,000, but now his stock is worth $13,000 <u>rather than</u>

$10,000! That is because he is no longer obligated to sell the stock for $100 once he buys the $100 call to close. The stock is worth $13,000, and the cash is reduced to $27,300 for a total account value of $40,300 — exactly the same as before the closing of the call.

If you exit a covered call position by buying the call to close, you are really *swapping cash for an unrealized capital gain in the stock*. In the last example, the investor surely lost $3,000 in cash in exchange for an unrealized gain of $3,000 in the stock.

So if you have new information on the stock and decide you want to keep it, buying the call to close is not the worst thing that can happen. You really don't lose anything at the moment you buy back the call — but you may if the stock falls afterward. Buying covered calls to close does not really destroy account value; it changes the values of the assets in the account.

If you decide to get out of a covered call position by buying back the call, be sure you are comfortable holding the stock at the current valuations.

Profit and Loss Diagram

In the profit and loss diagram, we are assuming an investor buys stock at $50 and writes a $60 call for $5. You can see the breakeven point has been reduced to $45, because he paid $50 for the stock but received $5 for the call, giving him an effective cost basis of $45. Also, we see that for any stock price above $60 — the strike — the profit is capped at $15, which is the maximum. Again, you must wonder why many professionals tell you this is the risk zone. It should be evident from the chart that the downside risk is that the stock falls. In fact, from a profit and loss standpoint, a covered call is the same thing as a naked put and the risk of a naked put is that the stock falls.

Covered calls are a highly useful strategy if used properly. If you use this strategy, make sure you are writing calls against stock you would hold regardless. Otherwise, treat the position as highly speculative and invest accordingly.

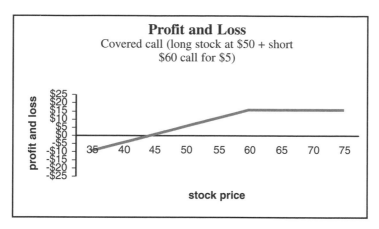

Profit and Loss
Covered call (long stock at $50 + short $60 call for $5)

Buy-Writes

A buy-write is simply a covered call — long stock plus a short call. The difference in the buy-write is in the way the order is handled.

Most investors who enter covered call positions buy the stock first and then sell the call at a later time. The problem with delaying the sale of the calls — even if it is a matter of only seconds — is that you will be exposed to market movement and downside risk in the interim.

Example: Say a stock is trading for $100 and a $100 call is trading for $5.

An investor wants to enter into a covered call position, believing that paying $95 for the stock and selling it for $100 over the next month will be adequate potential profit relative to the risk he is taking. So he puts in a market order to buy the stock, but gets filled at $101 because heavy trading caused the stock to move up (remember, price is not guaranteed on a market order). Then he immediately puts in the order to sell the call. The stock starts to fall and they sell the call for $4.50.

The five-point profit he was seeking has now been reduced to $3.50. He bought stock for $101 and sold the call for $4.50, effectively paying $96.50 for the stock instead of the desired $95 at the outset.

This is very common for people who enter covered calls in this manner. This is sometimes called "legging in" to a covered call because each of the "legs" — the long stock and the short call — is entered as a separate order.

To prevent this risk, known as *execution risk*, the investor could have entered a buy-write. There are two ways to enter a buy-write order: (1) as a market order or (2) as a limit order.

If the investor enters the buy-write "at market," this means the entire order — both the long stock and short call — must get filled *simultaneously*, and the investor is willing to take the prevailing prices at the time the order arrives to the floor or to market makers. In the example, had the investor entered a buy-write, he may have paid $101 for the stock but also may have received $5.50 for the call for a net debit of $4.50. This is still not the $5 point profit he was expecting, but certainly better than the $3.50 he got.

If the investor enters a buy-write as a "limit order," he will specify the price he wants to pay. The risk here is that the order does not get filled; however, if it does, you know the price will be at your limit or lower.

Example: Say we see the following quotes:

	Bid	Ask
XYZ Stock	$95.75	$100
XYZ Mar $100 Call Option	$5	$5.50

If the investor could be filled at the current prices, this buy-write would fill for a net debit of $95. This is because the investor can currently buy the stock for $100 (the ask) and sell the call option for $5 (the bid). This is also called "the natural" quote, because a debit of $95 is where the buy-write would be filled naturally if the trade could be executed immediately.

The investor may tell the broker, "I'd like to place a following buy-write and buy 500 XYZ and sell the Mar $100 calls for a net debit of $95." Now, the only way the trade can be filled is if the buy-write is filled at this price or lower.

Remember, this is the <u>net debit</u> the investor is willing to pay, so the order could come back filled as:

Stock purchased for	- $101
Call sold for:	+ $6
For net debit of:	$95

Or any other number of combinations of stock and option prices as long as the net debit does not exceed $95.

If you enter a limit order on a buy-write, it must always be entered as a net debit, because the price of the call can never exceed the price of the stock.

Placing a buy-write with the market maker is similar to trading in a car. If your car is worth $10,000 and you are trading it in on a $25,000 car, you may tell the dealer, "I want to buy that one and sell this one for a net cost (debit) of $15,000."

It should make no difference to you if they charge you $26,000 for the new car, as long as they give you $11,000 for your trade. Or the dealer may want to give you only $9,000 for your trade — but then must be willing to sell you the new car for $24,000. You are doing the same thing with the market maker on a buy-write limit order; you are specifying the net difference you are willing to pay for buying the stock and selling the call.

Of course, you may decide to try for a little better deal. Using the same quotes again, you may see the "natural" is $95 but tell your broker to place the order for a net debit of $94.75 instead. Regardless, any time you put in a limit order, you may not get filled. So you need to decide which is more important — getting filled or getting the price you want. You can guarantee only the execution or the price, not both.

By the way, if you do enter into a buy-write, you can close it out any time with a simultaneous order, too. Tell your broker to sell the stock and buy back the call (which is called an *unwind*). Unwinds will always be executed for net credits.

If you like covered calls, you should take the time to explore buy-writes. Market makers thrive on these orders, because you are giving them two of the three trades needed for them to complete a reversal (or to complete a conversion if you are unwinding a position). Because you will almost always get more favorable pricing for presenting two orders instead of one, the 1/4- and 1/2-point differences (or more) can make a huge difference at the end of a trading year.

Questions:

1) Someone tells you that covered calls are a conservative strategy and best for beginners with options. How would you comment?

2) From a profit and loss standpoint, which strategy is the equivalent of a covered call?

3) If you want to avoid execution risk on a covered call, you can buy the stock and sell the call simultaneously with which type of order?

4) What type of order allows you to get out of a covered call position without execution risk?

5) What is the risk of a covered call: having the stock rise and losing it, or having it fall?

6) You see a stock trading for $50 on the ask, and the $50 call is trading for $2 on the bid. What is the natural quote for a buy-write?

Sell-Writes

Many investors don't know this, but there is a trade opposite the buy-write, known as a sell-write. To enter a sell-write, the investor simultaneously shorts the stock (sells it) and then writes the put. The resulting position is a covered put; the sell-write is nothing more than a method of executing the two trades together to avoid execution risk.

If the stock falls, which is what the investor is betting on, he may be assigned on the short put and be forced to buy the stock. But this is what the trader must do at some point, and he can profitably cover the short position through the assignment of the put. As with the buy-write, the short option position is considered "covered" because the risk of the short put — the downside — is covered by the short stock. This does not mean this strategy is risk-free; the trader has *unlimited liability to the upside*. The short put just provides a little upside hedge.

Example: A trader is bearish on XYZ trading at $100. He decides to place a sell-write. What is the "natural" based on the following quotes?

	Bid	**Ask**
XYZ Stock	$95.75	$100
XYZ Mar $100 Put Option	$5	$5.50

The natural is $100.75, because the trader can currently sell the stock for $95.75 and sell the put for $5, for a total credit of $100.75. Notice what the sell-write accomplishes. The trader now has a *higher* net credit, which is what you want when you are short selling. If the trader were just shorting the stock, he would receive only $95.75, but with the sell-write, he receives $100.75. Remember, when short selling, you sell high and buy low, and the sell-write gives you a higher credit.

Because of this higher credit, the sell-write provides a little upside hedge for the trader. If the trader is wrong about the direction of the stock, he can afford for the stock to now move up $5 — the premium received for the put — to a level of $100.75 before heading into losses. The trader who only shorts the stock will be exposed to losses for any price above $95.75.

What if the stock falls? If the stock falls far enough, the sell-write trader may be forced to buy the stock at $95, because of the short $95 put. From the trader's perspective, that 's acceptable because he was going to have to buy it to cover the short anyway.

The tradeoff with this strategy is this: Say the stock crashes to a price of $50. The short seller would gain the full profit of $45.75 (short the stock at $95.75 and buy it back for $50). The sell-write trader, even though the stock is trading at $50, will be required to pay $95. The maximum the covered put writer could ever make, in this example, is $100.75 - $95 = $5.75.

Again, it is all about risk and reward. Neither strategy is superior.

There is another important point to consider with the sell-write. In the last example, we said the trader might have to pay $95 with the stock at $50. Remember, however, that the long put position dictates whether or not to exercise it. So while you may be ready to close out the sell-write, you don't have that choice. It is up to the person who is long the put. In cases like these, it is sometimes best to simultaneously buy back the put and buy the stock, or *unwind* the position, even though it will result in less profit.

I have seen investors enter a sell-write, watch the stock plummet, and then wait to be assigned on the stock, but they never are. In the meantime, the stock runs back up, sometimes into losses, and the investor never profitably closes out the trade.

Buy-writes and sell-writes are vital strategies to understand because they allow you to obtain more favorable pricing from market makers. After all, you are presenting them with two trades rather than one, so you definitely give yourself an edge.

Deep-in-the-Money Covered Calls

We have been saying how versatile options are and how they allow you to tailor risk-reward profiles to meet your specific needs. There is a variation of the covered call that most investors neglect, yet it can be one of the most significant strategies available to you. It involves the use of deep-in-the-money covered calls, which most investors never consider for incorrect reasons.

Most traders entering covered call positions buy the stock and then sell a call with a strike above the current stock price. For example, they may buy stock at $50 and then sell a $55 or higher strike call. Because these calls are out-of-the-money they do not carry much time premium, so they don't provide much of a downside hedge if the stock falls. In other words, selling out-of-the-money calls does not reduce your cost basis on the stock very much. Remember that falling stock prices are the risk of a covered call, and the downside hedge can be as important as the upside gains. Covered calls constructed with out-of-the-money calls are more of a revenue-generating strategy than a risk-reducing strategy.

Let's look at what deep-in-the-money calls can do for you. For example, assume a trader buys stock at $50 but sells a $40 strike call. I know some of you are thinking, "Wait a minute, why would I want to buy stock at $50 and give someone else the right to buy it for $40? That is a guaranteed loss!"

This way of thinking is exactly what keeps most beginning option traders from using deep-in-the-money calls against stock. The piece of the puzzle they are forgetting is the *time premium* of the call option. The $40 call in the above example may be selling for, say, $11. So even though it appears you may be taking a 10-point loss at expiration, the call buyer is paying for that up front. This $40 call has $10 intrinsic value and $1 point of time premium. It is the $1 time premium that the deep-in-the-money call writer is trying to capture. Deep-in-the-money call writers intend to have the stock called.

If the option were trading at parity (all intrinsic value and no time premium), then deep-in-the-money calls certainly would not be a good strategy. For example, if the $40 call is trading for exactly $10 (trading at parity), by entering the covered call position, you are buying the stock for effectively $40 (buying stock at $50 and selling the call for $10) and then selling your stock at a later date for $40. Effectively, you are giving up the interest on $40 through option expiration and paying two commissions. Clearly, options trading at parity are not a winning strategy for covered calls.

But as long as there is significant time premium on the deep-in-the-money call, the strategy changes. The deep-in-the-money call writer is putting the odds on his or her side that he will be assigned and be forced to sell the stock — *in exchange for the time premium.*

What makes this strategy appealing is that you are, in most cases, receiving a high rate of return *and* getting a huge downside hedge. You are getting the best of both worlds.

Now please do not misunderstand and think you will be over-compensated for the strategy. The markets will price them according to the relative risks involved. But if you are using this strategy on stock you like regardless, you will probably find this strategy to be one of the most appealing, especially when you see the balance between returns and downside protection.

Example: Extreme Networks (EXTR) is currently trading for $53.63. The December options with 16 days to expiration are quoted as follows:

Strike	Bid	Ask	Time premium
42.50	12.75	14	1.62
45	10.63	11.88	2
47.50	9.13	10.13	3
50	8.13	9.13	4.50
52.50	6.50	7.50	5.37
55	5.38	6.38	5.38
57.50	4.63	5.38	4.63
60	3.75	4.50	3.75

Say you buy the stock at $53.63 and sell a deep-in-the-money call such as the $45 strike. The net cost to you is:

Buy stock   = -$53.63
Sell $45 call = $10.63
Net cost   = $43.00

Effectively you are buying stock at $43 and putting the odds heavily on your side that you will sell it for $45. In fact, because the delta is currently 0.70, the markets are saying there is a 70% chance the sale will occur. If that happens, you earned 2 points (time premium) interest on a $43 investment for only 16 days of time. That is a simple return of 4.65%, an annualized return of more than 104%, and an effective compounded return of more than 178%.

So far, so good. Now let's look at the downside hedge. Because you received $10.63 for the call, the stock can fall by this amount, and you would be at breakeven. With the stock trading at $53.63, it could fall to $43 for nearly a 20% downside hedge.

If the stock is above $45 at expiration, you make an annualized rate of 104%; if it is down to $45, you are at breakeven. It is tough to beat, especially if it is a stock you do not mind holding and you're willing to assume the downside risk.

There are, of course, many ways to use the strategy. Maybe you are not so concerned with the downside risk and want more upside return. You may elect to sell the $47.50 or $50 strikes instead. If you are more concerned with downside risk, you may go for sale of the $42.50 strike with $1.62 time premium.

You should be seeing the benefits of using deep-in-the-money calls compared to the usual out-of-the-money calls used by most traders. Using the above quotes, many would be inclined to sell the $60 calls. Although that will yield a whopping 20.3% simple return and 6,273% compounded return if the stock is above $60 at expiration, it gives only $3.75 or a 7% downside hedge. Further, those returns are only realized if the stock is above $60 — there is a big chance that it will not be that high at expiration. The out-of-the-money call strategies are, for most investors, disproportionately stacked with upside returns in relation to their downside hedge.

Why Does This Strategy Work?

If you are still not clear why this strategy works, think about the following analogy.

Say you have a used car for sale for $20,000. A buyer comes to you with the following offer: He will give you $15,000 now and the balance in three months. If you take the offer, you are effectively loaning $5,000 to the buyer. Therefore, the only way you should accept the offer is to take additional money (interest) above the $5,000 payment he will owe you in three months. For example, you may take the offer for $15,000 now and $5,500 in three months.

Notice the similarity with the deep-in-the-money covered call strategy above. The buyer (long call position) is offering to buy your stock for $53.63. Instead of giving you the full amount up front, he is effectively asking to borrow $45 by purchasing the $45 call from you. In doing so, he can defer that $45 payment for 16 days.

Because he's borrowing $45 dollars, there is a net balance due of $8.63 ($53.63 stock less $45). However, as with the car example, you should not be willing to take the net balance without interest. How much interest is the market willing to pay for that deal? It's the $2 of time premium.

The $45 call buy will thus pay you $10.63 now and the balance in 16 days, effectively borrowing $43.

You are not taking a loss by purchasing stock at $53.63 and selling it for $45 any more than you are taking a loss by giving someone the right to buy your $20,000 car for $5,000. In both cases, the buyer is paying part of that future obligation now and paying you *interest* (time premium on the option) to float the balance. If the interest rate is appealing to you, you will take the offer.

You can add a little edge to deep-in-the-money covered calls by entering the trade as a buy-write. Because market makers love combinations of stock, calls, and puts to place them into locked positions (conversions and reversals), they will usually give you a break on the natural quote. For example, notice the spread on the $45 calls above: $10.63 to $11.88 for a $1.25 spread. It is very feasible to enter an order to buy the stock and sell the $45 call for a net debit of, say, $42.50. While this is only $0.50 better than the natural $43 debit we assumed earlier, look what it does to the returns. Now you are buying stock at $42.50 and potentially selling it for $45. That is a 5.88% simple return (compared to 4.65% earlier) and 262% effective annualized compounded rate (compared to 178%). What a difference a half-point can make.

You don't necessarily need to look at volatile stocks for this strategy to work, either. For example, take General Electric (GE), which is considered one of the "bluest" of blue chips. The stock is currently trading for $48.88, and the January $43.38 strike is trading for $7 on the bid and $7.25 on the ask. If you sell the call for $7, that is $1.50 of time premium with 51 days to expiration. You will likely be assigned on the short call; if so, you effectively paid $41.88 (paid $48.88 for stock and sold call for $7) and sold for $43.38 in 51 days. That is a simple return of 3.58% or an effective annualized compounded rate of 28.2%. Granted, it is not as impressive as the returns we saw earlier, but it's not as risky either. Your breakeven point would be $41.88 for a 14% downside hedge.

Two Warnings

If you trade in small lots (say 100 to 300 shares), make sure the commissions do not eat away your profits before entering the buy-write. To check, calculate the total net debit including commission to enter the position and the total credit for selling the position. If you are trading in small lots (or being charged very high commissions), it is not uncommon for the difference between your net credit from the sale and net debit from the purchase to be small or possibly negative. If that is the case, it is definitely not worth doing. Make sure there are significant dollars left over and that the amount is worth the risk.

The second warning is to make sure you are not being compensated at only the risk-free rate. We learned in Chapter 7 that an option's time premium approaches the risk-free rate the deeper in-the-money it goes. For example, in the GE example, we assumed the trader bought stock at $41.88. The trader is missing out on interest on $41.88 by entering the covered call. If we assume a risk-free rate of roughly 6%, the cost of carry for this position is $41.88 ∗ 6% ∗ 51/360 = 0.355, or about 36 cents. Because the time premium of $1.50 is significantly higher than 36 cents, this strategy will make financial sense as long as the commissions do not diminish the profits. If enough strikes were available, you could keep looking further in-the-money and eventually find one that is trading for exactly the cost of carry (where delta equals one). This will be true for all strikes below this strike.

To enter a deep-in-the-money covered call with options that exactly pay the risk-free rate of interest is like paying two commissions to enter the position, yet earning the exact amount if you had just left the money in the risk-free money market. Remember from Chapter 7, the deeper in-the-money you go, the less risky the strategy becomes. At a certain strike and below, the markets will view the deep-in-the-money covered position as nearly risk-free and will reward you only the risk-free rate.

A covered call can be a very rewarding strategy when you get the risk-reward ratios in proportion to your needs. If you feel that the out-of-the-money covered positions you've tried did not feel quite right, try deep-in-the-money calls for a revitalizing change.

Questions:

1) What is a buy write? A sell-write? Why would an investor use either?

2) Your friend tells you that selling in-the-money covered calls is a guaranteed loss because you are giving someone the right to purchase stock for less than you paid. How would you comment?

3) You are looking to write a deep-in-the-money covered call. The stock is currently $100, and the $80 call is trading for $20. Would it make sense to write this call? Why or why not?

Bull and Bear Spreads

In the past few sections, we have been looking at ways to combine options. We have seen long calls combined with long puts in the straddles and combined in different proportions in the strips and straps. Then we saw how options could be combined with long and short stock positions. Now we are going to take another step and examine long and short options held at the same time. If you buy one option and sell another, it is called a *spread* position. There are many types of spreads, and we will consider several. While this may sound complicated, it is really not any tougher than the buy-write and sell-write strategies discussed earlier. Instead of buying stock and selling a call as with the buy-write, we are buying a call and selling a call. In this way we are really using the long call in place of the long stock. We will see that it creates even more leverage than the covered call position because of the reduced price of the option compared to the stock.

Spreads were given their name because an investor, in fact, spreads the risk when he enters into one of these transactions. One of the positions, either the long or the short, acts as a hedge and either makes the position cheaper or acts as protection from a runaway stock. You are spreading the risk, and this — among other factors — is what makes spreads so popular and powerful.

In most situations, the trader is buying and selling an option in the same underlying stock or index. For example, long the Intel $30 call and short the Intel $35 call. These are collectively known as *intramarket* spreads, because they are spreading within the same market. If you are long Intel $30 and short Microsoft $45, this is an *intermarket* spread. The *intramarket* spreads are more common by far, and will be our only focus. Just understand that you do not have to be long and short the same underlying for it to be considered a spread.

The Four Basic Spreads

The most basic spreads are the bull spread and bear spread. Each can be accomplished by using calls or puts, for a total of four basic spreads. In other words, you can have a bull spread using calls or puts and a bear spread using calls or puts. Spreads are probably the most versatile and widely used among professional traders, and you will learn why these four spreads will add an invaluable set of tools to your arsenal of option strategies.

Bull Spreads

As the name implies, bull spreads need an upward movement in the stock to be profitable. Even though it may seem counterintuitive, bull spreads can be placed with calls or puts.

Bull Spreads Using Calls

The bull spread using calls is one of the most common spread strategies. This strategy involves the purchase of a *lower strike call* and the sale (equal number of contracts) of a *higher strike call* with all other factors the same (i.e., same underlying stock or index and time to expiration).

For example, a trader may buy 10 MRVC Jan $35 calls and sell 10 MRVC Jan $40 calls. This is sometimes referred to as a $35/$40 call bull spread.

We showed in Chapter 9 that the lower strike call would always be more expensive than the higher strike, with all else constant, so this trade will result in a net debit. To make up for this debit, the trader will need the stock to move higher, hence the name bull spread. This spread is also known as a debit spread, price spread, or vertical spread, and later we will show you an easy way to remember these names.

In this case, the trader is said to be *long* the $35/$40 bull spread. As with any position, if you buy it you are long, and if you sell it you are short. Because this trade resulted in a net debit (the trader paid for it), the trader is long the spread.

In a call debit spread such as this one, the short call (the $40 strike) acts as a way to bring in cash — it reduces the cost basis of the long $35 call. This is a great tool for option trading because it can allow you to buy lots of time without having to pay a lot of money.

Example: Say it is November, you are bullish on SCMR, trading around $64, and you want to buy 10 June $60 calls that are currently trading for $20.50. That trade will cost you $20,500 and could expire worthless. Because of the high price, many people avoid buying time in options and instead look at, say, a November $60 currently trading for $8. That call will cost you $8,000 for 10 contracts. Granted, you can lose less money with the November contract; however, you have a much higher probability of doing so. Is there a better way? Yes, and the bull spread answers this problem for many traders. Let's do a bull spread with SCMR and see the difference:

> Buy 10 SCMR Jun $60 = $20.50
> Sell 10 SCMR Jun $65 = $18.25
> Net cost   = $ 2.25

For only $2,250, you will own 10 contracts *but* have all the way until June (8 months) to profit from it. Your tradeoff is that you will not profit above $65. If the stock does get above $65 at expiration, this trade will be worth $5 for $2.25 down or a profit of 122%, or roughly 233% on an annualized basis. So by using the spread tactic, you reduce the time decay of the position and put the odds on your side that you will, in fact, get a very healthy profit.

Because options are so versatile, spreads can be versatile, too. If you want more upside potential, you could sell the June $70 call instead:

> Buy 10 SCMR Jun $60 = $20.50
> Sell 10 SCMR Jun $70 = $16.88
> Net cost   = $3.63

Here you will pay $3,625 for 10 contracts. Yes, you now have more money at risk, but you also get more reward in that you profit all the way to $70 instead of $65. You can tailor the spreads to meet your exact needs. If the stock reaches $70 or higher at expiration, this trader will make $10 points for $3.63 initial investment for a profit of 175% or 312% on an annualized basis.

So what does the position look like from a profit and loss standpoint?

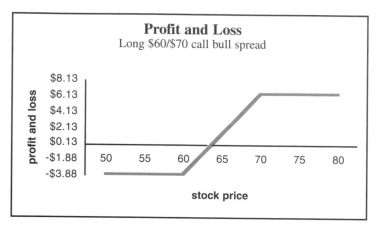

We can see that the most the trader can lose is the $3.63 — the amount paid. We also know from Chapter 9 that the most the spread can be worth is $10 points (difference in strikes), so the max gain must be the difference, or $6.37.

Where is the breakeven point? The trader needs to make back the $3.63 initially paid. If the stock is trading for $63.63 at expiration, the long call will be worth exactly $3.63 and the short call will be worthless; the breakeven is therefore $63.63, which can easily be found by taking the low strike and adding the net debit.

This trader will profit if the spread *widens*. In other words, he wants the spread to increase in value so that it can be sold for a profit. As the stock moves higher, the long position becomes more valuable, and the short position becomes more of a liability. Because the delta will always be higher for the lower strike call (all else the same), the value of the spread increases. The trader can buy the spread for one price and sell it for a higher price if the stock rises sufficiently.

No matter how high the stock goes above $70, the most this trader will make is $6.37. The bull spread has a limited downside as well as upside, which can be seen by the flat end on the left side of the profit and loss diagram. The trader is trying to capture the 10-point move between $60 and $70.

While using spreads may sound like a great strategy, it really requires the trader to hold the position close to expiration. Therefore, spreads are not good short-term trading tools. While the spread will certainly reduce your risk of the long position for day trading, its value will hardly change even if the stock is up a couple of points. The long call will gain more than the short call loses, but after commissions it may still be a losing trade. Enter spreads only when you are willing to hold on for the majority of time near expiration. For example, if you enter a one-month spread, you should be willing to hold that position for at least 20 to 25 days. The only exception is if the stock makes a remarkable upward move. But this is rare, so don't trade spreads with this expectation. If it turns out you can get out of the spread early, that's even better. But do not enter the spread with the intention of getting out in a few days with a profit, because it hardly ever happens.

Bull Spreads Using Puts

A bull spread with puts is a strategy where the trader buys a low strike put and sells a higher strike put in equal quantities. Because a higher strike put will always be worth more (all else constant), this trade will result in a credit to the account.

For example, a trader may buy ten MRVC $40 puts and sell ten MRVC $50 puts, which is a $40/$50 put bull spread. This spread is also known as a credit spread, vertical spread, or price spread.

This trader is said to be short the $40/$50 put bull spread because of the resulting credit to the account. This trader is hoping for the spread to "shrink" (as is any short seller) so that it may be purchased back later at a profit. How will a put bull spread shrink? If the stock moves up significantly by expiration (actually, this spread can also profit by sitting still; it just cannot move down) the put spread will make money — hence the name bull spread.

Example: Say you are bullish on MRVC trading at $39.50. You elect to do the following bull spread with puts:

Buy 10 Apr $40 puts = $12.50
Sell 10 Apr $50 puts = $16.25
Net credit   = $3.75

You will receive a credit of $3,750 to your account and will profit by this amount if the stock closes at or above $50. If the stock is $50 or higher at expiration, both puts expire worthless and the spread shrinks to zero — exactly what you want it to do.

Let's look at the profit and loss diagram for the short $40/$50 bull (credit) spread.

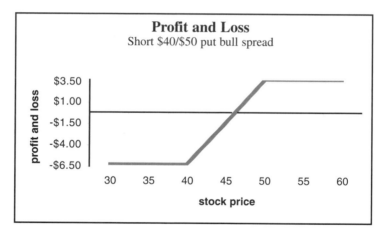

Based on the diagram, you will make $3.75 maximum; that is assuming the stock closes at $50 or higher on expiration. However, this $3.75 credit does not come for free. In exchange, you must be willing to assume a downside risk of $ 6.25. Remember, the higher strike put is more valuable, and that is the one you sold. If the stock falls, the higher strike put becomes more valuable to the owner and equally less valuable to you. But, if the stock continues to fall below $40, then your long $40 put starts to become valuable to you. So the spread can be worth a maximum of only $10 to the owner, or negative $10 to you, the seller. Because you brought in $3.75 for the initial trade, the most you can lose is $10 - $3.75 = $6.25.

Where is the breakeven point? You took in $3.75 initially, so the $50 put can work against you by this amount at expiration. So if the stock is trading at $50 - $3.75 = $46.25 at expiration, then your short $50 put will be worth negative $3.75 to you, and your long put will be worthless; you will just break even. To find the breakeven, take the high strike put and subtract the premium you received.

Notice that the two profit and loss charts have exactly the same shape. This is another way to identify a bull spread. They will always have this similar shape.

Which Is Better: The Credit or Debit Spread?

Many sources claim there is no difference between the two types of spreads. This is totally false. There is a big difference in the underlying assumptions, and depending on what they are, the call or put spread will be better suited.

We saw that for the debit spread, the trader <u>must have the stock move higher</u> because the trader must make up for the debit. The credit spread, however, <u>does not need the stock to move; it just cannot move down.</u>

Example: PWAV is currently $44.50. Let's compare the debit and credit spreads.

> **Debit Spread**
> Buy Dec $45 Call = $6.88
> Sell Dec $50 Call = <u>$4.25</u>
> Net debit   = $2.63

> **Credit Spread**
> Buy Jun $40 Put = $4.75
> Sell Jun $45 Put = <u>$6.75</u>
> Net credit   = $2.00

The trader using calls (debit spread) pays $2.63, while the one using the puts (credit spread) receives $2. If the stock sits still, the call trader <u>loses</u> $2.63, while the put trader <u>gains</u> $1.50. How? If the stock is still $44.50 at expiration, both calls are worthless; the long bull spread (debit spread) loses the entire $2.63 premium.

For the credit spread, if the stock is $44.50 at expiration, the short put is worth -$0.50, and the long put is worthless. The credit spreader will take a loss of $0.50 from the short position but keep the $2 from the initial trade, for a gain of $1.50.

So is the credit spread the best? After all, in this example, it seems like you get the best of both worlds. You get paid for the position and you do not need the stock to move to profit. Here is the catch: If you are wrong in your assumption about the direction of the stock and it falls, the debit spread sacrifices only the amount of the debit, or $2.63, while the credit spread loses $3.

The differences in the two types of spreads, either debit or credit, have to do with your assumptions about how quickly the underlying stock will move (yet another important reason to understand delta and gamma).

Cheap or Chicken

You may have noticed something about the two spreads we have been discussing. The debit trader is interested in purchasing the more valuable call. By entering the spread, the trader can <u>reduce the premium</u> he paid for this long position.

The credit spreader's goal is to short the more valuable strike and receive a premium; however, the trader is exposed to potentially higher losses if the stock moves against him. By entering the spread, the trader <u>hedges</u> himself in case the stock moves the other way.

There is a somewhat comical, although valuable, way of understanding the philosophies between credit and debit spreads. We can say the debit spreader is "cheap," since he doesn't want to pay a lot for the long call position by itself. Selling the higher strike reduces the price.

The credit spreader is "chicken," because his goal is to short the more valuable strike. But he is fearful of the unlimited downside risk, so buying another position gives him a hedge.

So remember "cheap" or "chicken" to help identify the underlying philosophies!

Bear Spreads

A bear spread, as the name implies, hopes the stock or index will fall. As with bull spreads, bear spreads can be executed through calls or puts.

Bear Spread Using Puts

This strategy involves the purchase of a high strike put and the sale of a lower strike put with all other factors the same.

Because you are buying the higher strike put, it will always be worth more and result in a debit. In order for the trade to make money, the stock must fall — hence the name bear spread.

Let's say you are bearish on INTC trading at $45; you think the price will fall. You could enter the following spread:

> Buy Apr $45 put = $6.50
> Sell Apr $35 put = $2.25
> Net debit   = $4.25

This trader would be long the $40/45 put bear spread. As before, this trader is long because a premium is paid.

This trader is interested in owning the $45 strike, because it is the most valuable of the two puts. However, he does not want to pay $6.50. By entering the spread, he can own it for only $4.25. Using our "cheap or chicken" method, this trader is "cheap." He is at risk for only $4.25, but the tradeoff is that he can profit to a stock price fall of only $35.

At expiration, if INTC is $45 or higher, this trader loses the entire premium of $4.25. If the stock is $35 or below, the trader will make the full spread of $10 (the difference in strikes) less the amount paid of $4.25, for a total profit of $5.75. To break even, the trader must be able to sell the long position for $4.25, which means the stock will have to be in-the-money by this amount, or $40.75. The formula would be high strike minus debit paid ($45 - $4.25 = $40.75). As with any debit spread, this trader wants the spread to widen so that it may be sold for a profit.

Let's take a look at these numbers on the profit and loss diagram:

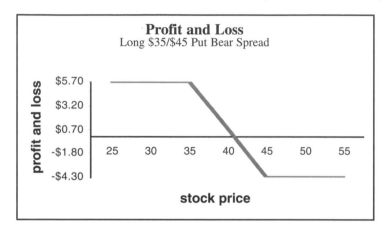

The chart confirms what we just figured out intuitively. Also notice that the bear spread profit and loss diagram is opposite that of the bull diagrams earlier. The bear spread profits from a downward move in the stock.

Bear Spread Using Calls

To create a bearish position with a "bullish" asset, we need to sell it and receive cash. If we sell the more valuable call, we will get cash and profit if the stock falls.

Assume Intel is still trading for $45. A trader who is bearish and wants to sell calls is interested only in shorting (selling) the $45 call. However, because of the unlimited risk to the upside with naked calls, the trader buys a $55 call for protection. This follows the "chicken" philosophy. Now it should be evident why the trader would spend the money to buy the $55 call; without it, he is at risk for all stock prices above $55. Notice the difference between the debit spread with puts and credit spread with calls. The put spread must have the stock fall whereas the credit spread does not need it to fall; it just cannot move higher. The put position needs movement (high gamma) and the credit spread needs slow or no movement (negative gamma).

For example, a trader could buy a $50 call and sell a $45 call. Because the lower strike will always be more valuable, this trade will result in a credit.

Let's use INTC again but with calls instead.

Sell Apr $45 call = $8.13
Buy Apr $55 call = $4.63
Net credit   = $3.50

If INTC is below $45 at expiration, both calls expire worthless and the trader will profit by the $3.50 credit. If the stock is above $55, the trader will lose $10 on the spread but will offset this loss by the initial premium for a net loss of $6.50. To break even, the trader can afford to have the lower strike call move $3.50 against him for a closing stock price of $48.50 at expiration. At this point, he owes $3.50 for the short position, which exactly offsets the original premium, so he breaks even. The formula would be lower strike plus premium received from the spread ($45 + $3.50 = $48.50)

The profit and loss diagram should confirm this:

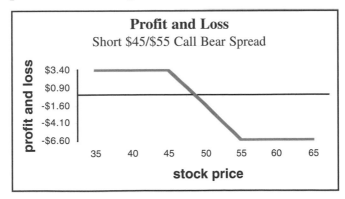

Again, as expected, this bear spread has the same shape as the previous bear spread. We see that the maximum profit is, in fact, $3.50, and the maximum loss is $6.50.

Because this trader received a credit from the initial transaction, he wants the spread to narrow so it can be purchased back cheaper or expire worthless. Either way will result in a profit.

How to Easily Figure Your Maximum Gain on Spreads

In Chapter 9 we learned that the difference in prices of any two options cannot exceed the difference in strikes with all else the same. Understanding this will make it easy to figure out the max gain and loss for spreads. Say you buy a $50 call for $3 and sell a $55 call for $1. The maximum this spread could ever be worth is $5. However, you paid $2 for it (paid $3 and sold for $1 for a net cost of $2), so the maximum gain is $3 on this spread. The maximum loss is the amount you paid, $2. It is really not that hard once you understand why the prices must hold. Always start by the maximum value the spread could be worth (the difference in strike) and then either add the credit or subtract the debit to arrive at your answer.

If you sell a $50 put and buy a $40 put for a credit of $6, the most you can make is $6. The maximum value of the spread, however, is -$10 (remember, it is a short spread) so your max loss is $4 (brought in $6 and lose $10 on the spread).

Do Not Forget About Risk-Reward

One of the biggest mistakes investors make using spreads is in failing to understand the risk-reward concept. This usually leads to unsuitable trades based on the investor's risk-reward profile or outlook on the stock. Let's look at an example:

INTC is now trading for $44.88 with the following quotes for December available:

$35/$40 spread = $4.25
$40/$45 spread = $3.38
$45/$50 spread = $2.50
$55/$60 spread = $0.69

Novice investors will look at quotes such as these and think the $55/$60 spread is the best because they pay only $0.69 and can make a maximum of $5 on the spread for a $4.31 profit. It certainly sounds better than paying $4.25 for the $35/$40 spread and making only $0.75 profit.

The reason the $55/$60 spread is relatively cheap is because it is an out-of-the-money spread; remember, the stock is trading at $44.88, so neither option is in-the-money. It is a higher-risk strategy, relative to the other spreads listed, so should be trading for a cheaper price and have a higher reward.

The $35/$40 spread is an in-the-money spread because both options have intrinsic value. This spread will grow to a maximum of $5 without the stock moving — just as long as the stock does not fall below $40 by expiration. It is much less risky than the other two spreads so should be trading for a higher price and have a lower reward.

When looking at profit and loss diagrams on spreads, you can immediately see the relative risk in strategies. Take a look at the profit and loss diagrams for the four spreads listed above:

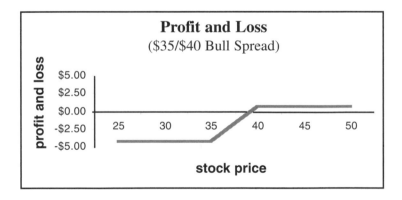

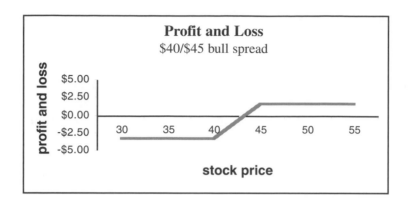

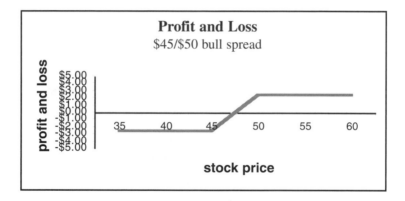

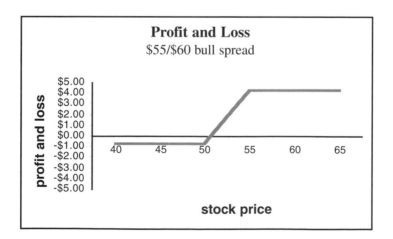

You can see the $35/$40 spread (graph on page 235) has a large loss area and a low reward area. As the spreads move more out-of-the-money, the profit and loss line shifts upward to reflect a lower loss and higher reward. For example, look at the $55/$60 spread (graph on page 236). It has only a $0.69 loss but a $4.31 reward, which certainly sounds appealing.

Again, most novice investors would immediately jump to the $55/$60 because of the amount of profit that can be made relative to the amount invested. Remember, you cannot get around the risk-reward relationship. With the $35/$40 spread, you will <u>probably keep</u> the $0.25 profit; with the $55/60 spread, you will <u>probably lose</u> the $0.69

It does not mean that either spread is right or wrong. Just be careful that you are picking the correct one that matches your opinion of the move in the underlying stock and not using it because it is cheap or that it has a high reward. Always consider the counterpart when looking at risk and reward.

One final note of caution. In the example, we looked at a $35/$40 spread that cost $4.75 and could yield $0.25 profit. Even though you will probably keep the 1/4-point, be sure to factor in commissions before entering into low-yielding spreads such as this. The commissions will, in many cases, lock you into a loss. Low profit spreads are common with floor traders because they may pay only a couple of dollars in commissions and they are really stacking the odds on their side that they will make a profit. For retail investors, you need to be sure the commissions are not too high. Technically, a broker should not even accept a trade from you that locks you into a loss such as this. They are bound by rules that require them to make sure there is some economic benefit to you in entering the trade. For example, there is really no benefit to you by entering a 5-point bull spread for a $4.88 debit, because the commissions will surely eat away the $0.12 potential profit. If a broker accepts a trade like this, you may have a case to have it removed. At the same time, if a trade is canceled for this reason, you should not be upset, because they are only looking out for your best interest.

Spreads that lock you into a loss are entertainingly called alligator spreads — you will never get out alive!

Bull and Bear Spreads — How Can I Keep All These Names Straight?

It can be confusing to remember which strategies are bullish and which are bearish, especially if you are new to spreads. Fortunately, there is a useful mnemonic device that will help you remember.

Whenever you BUY a LOW strike and SELL a HIGH strike, remember BLSH, which looks like "Bullish" and you will get the right answer. Of course, the reverse is also true. If you buy the high strike and sell the low strike, it is a bearish strategy. This method works for calls or puts and can be very helpful.

Examples:
Buy $40 call and sell $45 call.

You are buying the low <u>strike</u>, selling the high <u>strike</u>, so it is a bull spread.

Buy $120 put and sell $100 put.

You are buying the high <u>strike</u> and selling the low so it is a bear spread.

Buy $40 put and sell $45 put.

You are buying the low <u>strike</u> and selling the high so it is bullish.

Buy $50 call and sell $40 call.

You are buying the high <u>strike</u> and selling the low for a bearish position.

Be careful with this method though. A lot of people remember the "BLSH" mnemonic but often forget that it is in relation to the strike prices. It is very easy to look at the price of the option, and this is incorrect; in fact, it will get you the exact opposite answer!

Example: Earlier we looked at the following trade:

Buy 10 SCMR Jun $60 = $20.50
Sell 10 SCMR Jun $65 = $18.25

It is easy for investors to look at the prices of the options instead of the strikes. In this case, they may think we are buying high ($20.50) and selling low ($18.25) and think it is a bearish strategy — exactly the opposite.

So just be careful and remember that the BLSH method works great — for calls or puts — if you use it in relation to the <u>strike</u> prices.

How to Remember the Different Kinds of Spreads

There are many names for spreads and some are used inter-changeably. If you understand where these names come from, it will help you to identify the type of trade. For example, you may hear the following names for different spreads: price, time, vertical, horizontal, calendar, time, and diagonal, to name just a few. So how do you remember them?

If you look at option quotes in your local paper, you will most likely see a similar grid with the months across the top and the strikes down the side; in fact, this format was originally used on the exchanges to quote options:

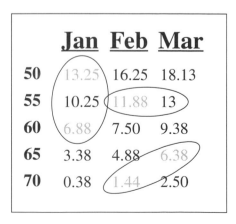

	Jan	Feb	Mar
50	13.25	16.25	18.13
55	10.25	11.88	13
60	6.88	7.50	9.38
65	3.38	4.88	6.38
70	0.38	1.44	2.50

Now, look at the Jan $50 and Jan $60 quotes. Depending on which one you buy and sell, it could be either a bull or bear spread. Because it is also spread on the vertical axis, it can be called a *vertical spread* or *price spread* because the prices are being spread.

So all the bull and bear spreads that we have talked about are also vertical spreads or price spreads.

If you spread horizontally such as the Mar $55 and Feb $55, then this is known as a *horizontal spread, calendar spread,* or *time spread* because we are actually spreading time, not price.

Last, if we spread time and price such as the Mar $65 and Feb $70, then it is a diagonal spread.

As always, if any of these spreads results in a net debit, the trader is said to be long the spread and short if it results in a credit.

Questions:

1) If you buy a $50 call and sell a $55 call, are you bullish or bearish?

2) What are the benefits and drawbacks to spreads? Consider time decay, risk, and costs.

3) If you buy a high strike put and sell a low strike put, are you bullish or bearish?

4) A friend tells you that a 5-point spread for $1 net debit is obviously better than a 5-point spread for $3 debit with all else constant. He reasons that it is better to pay $1 and potentially make $5 rather than pay $3 and make $5. How would you respond?

5) You purchase a $60 call and sell a $70 call. Is this bullish or bearish? Will this result in a net debit or credit? Why? What is the maximum you can make?

Synthetic Options

One of the most powerful tools an option trader can have is an understanding of synthetic options. Synthetic options are not a specific type of option such as calls or puts. Instead, they provide a method of combining stock, calls, and puts in such ways so that they behave like another asset. When we say "behave," we mean their profit and loss diagrams will be identical. For example, if we combine long stock with a long put, those two positions together will behave like a long call option from a profit and loss standpoint. We would then say that long stock combined with a long put is a synthetic call option.

Understanding synthetic options will benefit you in many ways. First, you will gain insights into option pricing theory. At first thought you may wonder, "Who cares about theory?" After all, the only thing that matters in the real world are the actual prices — not what the prices ought to be. However, there are times when theory answers questions that otherwise would not be known. For example, perhaps you will buy an at-the-money put and selling an at-the-money call in the next month. Will you need to set aside a sizable amount of money to pay for it? No, since an at-the-money call is always more expensive than an at-the-money put, so that trade will always result in a net credit. This can be shown by synthetic pricing relationships. You will understand how options are created and why the market makers are quoting options the way they are.

A second benefit of synthetics is that you can locate trades that result in a statistical advantage to you. Synthetics will also help you to hedge positions masterfully rather than using the roundabout, inefficient methods often used by new traders.

A third advantage is that it will allow you to *effectively* do things many traders will tell you cannot be done such as shorting stock on a downtick (or even when no stock is available), buying calls or selling naked puts in an IRA, buying stock for virtually no money down and a host of other imaginative strategies.

If you wish to master options trading, understanding synthetic equivalent positions is essential.

What Is a Synthetic Equivalent Position?

The name sure sounds intimidating, but synthetic options are actually fairly easy to comprehend and are truly a fascinating and useful part of options trading. In order to understand these mysterious sounding assets, you need to understand one of the most fundamental concepts of option pricing known as *put-call parity.*

Put-Call Parity

Parity is just a fancy word for equivalence. There are many "parity" relationships in finance, and they all show some type of mathematical tie between one asset and another asset or group of assets. Put-call parity is a relationship showing that put and call prices are very dependent on one another as well as the price of the underlying stock and interest rates. The prices of puts and calls are not just arbitrarily chosen by market makers, contrary to what many people believe. In order to understand the put-call parity equation better, it's best to show how orders are filled on the floor of an exchange. Here's an example of how it works with a simple hypothetical trade:

Trade:
Buy to open 10 ABC $50 calls (one year to expiration) at market. *Note: We will assume that ABC stock is trading at $50.*

When this buy order is received on the floor, the market maker must become the seller so that the transaction can be completed. This means the market maker must be willing to sell or *short* a call. Now, while you may be totally comfortable in speculating by buying 10 calls, the market maker may not be so eager to be on the short side. The reason is this: Market makers are in the business to take 1/8 or 1/4 of a point on a large number of trades; they are not really too interested in holding open speculative positions over long periods of time — especially short calls that have unlimited upside risk!

Market makers prefer to fully hedge themselves for guaranteed small profits but do so over a large number of trades.

How Does the Market Maker Create a Short Call?

If the market maker is to be short a one-year call, his risk will be that the stock moves higher. So in order to protect himself from this risk, he will purchase 1,000 shares (since 10 contracts control 1,000 shares) for $50,000. Now, no matter how high the stock moves, he will always be able to deliver 1,000 shares of stock at expiration. By purchasing the stock, all of the upside risk has been removed.

However, now there is a *new* risk— the stock may fall. So to protect himself from this, he will buy 10 $50 puts with one year to expiration. We're going to assume he pays $5 per put, although it doesn't really matter what the price is. As we will soon see, the price he pays for the put will be reflected in the price he charges you for the call, just as any business will price their products above cost. Purchasing the stock and put option are part of the market makers cost in creating a long call for you. By purchasing this $50 put, all of the downside risk has now been removed.

So our market maker is now long 1,000 shares of stock and long 10 $50 put options, which puts him in a no-risk situation of being short a call. He can now fill your order for 10 long calls, but what price should he charge? Please keep in mind as we move forward that the market maker is now long the stock, long the $50 puts, and short the $50 calls. You are long the $50 calls.

In order to understand how the market maker will price your call options, it's necessary to understand that the three trades he places — long stock, long put, and short calls — provide a perfect hedge. A perfect hedge means that all risk has been removed from the position and he does not care one way or another whether the stock sits flat, runs to the moon, sinks to the ground, or settles at any price in between. There is no risk to the market maker! How can that be?

Well, the stock price can do one of three things between now and expiration of the call option one year from now. It can stay the same, go up, or go down. If the stock stays exactly at $50, the $50 call and $50 put expire worthless and the market maker's position is worth exactly $50,000, which is the amount he originally paid for the stock. If the stock closes above $50, the long put will expire worthless and the market maker will get assigned on the short call and lose the stock; however, he will be paid the $50 strike and receive exactly $50,000. Likewise, if the stock closes below $50 at expiration, the short call will expire worthless and the market maker will exercise his put and receive $50,000. These actions are summarized in the following box:

At Expiration:

If stock is at $50:
   The market maker's long $50 put and short $50 call expire worthless. His position is 1,000 shares of stock at $50 for a total of $50,000.

If the stock is above $50:
   The market maker's long $50 put expires worthless. He will be assigned on the short $50 call and be forced to sell his shares for $50, which means he will receive a total of $50,000.

If the stock is below $50:
   The market maker's short $50 call expires worthless. He will exercise the long $50 put and sell his shares for $50, so he receives a total of $50,000.

   Note that no matter what happens to the stock price, the market maker's position is guaranteed to be worth $50,000 in one year.

So with the long stock at $50, long $50 put and short $50 call, the market maker is now <u>guaranteed</u> to receive $50,000 in one year. It is kind of ironic that by using these speculative derivatives of puts and calls we can actually create a risk-free portfolio.

Now, if any financial asset is guaranteed to be worth a certain amount in the future, then its value today must be worth the *present value* discounted at the risk-free rate of interest.

Present Value and Future Value are "time value of money" concepts used throughout the financial industry to describe the value of assets at different points in time. The concept of time value says that a dollar today is worth more than a dollar tomorrow because the dollar today can be invested and earn interest. For example, if you deposit $100 into an account that pays 5% interest, you will have $100 (1+5%) = $105 in the future. So the *future value* of $100 today is $105 if interest rates are 5%.

Similarly, if someone owes you $105 one year from now and interest rates are 5%, then you should be willing to accept $105/(1+5%) $100 today. In other words, it should make no difference to you whether you wait one year and receive $105 or collect $100 today. That's because you can take the $100 today, invest it at 5% for one year, and still have $105 a year from now. So the *present value* of $105 one year from now is $100 (if rates are 5%). To calculate the present value, we simply take the future value of the asset and divide it by 1 + risk-free interest rate.

We just showed that the market maker is guaranteed to receive $50,000 in one year regardless of the stock price. What is this position worth? If it's guaranteed to be worth $50,000 in one year, then the value today must be the present value, which is $50,000/ (1.05) = $47,619. This means the market maker should pay $47,619 today for the three positions. If he pays $47,619 and receives $50,000 in one year, his return on investment will be 5%, which is exactly the interest rate he should receive for a risk-free investment. We can check this by taking $47,619 * 1.05 = $50,000.[1]

The market maker will spend $50,000 for the 1,000 shares of stock trading at $50. He also paid an additional $5,000 for the put for a total cash outlay of $55,000. We already figured that the fair price for this package of long stock, long put and short calls should be worth $47,619 yet he's already laid out $55,000 for it. He will need to offset this high price from the sale of the calls he's selling to you.

---

[1] This doesn't work out to exactly $50,000 because we rounded the present value down to $47,619. The true present value is slightly less than $47,619.05.

The market maker therefore needs a credit of $55,000 - $47,619 = $7,381. He will need to bring in a credit for this amount, so he will fill your order on the 10 $50 calls for roughly $7.38. Doing so, he will receive the necessary credit to make his $55,000 cash outlay equal to $47,619. Of course, the market maker will try to make a 1/8- or 1/4-point profit so your order would probably be filled around $7.50.

To summarize, the market maker's initial position looks like this:

The Three-Sided Position of the Market Marker:

Buy 1,000 shares at $50   = -$50,000
Buy 10 $50 puts at $5   = -$5,000
Sells 10 $50 calls at $7-3/8 = +$7,381

Equals -$47,619 cash outlay by market maker

This three-sided position (long stock + long put + short call) established by the market maker is called a ***conversion***. If he had done the reverse (i.e. short stock + short puts + long calls) then it is called a ***reversal*** or *reverse conversion*.

It is imperative to understand conversions and reversals since they are the building blocks of synthetic equivalent trades.

The Put-Call Parity Equation

We have shown that the market maker's three-sided position (conversion) is guaranteed to be worth the exercise price of $50 at expiration. Because he's guaranteed this strike price, the conversion must be worth the present value of the exercise price. We can rewrite this using S for stock price, P for put price, C for call price, and E for exercise price as follows:

Equation 1.1, The Put-Call Parity Equation:

S + P - C = Present Value E

And in this little equation lies the magic behind synthetic options!

Equation 1.1 is known as put-call parity. If you know the value of any three of the four values (stock, put, call, present value of exercise price) you can immediately figure out the value of fourth.

Notice the notation with the plus and minus signs. Starting at the left, the S has no sign so is assumed to be positive. Next, the long put position is denoted by a "+" sign and the short call is denoted by "-". This is telling us that a long stock position plus a long put plus a short call must equal the present value of the exercise price. This notation of plus and minus signs to represent long and short positions will be important to remember later.

To make things a little easier to understand, we know the present value of E (the right side of the equation) is guaranteed to grow to E so it behaves like a risk-free investment such as a T-bill (or Treasury bill, Treasury note or Treasury bond). We can therefore rewrite the above equation as:

Equation 1.2:

S + P - C = T-bill

With some very basic algebra, we can create many interesting positions, which you've probably guessed will be called synthetic positions.

One Small Adjustment

Before we can continue with some examples, there is one small adjustment we need to make to the formula and is best shown with an example. Let's say we are interested in seeing what a long stock + long put position are equal to. The trick to using the equation is to isolate the asset or assets on one side of the equation with the correct sign.

In this example, we need to get the stock and the put on one side of the equation so that both have plus signs. By looking at equation 1.2, we can see that the long stock and long put are already together on the left hand side. In order to isolate them, we need to move the short call to the right hand side by adding C to both sides. Once we do, we have a new equation:

S + P = C + T-bill

What does this mean? It means that someone holding long stock and a long put in a portfolio (the left side of the equation) will have <u>exactly</u> the same portfolio balance at option expiration as another person holding a long call plus a T-bill (the right side of the equation).

Let's see if it holds true:

Assume we are interested in one-year $50 options and interest rates are 5%:

Investor A holds stock at $50 and a $50 put (left side of equation). Investor B holds a $50 call and a T-bill (right side of equation). Investor B will pay $50,000/(1.05) = $47,619 for the T-bill.

At expiration:

Stock price	Investor A			Investor B		
	Stock	$50 put	Total value at expiration	T-bill	$50 call	Total value at expiration
35	35	15	50	50	0	50
40	40	10	50	50	0	50
45	45	5	50	50	0	50
50	50	0	50	50	0	50
55	55	0	55	50	5	55
60	60	0	60	50	10	60
65	65	0	65	50	15	65
70	70	0	70	50	20	70
75	75	0	75	50	25	75
80	80	0	80	50	30	80
85	85	0	85	50	35	85

Regardless of where the stock closes, investor A will be worth exactly the same as investor B. There are no differences in the two portfolios as shown by the "total value at expiration" columns for each investor — they are exactly the same. Why does this happen? Portfolio A can never fall below $50, which is the strike of the put. However, if the stock rises, investor A will participate fully in the rally. Portfolio B, on the other hand, must *grow* to a value of $50 because that is the T-bill portion and is guaranteed. Portfolio B, like A, can therefore never have a value below $50. If the stock rises, investor B's call will start to increase in value by the same amount as the increase in stock in A's portfolio, so both A and B receive all of the upside potential in the stock.

Portfolio B is said to be the synthetic equivalent of portfolio A. Likewise, A can be said to be the synthetic equivalent of B.

So a synthetic equivalent is any position that has exactly the same profit and loss, *at expiration*, as another position using different instruments.

Now here's the one small adjustment I was referring to at the beginning of this section. By definition, synthetic positions only track the *changes* in portfolio values and not the total values. For example, in the above example with investors A and B, the total value of B's portfolio is the same as A's. To have the synthetic equivalent, we only need to track the changes. If B just held the $50 call option and not the T-bill, he would exactly reflect the changes in A's portfolio.

For example, if A buys the stock for $50 and it falls to $40, A can exercise the put and receive $50 — so A starts with a value of $50 and ends with $50 and therefore has no change. Portfolio B would also reflect no change as well since the call would expire worthless. If the stock is trading at $60 at expiration, portfolio A will be worth $60 reflecting a change of $10 from the beginning $50 value. Portfolio B will also change by $10, as the $50 call will now be worth $10.

The whole point of all this is that, with the original equation S + P - C = T-bill, we can ignore the T-bill on the right hand side, as it helps to account for total value but not for the changes in portfolio value.

Now our equation is even easier. All you need to know is:

Equation 1.3:

S + P - C = ?

Using this equation, we can figure out any synthetic position. Notice that there are only three assets in the equation: stock, puts, and calls. Before we get into the details of figuring out synthetic positions, it is important to understand a very simple property: The synthetic equivalent of any one asset will be some combination of the other two. In other words, stock can be formed by some combination of puts and calls. Calls can be replicated by some combination of stock and puts.

Remember, any one of the assets in equation 1.3 can be replicated by some combination of the other two. This basic property serves as an initial check for your answer.

Another way of looking at it is this: The synthetic equivalent will never include the asset you're trying to replicate. For example, a synthetic long call will not include a call option in the answer. If you come up with that, a mistake has been made. The only thing left now is to figure out whether those combinations are long or short.

We will take it slow with lots of examples, so hang in there!

Synthetic Positions

Now that you have equation 1.3, let's work through some examples to see how to figure out — and understand — synthetic options.

Let's start with a synthetic long call. Remember, the answer we come up with should be a combination of assets that behaves just like a long call option at expiration, and it will be some combination of stock and puts.

Synthetic Long Call

To find out the specific combination of assets that behave like a long call, all we need to do is reference equation 1.3:

S + P - C = ?

and it will be easy. To start, we need to get the asset that we're trying to replicate (either the stock, put, or call) by itself and with the correct sign. Since we are trying to find out the synthetic value of a <u>long</u> call, we need to get a +C (remember, we are using "+" to denote a long position) on one side of the equation. Using some basic algebra, if we add C to both sides of the equation we get S + P = C, and there's the answer; long stock plus long put (left side of the equation) will behave just like a long call (right side of equation). Therefore, if you hold long stock and a long put, you have a synthetic call position.

Shortcut Method:

Rather than adding or subtracting variables in the equation, it's easier to just imagine that you are moving the letters (assets) to one side of the equal sign or the other. If you change sides of the equal sign, the sign of the asset will change:

Using the above example, we were trying to get C by itself:

S + P - C = ?

The quickest way to envision that is to move the C from the left side of the equal sign to the right side:

S + P = +C

Because the C moves to the other side of the equal sign, its sign will change, too. In this case, it changes from negative to positive.

Let's check the profit and loss diagrams to see if we're correct:

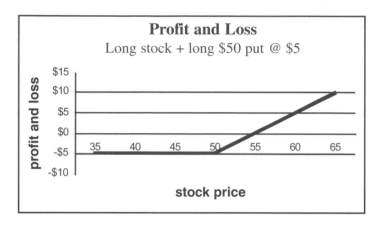

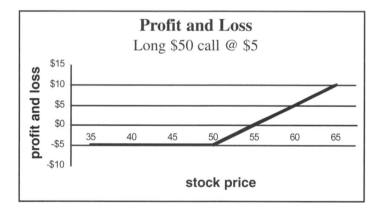

We can easily see there is no difference between long stock + long $50 put purchased at $5 (top chart) and long $50 call purchased at $5 (bottom chart). The person holding the long stock and long put raised the cost basis of their stock from $50 to $55. That's why their breakeven point is now $55, which is the point where the profit and loss line crosses the $0 profit and loss mark. However, they still participate in all of the upside movement of the stock. What if the stock falls? The investor is protected for all prices below $50, which is the strike of the put. The worst that can happen is for the stock to fall to zero. This investor will exercise the put and receive $50, effectively only losing on the $5 he paid for the put; therefore the maximum loss is $5.

For the call holder, he paid $5 so his maximum loss is also $5 but he also participates in all the upside of the stock. The stock will have to be $55 at expiration in order for the call holder to break even since he has the right to buy stock at $50 but paid $5 for that right. This effectively makes his breakeven price $55 as well.

It should now be apparent that call owners get <u>downside</u> protection as well as put holders; the call keeps you from losing value in the stock because you are not holding the stock.

We can use this information to gain some trading advantages. For example, most firms do not allow investors to buy call options in their IRA (Individual Retirement Account) but now you know that it can be done in a roundabout way with synthetics. You simply buy the stock and put, so you are effectively long a call option. Now, your return on investment will be much lower using long stock plus a long put as compared to the person who buys only the call. This is due to the difference in capital required to purchase the stock, but the two positions will behave the same in terms of net gains or losses at expiration.

<u>Examples</u>

1) A stock is trading at $60 and you wish to own a $50 call in your IRA. You find that your brokerage firm does not allow long calls in IRAs. How do you effectively buy a $50 call?

Answer: Buy the stock and buy the $50 put. Long stock + a long $50 put will behave (have the same profit and loss diagram) like a $50 call option.

2) What if you wanted to buy an out-of-the-money call such as a $65 strike? Which trades would you place?

Answer: Buy the stock and buy the $60 put.

We just saw that a long call is synthetically equal to long stock plus a long put. What do you suppose is the equivalent of a short call? A short call is synthetically equal to short stock plus a short put. Just change the signs and you have the opposite position:

+ Stock + Put = Synthetic long call
- Stock - Put = Synthetic short call

Synthetic Long Stock

Can we use equation 1.3 to see if there's a way to own stock synthetically? Without looking ahead, see if you can use the equation $S + P - C = ?$ and solve it for long stock. Hint: Just get S by itself with a positive sign and move the put and call to the other side taking note of their sign change.

Because we have +S on the left side already, let's move the C and P to the other side, which changes their signs. To do this we need to add C and subtract P from both sides. If you did it correctly you should find that $S = C - P$. Now you know that a trader holding a long call and short put (right side of equation) is actually holding synthetic stock (left side).

Looking at the profit and loss diagrams for each:

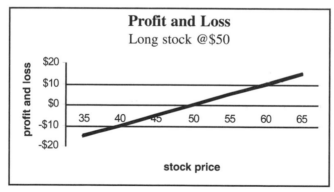

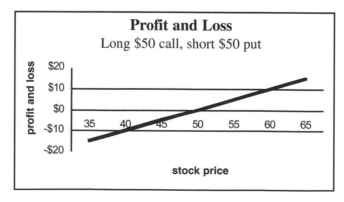

We see there is no difference between the two positions. The long stock purchased at $50 (top chart, page 254) will gain and lose point-for-point to the upside as well as the downside. The same holds true for the long $50 call and short $50 put (bottom chart, page 254). The $50 call will gain point-for-point at expiration while the short put will become a liability (loss) point-for-point if the stock should fall.

So synthetic stock is just a long call plus a short put. What would synthetic short stock be? Once again, all we have to do is change the signs of our previous answer and find out that a long put plus a short call will behave just like a short stock position. This is great to know for all traders involved in short selling. Now you know how it is possible to short stock without an uptick or when stock is not even available for shorting — use synthetics!

Question:

You wish to short a stock trading for $100. Your broker informs you that the stock is not marginable and therefore cannot be shorted. How can you effectively enter a short sale?

Answer:

Sell the $100 call and buy the $100 put, which is synthetically the same as short stock.

How much will it cost to short synthetic stock? As stated at the beginning of this report, the synthetic equation will lend insights into option pricing, and we can certainly use it to answer this question. The answer is that you should receive a slight credit. This can be shown by the original equation (1.1), which is S + P - C = Present value of E. If we rearrange it to find the value of a long call minus a short put, we'd get:

C - P = S - Present value of E

If S and E are equal (in other words, at-the-money), then S - Present value of E can be rewritten as S - Present value of S. We now know that the right side of the equation must be positive since the Present value of S has to be smaller than S. We also know that C - P is equal to the right hand side, so C - P must be positive as well.

The only way for that to happen is if C is more expensive than P. Realistically though, because of bid-ask spreads and commissions, it may cost you a slight debit. Regardless, it will not be a major cash outlay to enter this position (please keep in mind that there will be significant margin requirements to do so). However, they should not exceed (and will usually be much less) than the Reg T requirement of 50% required to short a stock. So not only can synthetics allow trades that otherwise cannot be done, they usually allow it to be done more efficiently by requiring less capital to take the same position.

Example

Recently, between May 17 (shown by the dotted vertical line on graph, pg. 16) and June 3, 2002, the OEX took yet another plunge. While there is usually no way to short the OEX index through the stock market, you could have done it synthetically. On May 17, the index was trading at 550 and the 550 calls were $13.00 with the 550 puts at $11.80. As we showed earlier, an at-the-money synthetic short will usually result in a slight credit, which was the case here. Selling 20 calls and buying 20 puts would result in a net credit of 20 contracts * 100 * $1.20 credit = $2,400. Just 17 days later, at the close of trading, the puts were worth $38.20 and the calls 0.80. The synthetic short position could have been closed out for a credit of $37.40 * 20 * 100 = $74,800.

For no money down (in fact, a credit of $2,400) you could capture a $70,000 profit in just no time. Of course, this trade does not come without risk. The risk is that the index trades higher, which leaves you in for a loss. Regardless, synthetics allow you to initiate positions that others will tell you cannot be done. The more agile and efficient you are at establishing positions, the better trader you will become. Synthetics give you those abilities.

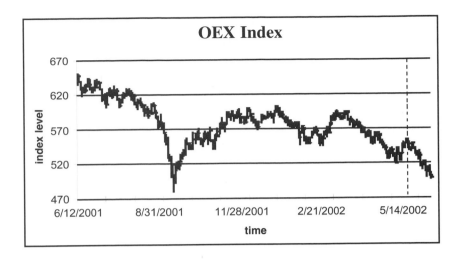

Synthetic Covered Call

What is a synthetic covered call? We know a covered call is long stock plus a short call, so it would be represented by S - C in our equation. Looking at the equation S + P - C = ?, we need to get S and -C on one side. In order to do that, we can just move P from the left to the right and get S - C = -P. A covered call position is therefore synthetically equivalent to a short put.

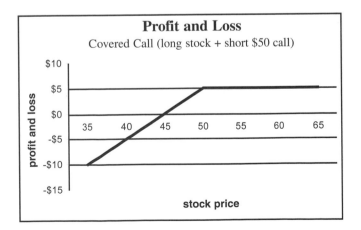

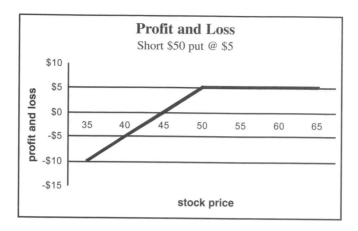

As expected, the profit and loss diagrams are exactly the same. For the covered call position bottom chart, page 257), the investor buys stock at $50 and sells a $50 call for $5, effectively giving the stock a cost basis of $45, which is shown to be the breakeven point. If the stock rallies above $50 at expiration, the investor will be forced to sell it for $50 regardless of how high the stock moves. The investor cannot profit above a stock price of $50, which is why the profit and loss line flattens out at $50 and higher.

The short put above chart) is at risk for all stock prices below $50 which is offset by the $5 premium received, which gives a break-even point of $45. The short put seller keeps the $5 premium for any stock price above $50, which is why the profit and loss line flattens out above $50. However, if the stock falls below $50, the short put seller starts to head into losses — just like the covered call writer.

Question:

You wish to sell a naked put in your IRA but your broker says it's against policy to do that. How can you do it synthetically?

Answer:

You one can buy stock and sell calls, which is exactly the same thing from a profit and loss standpoint. So while your broker will probably not allow naked puts (unless cash secured), you can always use covered calls.

Understanding synthetics also allows investors to gain insights about the risks of their own trades. How many times have you heard that covered calls are "conservative" and that naked puts are "high risk"? Once you understand synthetics, you'll know there is no difference between the two. It is ironic that most brokerage firms require level 3 option approval to short puts yet require only level 0 to enter covered call positions. If you wouldn't short a put on a particular stock, you shouldn't enter into the covered call either.

Added Insights Into Synthetics

We said earlier that the market maker using a conversion was perfectly hedged against all risk. Now that you understand synthetics, it will be easier to see why. Recall that the conversion was:

S + P – C = Present Value E

We can see in the formula that the market maker is long stock, which is denoted by the positive S. What position do you suppose would offset a long stock position? Hopefully you guess it would be a short stock position. If you are long stock and are also short the same stock you have no risk. Now look back at the equation and, aside from the S, we see the market maker also has a long put and a short call — a synthetic short stock position. Effectively then, the market maker is long stock and short stock, so he has eliminated all risk. Remember though, that he did this for a profit at some level higher than the Present value of E! In this sense, market makers act like banks and can borrow at one rate and lend at another, and thus profit by the spread.

We could also look at the equation and say that the market maker is long a put option, which is denoted by the +P. You should now understand that a short put will exactly offset a long put and eliminate all risk. The remaining +S and –C are exactly a short put.

It turns out that no matter which asset you pick, the other two are the synthetic opposite and fully hedge the risk. We could also pick any two assets and know that the third will fully hedge those two.

We can use synthetics to better understand why multiple trades such as buy-writes are valuable. A buy-write is simply a covered call but is executed simultaneously. For instance, rather than buying the stock and then selling the call as a separate order, you can instruct your broker to enter a buy-write; you'd buy the stock and simultaneously sell the call. What's the difference? The difference is that the market maker receives two of the necessary three positions to fully hedge himself so he can offer you a better price! Use multiple order entries whenever possible.

All Combinations of Synthetics

It is great practice to run through equation 1.3 and figure out the various combinations of synthetic trades. If you are really motivated, try to draw the corresponding profit and loss diagrams. All of the combinations are listed below for your reference. Note that the short positions are exactly the opposite of the long positions.

Long stock = long call + short put
Short stock = short call + long put

Long call = long stock + long put
Short call = short stock + short put

Long put = short stock + long call
Short put = long stock + short call

How Do Market Makers Arrive at Their Option Quotes?

Market makers must balance the demand for calls and puts by raising and lowering prices. However, they cannot just arbitrarily raise stock, call or put prices as they are all tied together by the put-call parity relationship. At the beginning of this report, we showed that a one-year $50 call option would theoretically be worth about $7.38 if the stock were $50, the $50 put was $5, and interest rates were 5%. In that scenario, we would say the "fair value" of the call option is $7.38. The market maker, however, will try to make a profit whether he's buying or selling. He may, using this example, post an asking price of $7.50 for the call (the price he's willing to sell) and a bid of $7.25 (the price he's willing to pay). Likewise, we saw that the market maker could accomplish this conversion by paying $5 for the put. Therefore, he may bid $5 for the put and ask $5.25. No matter which trade comes across his desk, he can fully hedge it for a profit. Market makers just "straddle" the fair values of calls and puts; they bid low and offer high. While this may sound like a great business arrangement, keep in mind that it is extremely competitive and that the option prices are usually not too far above or below fair value.

Finding Optimal Trades

Synthetic pricing relationships can also allow you to become more efficient because they allow you to understand various equivalent trades and to pick the best one for your situation.

A quick insight gained from synthetics is that the market makers will bid below the fair value and offer above fair value. Therefore, if you continually buy at the asking price and sell at the bid, you are significantly stacking the odds against you. Trading "in between" the bid and ask can greatly improve your results. Please don't confuse this to mean that you should never buy at the ask or sell at the bid. There are certainly times when it makes sense to do so. What's important to understand is that you have a mathematical disadvantage by doing so, because the market makers will tack on a profit to the fair value of the option. Once you pay above (or sell below) the fair value, you are statistically disadvantaged.

Let's look at another use. Assume you wish to buy a call option. Are you better off buying the call or taking the synthetic equivalent and buying the stock and buying the same strike put? Check the quotes for each trade and you will see that there is often a slight difference, which makes one better than the other — especially if it is a large trade. For example, most beginning investors tend to stick with covered calls. But this trade requires two commissions and two bid-ask spreads that both work against the investor, since he buys the stock at the ask and sells the call at the bid. Most market professionals, however, tend to use naked puts since there is only one commission and one bid-ask spread. The risk profile is the same in either case, but the naked puts are a more efficient way of doing it.

Synthetic trades may seem complex at first, but they are actually quite simple. Many think they are a needless academic exercise and of no practical use. Nothing could be further from the truth. If you plan to actively trade options, it is crucial to understand synthetics. Market makers make their living with the put-call parity relationship, so don't think it's a waste of your time to gain a basic understanding. A little time spent learning will make option investing worth your time.

The Box Spread

Market makers use many tools to hedge risks either partially or fully. One of the most powerful tools is called a box spread. While this particular strategy is not widely used by retail investors, it is very useful in determining if your vertical spread is priced fairly.

If you understand the box spread, you will be able to immediately determine if there is any room for the market makers to work with your order. So if you use spread orders, understanding box spreads will be a very helpful tool!

The Box Spread

A box spread is a relatively simple strategy. To enter into a long box position, all you need to do is to buy the bull spread and buy the bear spread with the same strikes and all other factors the same.

For example, say a stock is trading at $50. A trader could buy the Jan $50 call and sell the Jan $55 call (bull spread), and also buy the Jan $55 put and sell the Jan $50 put (bear spread).

This trade will result in a debit for both spreads. What is interesting about this position is that it is now <u>guaranteed</u> to be worth the difference in strikes at expiration, which is $5 in this example. Keep in mind this is a theoretical price and, in the real world of trading, the bid-ask spreads will probably make the value slightly less than $5 at expiration.

How is it guaranteed to be worth the difference in strikes? No matter where the stock closes, either the $50 call or the $55 put will be in-the-money. Because these are the two long positions of the box spread, the trader who buys the box spread is guaranteed to have a position worth $5 at expiration.

For example, if the stock closes at $53, the long $50 call will be worth $3, and the long $55 put will be worth $2 for a total of $5. The short $55 call and short $50 put will expire worthless. If the stock closes at $51, the $50 call will be worth $1, and the $55 put will be worth $4 for a total of $5. Again, the two short positions expire worthless.

If the stock closes outside these ranges at, say, $30, the $55 put will be worth $25, and both calls will expire worthless. However, the short $50 put now has value. In fact, it will be worth $20, which is an obligation because the trader is short. So the total value of the position is +$25 - $20 = $5.

You cannot get around it. No matter where the stock closes, the position will be worth the difference in strikes, in this case, $5.

Pricing a Box Spread

Now that we know the mechanics of the box spread, how can we use it to help with our trading?

It is now October 31 and you are bullish on SCMR, which is currently $58.38, with the following quotes available for options:

	BID	**ASK**
Dec $55 Call	$12.88	$13.88
Dec $65 Call	$8.88	$9.63
Dec $55 Put	$8.75	$9.50
Dec $65 Put	$14.75	$15.75

Let's say you want to place a $55/$65 call bull spread:

Buy Dec $55 Calls = $13.88
Sell Dec $65 Calls = $8.88
Net debit   = $5.00

Is this bull spread being priced fairly? Is it likely we will be filled if we place a limit order of $4.75 debit?

To answer these questions, let's look at the other side of the box spread:

> Buy Dec $65 Puts = $15.75
> Sell Dec $55 Puts = $8.75
> Net debit   = $7

You will pay $5 for the bull spread and $7 for the bear spread for a total debit of $12, which is guaranteed to fall to a value of $10 at expiration! So with the current bid-ask spreads, this box is not being priced fairly. In fact, this is most often the case and is the primary reason the box spread is not a popular tool for retail investors.

Let's see what the market makers are trying to do. Remember, the bid represents what they are willing to pay, and the ask is the price at which they are willing to sell. So from the market maker's perspective, here is how the box spread looks:

> Buy Dec $55 Calls = $12.88
> Sell Dec $65 Calls = $9.63
> Net debit   = $3.25
>
> Buy Dec $65 Puts = $14.75
> Sell Dec $55 Puts = $9.50
> Net debit   = $5.25

The market makers want to complete the box spread for a total of $8.50, which is guaranteed to grow to a value of $10.

On the surface, it appears to be a pretty good deal. Let's see just how good it is.

Remember, it is October 31 and we are looking at December options, which will expire in 45 days. That actually works out to be 17.6% simple interest or a whopping 141% annualized rate of return — which certainly beats the guaranteed rates on T-bills.

So, to answer the second question, yes there is certainly a lot of room to work with on the bull spread.

Let's go a step further and see just how much room there is. One method is to start with what the spread "should" cost. If the spread is guaranteed, it should earn the risk-free rate, which we will assume is roughly 6%. So the value of $10 guaranteed in 45 days is about $9.93, which is roughly $1.42 above the $8.50 price the market makers are trying to pay.

In a case like this, it is very feasible to get 1/2-point or maybe more off of this spread.

Please remember, any limit order, no matter how close to the market, is not guaranteed to fill. So, if you really need to get into or out of a trade, use caution in applying this method. This pricing method is a great tool for analyzing the potential for all traders who like to use limit orders.

Uses of the Box Spread

Why would a market maker enter into a box spread? The box spread is a way for market makers to borrow or lend money. If market makers sell a box spread, they are effectively borrowing money. They receive a credit and must pay back the value of the box at expiration. Similarly, if they buy a box spread, they are loaning money. They will pay money but receive a guaranteed return at expiration. Of course, the market makers will price the boxes in their favor and either buy it below or sell it above the theoretical fair value.

For example, say a $90/$100 *box* is priced at $9. If the $90/$100 *put spread* is priced at $4, the $90/$100 *call spread* should be worth $5. The call spread and put spread will total the box spread. However, the market maker may bid $4.75 and ask $5.25 for the call spread. In this way, regardless of whether the market maker buys or sells the call spread, he is either borrowing at less than the current risk-free rate by completing the box or loaning for a higher rate. For instance, if he buys the call spread for $4.75, he will buy the put spread for $4, thus paying only $8.75 for a box position worth $9 and effectively loaning money for higher than the risk-free rate. Likewise, if he sells the bull spread for $5.25, he will sell the bear spread for $4, thereby completing the box for $9.25. Now the market maker has sold a box worth $9 for $9.25 and has effectively borrowed money for less than the risk-free rate.

Another View of the Box Spread

We said earlier that a long box spread could be viewed as a long bull spread matched with a long bear spread. There are two other ways to view boxes. Depending on your situation, one may be more helpful than the other.

One way is to see it as a conversion at one strike and a reversal at another. For example, if a trader is short stock at $50, long $50 calls, and short the $50 puts, he has a reversal at $50. If he subsequently buys stock at $60, with long $60 puts, and short $60 calls, he has a $60 conversion.

Notice that the long and short stock positions cancel out, leaving the trader with long $50 calls and short $50 puts with long $60 puts and short $60 calls (synthetic short position).

$50 reversal	$60 conversion
~~Short 1,000 shares at $50~~	~~Long 1,000 shares at $60~~
Long 10 $50 calls	Long 10 $60 puts
Short 10 $50 puts	Short 10 $60 calls

The long and short stock positions cancel each other out. The remaining positions are a synthetic long position at $50 and a synthetic short position at $60. Notice the embedded bull and bear spreads (long $50 call and short $60 call, long $60 put and short $50 put).

Naturally, a synthetic long position (long $50 calls and short $50 puts) matched with a synthetic short position (long $60 puts and short $60 calls) cancels each other out. The trader who is synthetic long at $50 and synthetic short at $60 has effectively purchased stock at $50 and sold at $60. This is not as good as it seems, because the trader was also short stock at $50 and long at $60. The profits or losses come for the total reversal and conversion prices.

If you trade spreads, take the time to really understand box positions, because it will make all the difference in your understanding of spread pricing. Once you have a handle on that, you will be able to make more knowledgeable decisions as to which limits to use with your orders.

Questions:

1) You are thinking of buying a six-month $75 call and selling the six-month $80 call, which is currently quoting a net debit of $3.50 for the spread. You would like to put in a bid at a lower price. How would you determine how much room there is to negotiate? Assume the six-month $75/$80 put spread is trading for $1.88 and interest rates are 5%.

2) If you buy a bull spread and buy a bear spread, what is this position called? What is the risk of the position?

Equity Collar

The *equity collar* or sometimes just *collar* is a popular strategy among institutional and floor traders. It can also be a great strategy for retail investors, although most are unfamiliar with it.

Equity collars involves long stock paired with a long put and short call to provide <u>limited</u> upside profits in exchange for <u>limited</u> downside losses.

Equity Collar Example

Assume an investor is long 1,000 shares of stock at $100. He is willing to sell the stock at $105 but is also worried about the downside risk. He could sell the $105 calls and use those proceeds to finance the long $95 puts. These three positions, long stock, short calls, and long puts, make up an equity collar.

There is no reason this investor must sell the $105 call and buy the $95 put. Instead, he could sell the $100 call and buy the $100 put (which would be the same as a conversion), or sell the $110 call and buy the $100 put. There are many ways to position the collar, including out-of-the-money, at-the-money, and in-the-money options. Each has a unique set of risks and rewards and we will review many variations.

First, notice a couple of things about the collar. The above investor was long stock and then sold the $105 calls — a covered call position. However, the risk of a covered call is to the downside. To reduce the downside risk, the investor used the proceeds from the sale of the calls to buy the puts.

If the stock rises above $105, he will be forced to sell his stock for $105 per share, regardless of how high it goes. But if the stock falls, he can sell the shares for $95 per share (or just close out the puts thus using them as a hedge).

From a profit and loss standpoint, the collar looks like this:

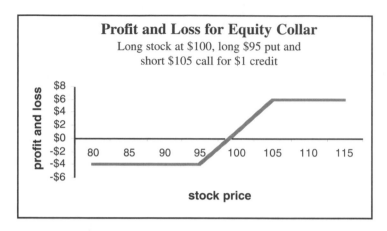

We are assuming this investor paid $100 per share for the stock, sold the calls, and bought the puts for a credit of $1, leaving the investor with a cost basis of $99 per share. If the stock falls below $95, he will exercise the put and receive $95, for a total loss of $4 per share. If the stock rises above $105, he will be assigned on the short calls and be forced to sell the stock for $105 and yield a $6 profit.

You may have noticed the above profit and loss diagram looks very much like a bull spread. If you understand that collars are the equivalent of bull spreads, the profits and losses become much easier to calculate. In the above example, there is a $10 difference in strikes. Once you calculate the maximum loss as $4, the maximum gain can be only $6 because the maximum value of a spread cannot exceed the difference in strikes, as shown in Chapter 9.

If you are still not sure why a collar strategy is the same as a bull spread, remember that a bull spread with the above positions would be long $95 call and short $105 call, which is exactly what is being shown in the profit and loss graph.

Collars for Credits or Debits?

Many investors believe the best strategy with collars is to execute them for credits. After all, why not get paid to have the long put and short call position?

Investors who believe this do not understand profits and losses with the total position. If you execute a collar for a credit versus a debit with all else the same, you open the doors to a larger loss. Once you understand synthetics, you will see that you are <u>paying</u> for the credit synthetically by allowing a larger loss potential. This is not to say that it is not a good strategy to execute for credits. But be sure that you understand the total picture and that it is in line with your expectations on the stock. In other words, do not execute for credits if your bigger concern is the downside risk of the stock.

We are going to run through several examples to make sure you understand it.

Corning (GLW) is currently trading for $59.75 with the following option quotes for January (approximately 2 months to expiration).

	Calls		Puts	
	Bid	**Ask**	**Bid**	**Ask**
Jan $50	13.63	14.38	4	4.38
Jan $55	11	11.75	5.88	6.38
Jan $60	8.50	8.75	8.25	8.75
Jan $65	6.25	6.75	10.88	11.63
Jan $70	4.75	5.13	14.13	14.88

Same Strike Collars (Conversions)

Say an investor buys 1,000 shares and sells ten $60 calls and buys ten $60 puts — a collar with both strike prices the same, which is a *conversion*.

The investor will pay $59.75 for the stock, receive $8.50 for the call (the bid), and pay $8.75 (the ask) for the put. The options (not counting commissions) cost $0.25 (pay $8.75 and receive $8.50). The most this investor will gain on the stock is $0.25 if the stock rises above $60 at expiration. But because it cost $0.25 to establish the collar, there is no net gain from the position; it is effectively locked at $60.

This investor is guaranteed to receive $60 at expiration in two months. If the stock is above $60, he will be assigned on the short calls and receive $60; if it closes below $60, he will exercise the puts and receive $60.

Notice that the investor's cost basis is also raised by $0.25. He paid $59.75 and paid $0.25 for the options, for a total of $60.

What does this cost? If interest rates are roughly 5%, then $60 $*$ 5% $*$ 2/12 years = 50 cents (or 1/2 point). So strictly from a monetary standpoint, this collar is not a good strategy, because it will cost you 1/2-point in lost interest. Basically, this investor is buying stock today for $60 and guaranteeing the sale in two months at $60 for no money. He will be losing out on interest he could be earning if he sold the stock today.

You may recall that the equity collar is the same three-sided position used by market makers in Chapter 8. There we said that conversions are generally not good strategies for retail investors because of bid-ask spreads and the three commissions involved. This example proves the point. This does not mean it is not a valid strategy to know. In this example, we are assuming you purchased the shares for the *current* $59.75 price, which makes the strategy unsuitable with the current option prices. But what if the stock were purchased previously for a lower price such as $45? With the current option quotes, the collar can be a powerful strategy in times of uncertainty.

This may be a good strategy for someone who is deferring sale of stock. In the past, this was done with a box position where the investor would short 1,000 shares against their long 1,000, effectively locking in the current price, as did our collar trader above. Recent tax law changes have effectively eliminated the box position as a tax-advantaged trade. But we can still execute it synthetically. Notice that the trader is long shares at an effective price of $60. The short $60 call and long $60 put constitute a synthetic short position. So the investor truly is long and short the same stock — a box position. This is exactly why our trader will not profit — or lose — anything from the above collar.

Collars for Credits

Say instead our same investor chose to sell the $60 call for $8.50 but buy the $55 put for $6.38 (the ask). Now he has a credit of $2.12, effectively reducing the cost basis on the stock by this amount to $57.62 ($59.75 - $2.13 = $57.62). Notice though, that his "insurance" from the put does not start until $55, so he can still lose $2.62 (he pays $57.62 and sells for $55) if he exercises these puts. This is what we were referring to when we said traders who execute collars for credits wind up paying for it by additional downside risk. Because there is a $5 difference in strikes, the maximum gain from this collar is $2.38. We can check the math and see that $2.38 max gain + $2.62 max loss = the $5 difference in strikes.

The trader who executed the collar for a net zero had no downside risk. But when executed for a credit, he now has a $2.62 risk. This is exactly why the market will "pay" you credits for this type of collar. Effectively this credit trader is assuming a "deductible" of $2.62. Also notice that the market paid him only $2.12 for it. Again, the credit collars do not come for free.

This is a great strategy if the trader is very fearful of downside risk below $55, yet willing to sell his stock for $60. At expiration, he will profit by the $2.12 credit if the stock sits flat, make $2.38 if the stock is above $60, and lose a maximum of $2.62 for any stock price below $55.

Collars for Debits

Let's assume the trader sells the $70 call for $4.75 (the bid) and buys the $60 put for $8.75 (the ask) for a net debit of $4. The cost basis on the stock is raised from $59.75 to $63.75. In exchange, he can sell his stock for $60 for a $3.75 loss, but may be forced to sell the stock for $70, realizing a $6.25 profit. Again, the $3.75 loss + $6.25 gain = $10 difference in strikes.

With this spread, the trader is allowing a larger loss — $3.75 instead of $2.63. Why did this happen when he paid a debit to begin with? Because that $70 out-of-the-money call was sold. The trader wants more profit if the stock rises. Because, all else being equal, all investors would rather have more profit than not, the markets will effectively charge you for that privilege.

Notice that <u>no</u> collar combination will prevent a loss. This is because the markets will not assume the risk for free. If you buy the stock at $59.75, no matter which combination of short calls and long puts you choose, you must accept some downside risk after accounting for the debits or credits from the collar. If you buy the $60 put for $8.75, you just bumped your cost basis to $68.50. True, you are guaranteed to be able to sell your stock at $60, but this leaves a loss of $8.50. By selling calls against the long put position, it will <u>decrease</u> the expense of the put but never to the point of no loss. Even with the zero debit at-the-money collar we looked at earlier, the trader still lost on foregone interest and retained no upside potential in the stock.

The only time a collar can lock in a profit is if the trader had purchased the stock previously at a lower price, say, $50. With the above prices, he can now execute a number of collars to guarantee a profit and still leave upside potential. But this still is not free, either, because the trader was holding the stock for some time and assuming all of the downside risk. Now that the stock has moved in his favor, he may be able to lock in gains with a collar.

This is when collars are especially attractive. Consider using them when you have significant profits, especially if a big announcement is pending, such as earnings that may cause the stock to plummet. The collar can still yield healthy upside potential while greatly reducing downside risk.

Collar Comparisons

The following chart shows four of many possible combinations of collars that could be constructed from the above option quotes. There are two important points to notice: 1) None of the collars prevent a loss, and 2) The higher the debit, the <u>lower</u> the loss and the <u>higher</u> the reward. This confirms what we said earlier: A trader who places collars for credits is allowing for more downside risk.

Notice in the chart how the trader receiving the $6.63 credit has the lowest profit and highest loss. Again, this does not mean that it's not a good strategy to execute for credits. Just be sure you understand that it is not free.

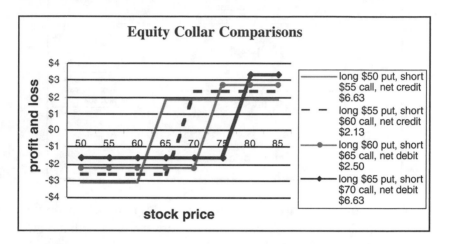

Equity Collar Comparisons

Legend:
- long $50 put, short $55 call, net credit $6.63
- long $55 put, short $60 call, net credit $2.13
- long $60 put, short $65 call, net debit $2.50
- long $65 put, short $70 call, net debit $6.63

(y-axis: profit and loss, x-axis: stock price)

Reverse Equity Collars

We mentioned earlier that equity collars are actually bull spreads. This allows the investor, in most cases, to participate in additional upside in the stock as well as reduce the downside exposure. What if the investor's main concern is the downside? Is there a way to hedge that portion in exchange for the upside gains? Yes, by using a *reverse equity collar*.

To execute a reverse equity collar, you need to buy the higher strike put and sell the lower strike call — an in-the-money collar. Notice that up until now, we have always purchased the put with a lower strike and sold a call with a higher strike. This will always net a synthetic bull spread. A synthetic bull spread is a position that behaves like a regular bull spread (such as buy a low strike call and sell a higher strike call) but is constructed differently. If we execute the reverse, we end up with a synthetic bear spread.

Using the option quotes in the above box, let's assume a trader buys stock at $59.75, buys the $65 put for $11.63, and sells the $55 call for $11, for a net debit of $0.63. The following chart shows the profit and loss diagram for a reverse equity collar:

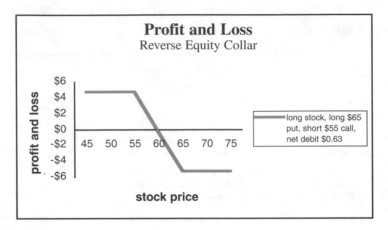

Notice how the chart favors the downside; that is, it becomes more profitable as the stock falls, which is not the case with a regular collar. The max gain, in this example, is $4.62 and the max loss is $5.38. Once again, this shows just how versatile options can be and why all investors should take the time to understand them.

Collars are fairly complex because they require three positions. Be careful when calculating net gains and losses, and be sure to include commissions to make sure the trade is worthwhile.

Bear Spreads in an IRA?

Most brokerage firms will require a basic option approval level to place a collar, and they can be used in an IRA — including the reverse equity collar. In fact, the reverse equity collar is a synthetic means to trade bear spreads in an IRA, which is something your broker will tell you cannot be done. The reason they will tell you this is that they probably do not understand synthetics, and they immediately think about debit or credit spreads such as with a long put and short put — or long call and short call as we talked about earlier. These types of bear spreads are generally not allowed in an IRA.

However, brokerage firms that allow you to trade options in an IRA account usually allow only covered calls and protective puts (long puts to protect a stock position). If you look at the individual pieces of the reverse equity collar, you will see that the trader is long stock and short a call (covered call), which is certainly allowed. Then a put is added to protect the long stock position with a strike price higher than that of the call, which is certainly allowed.

If you are ever bearish on a stock and want to trade bear spreads in your IRA, you now know how to do it. If your broker tells you that bear spreads cannot be placed in an IRA, just enter the three positions through him and be happy you understand reverse equity collars.

Questions:

1) What is the upside and downside risk of an equity collar position?

2) Somebody tells you that you should always enter collars for credits because you receive money instead of paying money to enter the position. How would you respond?

3) Can collars generally be used in an IRA with option approval?

4) Which position is the same as a collar from a profit and loss standpoint?

5) You bought stock at $100 per share, sold a $105 call for $3, and bought a $95 put for $2. What is your cost basis on the stock? What is your maximum gain and loss?

The Butterfly Spread

As you become more involved in trading options, you will no doubt hear about a strategy known as the "butterfly spread."

The butterfly spread is one of many strategies that belong to a family collectively known as "wing spreads," which get their name from the shape of their profit and loss diagrams.

The butterfly spread is avidly written about in many options books. It attracts traders who want to venture into new strategies. But because the strategy involves three or four separate commissions to open (and sometimes more depending on how the spread is constructed) and the same number to close, it is very costly and typically not a good strategy for the retail investor.

The butterfly spread is really designed for floor traders to take advantage of pricing discrepancies between spreads. While it is not an arbitrage play, it stacks the odds in their favor largely because they are not paying retail commissions.

The Long Butterfly Spread

A basic butterfly spread involves three strike prices, which we shall generically call low, medium, and high. For the long butterfly, the trader will buy one low strike, sell two medium strikes, and buy one high strike, all with the same expiration dates. The butterfly can be executed with either calls or puts (or a combination). The high and low strikes must be the same distance from the medium option.

The butterfly spread is designed to be a limited-risk neutral strategy, meaning that it profits if the stock sits still and is not exposed to high risk regardless of stock direction.

Example: A stock is trading at $100, and a trader wants to place a butterfly spread. The trader may buy one $95 call, sell two $100 calls, and buy one $105 call. Notice how the high and low strikes are the same distance, in this example $5, from the medium strike. This would be called a $95/$100/$105 butterfly. Sometimes traders will refer to only the "body" of the butterfly and call it simply a $100 butterfly.

The long butterfly spread is always executed in a 1-2-1 pattern — buy 1, sell 2, buy 1. Of course, you could elect to do multiple spreads, in which case your pattern would be 2-4-2 or 3-6-3 or any other combination, as long as the middle strike is always double the number of contracts as either the high or low. If you execute a 2-4-2 pattern, this is considered two butterfly spreads; a 3-6-3 is considered to be three spreads.

Understanding the Butterfly

There are many ways to view a butterfly spread. In fact, there are probably an infinite number of ways to construct one; although most investors vaguely familiar with them will tell you there are only two ways (either with calls or puts) and always three strikes. A trader can use calls, puts, combinations of the two, and synthetic versions of each piece of the butterfly to create the same profit and loss diagrams. All ways are equally correct as long as the profit and loss diagrams look the same.

One of the easiest ways is to view the long butterfly as the combination of a long bull spread and a long bear spread. For example, the trader in the above example went long one $95 call, short two $100 calls, and long one $105 call. We can look at that trade in another way as follows:

> Long $95 call   **(This is the bull spread)**
> Short $100 call
>
> Short $100 call   **(This is the bear spread)**
> Long $105 call

We see that the long bull and long bear spreads consist of exactly the same pieces as the butterfly spread: long one $95, short two $100, long one $105.

If you understand the butterfly spread in this way, it will also help if you understand why it is so useful to floor traders.

Why Floor Traders Love Butterflies

Floor traders ideally love to get into "flat" positions that guarantee profits. The business of market making is often humorously described as "picking up nickels in front of bulldozers." This points out that market makers love to make quick, small profits and then get out of the way. They are not interested in holding high-risk positions for lengths of time. Because of this, market makers are always scanning quotes on their monitors for any mispricings (arbitrage) or prices that may give them a theoretical edge. The butterfly is one of many strategies that market makers use to scan for option mispricings.

Let's assume a stock is trading for $101 and we see the following quotes on some call options:

Option	Quote
$95 call	$10
$100 call	$8
$105 call	$6

We know from basic option pricing in Chapter 11 that the $95 call should be more than the $100 and the $100 more than the $105. In addition, the differences in prices do not exceed the differences in strikes so there are no readily apparent mispricings there.

However, after checking these basic relationships, market makers will, in addition, check spreads and straddles for other possible mispricings.

The $95/$100 bull spread becomes more valuable as the stock rises. In fact, the maximum profit is achieved if the stock price is above $100 at expiration. With the stock currently at $101, the bull spread is at maximum profit if the options expire immediately.

Now let's looks at the bear spread. The bear spread consists of the short $100 call and the long $105 call. This spread will become more valuable as the stock falls; in fact, the maximum profit here will occur if the stock is below $100 at expiration. The bear spread, unlike the bull spread at this point, is below maximum profit if the options expired instantaneously.

So if you had to pick a spread to be the winner, which would it be? Obviously, it should be the bull spread, because it is theoretically worth more. But look at the quotes again — we see both spreads are priced at $2.

The bull spread consists of the long $95 and short $100 for a net debit of $2. The bear spread consists of the short $100 and long $105 for a net credit of $2.

With the stock at $101, the market maker knows the bull spread should be more valuable relative to the bear spread, so he will buy the bull spread and sell the bear spread — a butterfly spread.

Notice that this does not guarantee a profit — the stock could dip below $95 or rise above $105 — so is not an arbitrage play. It does, however, allow the market maker to take advantage of a mispricing and put the odds on his side that the trade will be profitable. This is one of many trading situations known as a pseudo-arbitrage, because it does not guarantee a profit but is traded solely from a theoretical mispricing viewpoint; it is an arbitrage on theoretical odds.

What Does a Butterfly Spread Look Like?

The profit and loss diagram for the above butterfly looks like this:

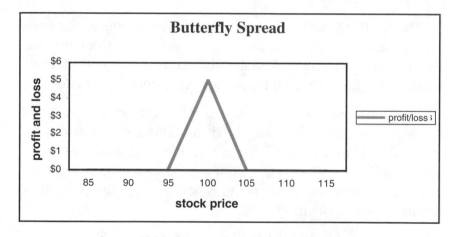

Notice how there is no loss area; the lowest this spread can go, in this example, is zero. This is because it was constructed with the bull and bear spread priced the same so there was no cash outlay

— the market maker paid $2 for the bull spread and received $2 for the bear spread. Realistically, there will be a slight debit, especially after commissions, so it will actually look more like this:

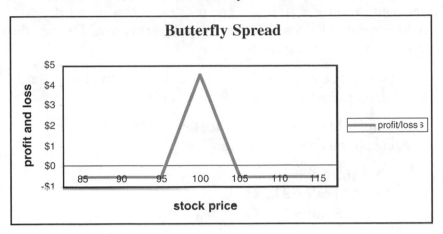

The point is that with a butterfly (assuming a very low debit or low commissions) you have a very little loss area but a high profit area, albeit over a small range of stock prices. In many ways, it's like playing the lottery. The market makers think they have little to lose but a lot to gain. The maximum profit will be achieved at the strike price of the short, in this case, $100.

If you use your imagination, the profit and loss diagram looks like the body and wings of a butterfly (*really* use your imagination!) — hence the name butterfly spread.

Iron Butterfly

Another way to view the spread is that it is the combination of a short straddle and long strangle. If a trader executes a short straddle and long strangle, it is a special variation of the butterfly known as an *iron butterfly*. The trader of an iron butterfly wants the stock to fall, so the profit and loss diagram is actually a *short iron butterfly* or *long butterfly*. The short straddle is easy to see; it is the part that forms the upside down "V" in the diagram. The long strangle (long $95 put and long $105 call) provides protection from further losses if the stock falls below $95 or rises above $105. It is the long strangle that forms the protective "wings" to the left and right of the diagram. If a butterfly spread is constructed in this manner, there will be four commissions to open and four to close.

If you can ever execute a butterfly for a very low debit, you may want to consider it. If you can ever execute it for a net credit (including commissions), do not pass it up. This would be an arbitrage situation, and you cannot lose!

Let's look at some real numbers and see why retail investors should think twice before entering a butterfly spread.

Example: MSFT is currently trading for $68.75 with the following option quotes available:

>   Dec $65 call = $6.50 ask
>   Dec $70 call = $3.38 bid
>   Dec $75 call = $1.75 ask

Let's trade the $65/$70/$75 butterfly and see what happens:

>   Long one $65 = -$6.50
>   Short two $70 = +$6.76
>   Long one $75 = -$1.75
>   Net debit   = $1.49

Now, to make it more realistic, let's say you pay a commission of $100 for the three strikes, which may be a conservative number, which means you must add $100 to the cost. Remember that we are dealing with three different strikes, so there will be three separate commissions — and that's just to buy it.

Now our net debit is $2.49, and the maximum we can make is $5. Here is our profit and loss diagram so far:

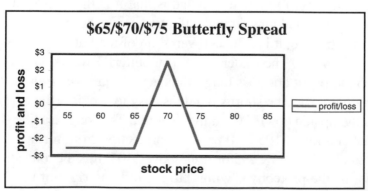

It already looks much different from the market maker's above. Notice just how much more "loss" area there is in this diagram.

Now, our breakeven points are $67.49 and $72.49. If the stock closes below $67.49 or above $72.49, the trade will incur losses, and we haven't even considered the commissions to get out.

Already it is a pretty narrow range to be profitable — a five-point range between breakeven points. Let's assume the stock closes at exactly $70, which is the point of maximum gain. We make $250 but have to pay another $100 in commissions for a total gain of $150.

Now, it still may not seem like such a bad deal; after all, $150 bucks is $150 bucks. But this was assuming the stock closed at exactly $70. Just how much room do we have to work?

Taking the sell commissions into account, here's how the trade looks now:

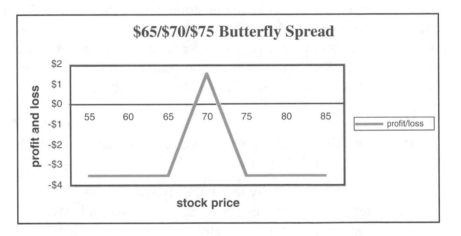

The stock must close above $68.49 or below $71.49 to get anything. To get the full $150, we need the stock at exactly $70. If you can call the stock closing prices within this close of a range, you are better off selling naked calls, puts or straddles.

Butterfly spreads are an interesting combination strategy, which you will no doubt hear about as you continue with your options trading. Over the past seven years, I have seen many retail investors attempt butterfly spreads, and not one of them made a dime.

If you decide to try a butterfly spread, you may want to check with your broker regarding commissions and breakeven points. My guess is that you will decide against it.

This does not mean that butterfly spreads should not be learned. A butterfly spread can be used as a great subsequent trade on an existing position. For instance, you may have a long strangle and think the stock is going to sit still. It may be possible to sell the straddle and recoup your costs plus a profit and leave you in a guaranteed winning trade. Keep in mind this is not arbitrage, because the position was not guaranteed to make money with no risk. You held the strangle for a period of time by itself, and the trade happened to move your way. Nonetheless, the butterfly provided a means to capture a profit.

Another reason why you should learn butterflies is because they emphasize the type of thinking required to become good at options trading. Notice how we broke the position down into either bull and bear spread or straddles and strangles. Many advanced option strategies are simply making use of other advanced strategies. Once you learn to break option strategies into component parts, you will become a much stronger — and profitable — options trader.

Questions:

1) A butterfly spread can be viewed as combination of which two strategies? Any others?

2) You hear someone say that butterfly spreads are a great strategy for retail investors because they have a low cost and potential high payout. How would you comment?

3) Why do market makers use butterfly spreads?

Option Repair Strategy

If you have been buying stocks for any length of time, you have probably been in the situation every investor dreads — seeing your stock down 20 percent or more from your purchase price.

Some of you may be thinking that will not happen to you, because you use stop orders to prevent such losses. As we learned in Chapter 4, even if you use stop orders, large losses can occur between trading days. For example, a stock can close at $75 one night and open the next day at $60. If you have a stop order in at $75, you will be filled at $60. If you have a stop limit at $75, you will not be filled at all. In either case, the stop did not work as expected, and you are down!

Fortunately, with the use of options, we can sometimes get out of these precarious positions with ease. To do so, you need to understand the option repair strategy. This strategy is a very clever, yet simple strategy. Many investors would not think to do it, which is what makes it a powerful tool to add to your list of strategies.

The repair strategy is helpful to any investor at one time or another. If you have ever purchased a stock only to watch it fall 20% or more, in most cases, you probably viewed it as a "long-term hold" and held on for a long time (sometimes years) before you got your money back. The option repair strategy is designed to get you out of a bad situation such as this much sooner.

The repair strategy does make a couple of assumptions. First, you must be at least moderately bullish on the stock over the short term. If you think the stock is heading south, you are probably best selling at a loss or buying puts to hedge the position. Second, you are assumed to be trying to get out of the position by just breaking even (or close to it). In other words, this is not used as a high-profit strategy; it is designed to get you out of a bad situation for nearly breakeven. So if you are in a losing stock situation and thinking, "Just get my money back and I'll walk away," then this may be the strategy for you.

With the above assumptions, we can complete a breakeven with the repair strategy. Here is how the strategy works:

Say you buy 1,000 shares of stock at $50 and it is now trading for $40 — down 20%.

You think the stock will rise to $45 but not much past that; again, you must be somewhat bullish in order for the strategy to work. The way to design a repair strategy under these assumptions is to look for a ratio call spread you can write for no money down. Ratio spreads are similar to the spreads we discussed earlier, except you are selling more contracts than you purchase. In our example, we may buy ten $40 calls for $5 and write twenty $45 calls for $2.50. Here are the transactions:

> Buy ten $40 calls for $5   = -$5,000
> Sell twenty $45 calls for $2.50 = $5,000
> Net cost   = $0

Notice that we bought ten and sold twenty — a ratio call spread. Normally, a ratio writer is subjected to unlimited upside risk, because he is short more contracts than long. But because you already own shares, you can cover ten of the short $45 calls with your stock and the remaining ten contracts with the $40 call. Effectively you are writing ten $45 contracts as a covered call plus entering ten $40/$45 bull spreads. Because you can write twice as many calls as you need to purchase, the long $40 calls cost you nothing.

In most cases, you will be limited to no more than a five-point difference in strikes. In other words, this strategy will usually not work by buying the $40 and selling the $50 calls because that is a ten-point difference in strikes.

Now, if the stock does move to $45 at expiration, the long shares will be worth only $45 (the short $45 calls will expire worthless). The $40/$45 bull spread will be worth $5, for a total of $50.

Here are the transactions in detail:

Transaction	Account Value
Buy the stock at $50	$50,000
Stock falls to $40	$40,000
Buy 10 $40 calls, sell 20 $45 calls for $0	$40,000
Stock rises from $40 to $45	Long stock now worth $45,000
	Long $35/$40 spread worth $5,000
	Total account value = $50,000

In effect, we have leveraged the account for an upside move for no money down and no additional risk. Our tradeoff is that we cap our upside returns. But if you are not long-term bullish, then capping the upside in exchange for breakeven may make perfect sense for a particular situation.

In the example above, does the stock need to close at exactly $45 for the strategy to work? No, it will work as long as the underlying stock rises to $45 or higher. Say the stock rallies all the way back to $50 at expiration. Now your long stock is worth +$45 (remember, you have a $45 covered call against the shares), and your long $40/$45 calls spread is worth +$5, for a total of $50. Any stock price above $45 at expiration will result in the total position being worth $50.

It is also helpful to look at the various option strikes and months to help make your decision about which options to buy and sell. You can get these through most brokerage firms or from CBOE's Web site at www.cboe.com.

The option repair strategy is yet another demonstration as to the versatility of options. We have taken these "risky" assets and used them in a way to leverage our returns for no money down.

Chapter 16: No Options for Me!

By now you know that options are an important, if not necessary, tool for today's investor. Despite all the benefits and strategies that have been covered, many investors adamantly refuse to buy or sell options and insist on holding only stocks. *But if you refuse to use options, you are speculating.* As we have shown, options were created as hedging tools. Whenever you hedge, you give up some upside profits in exchange for some downside protection (the opposite if you are short the stock). So if you buy stock and refuse to buy or sell options, you are speculating that nothing will go wrong with your long stock position. You are willing to hold out for more profit at the expense of downside exposure to a theoretical price of zero. In fact, it can be argued that investors who do not use options are among the most speculative of all.

If you are still in doubt, would you believe that your long stock is an option?

Valuing Corporate Securities as Options

When Black and Scholes developed their famous option-pricing model, they were certain there were many uses for it other than just valuing call options. One of the uses they suggested was valuing corporate securities.

Consider a firm that has issued one zero-coupon bond that matures to a value of $1 million in five years. With this money, the firm produces products and hopes to have a value in excess of this $1 million in five years and pay off their debt, leaving the stockholders with whatever remains in value. However, if the firm's value is less than $1 million at the bond's maturity, the stockholders will simply turn over the assets to the bondholders and will be free of further liability.

Let's look at the payoffs for stockholders and bondholders at maturity:

If value of the firm is *less* than $1 million, say, $800,000:

> Bondholders get: $800,000
> **Stockholders get: $0**
> Total value of firm = $800,000

If the value of the firm is *greater* than $1 million, say $1.5 million at maturity:

> Bondholders get: $1 million
> **Stockholders get: $500,000 (excess value)**
> Total value of firm = $1.5 million

We see with the above payoffs that the total value of the firm is partitioned between the stockholders and bondholders. Notice how the stockholders receive nothing at expiration if the value of the firm is below the value of the matured debt. But if the value of the firm is greater than the matured debt, stockholders receive the *excess value*.

Now compare this to options.

You own a $100 call option that someone has written as a covered position:

At expiration, if the value of the stock is less than $100, say $80:

> Call writers get: $80
> **Call owners get: $0**
> Total value to the investor = $80

In other words, if the value of the stock is below the strike at expiration, the covered call writer is left with the stock at its current value of $80. The long call position receives nothing.

If the value of the stock is greater than $100, say $150 at expiration:

> Call writers get: $100
> **Call owners get: $50 (excess value)**
> Total value to the investor = $150

If the value of the stock is above the strike at expiration, the covered call writer will be assigned and receive the $100 strike price.

The call owners will receive the stock and pay the strike for a value of the stock price minus the strike price. The stockholders, in this case, receive what is left over after the bondholders are paid.

If you look closely, you will see that the payoff for this call option exactly resembles the payoffs to the stockholders for the corporation discussed earlier.

Using the Black-Scholes Model

It can be shown that the stock price + put price - call price must equal the present value of the exercise price, which is referred to as put-call parity:

Stock + Put - Call = Present value of the exercise price

We can rewrite put-call parity for the above corporation as:

Stock + Put - Call = Present value of the debt

Which can be rewritten *at maturity* as:

Stock - Call = Value of debt - Put

The Black-Scholes Option Pricing Model tells us the value of the covered call position (left side of equation) in our hypothetical firm is equal to the debt at maturity with a put written against it (right side of equation).

This means that the bondholders have, in essence, written a put against the firm. In other words, if the value of the firm is less than the debt that is due at maturity, you "put" the firm back to the bond-holders and walk away losing only what you paid for the stock — just as when you buy a call option.

The value of this put is part of what gives your *stock* its value!

If you like owning stocks because of the limited risk they offer, you should consider using options in some fashion. Options allow you to do exactly what you are doing with stock — but for a lot less money. They can also be used to create downside hedges in exchange for upside profits. Because of these uses, you can create better risk-reward profiles that are simply not possible with stock alone.

There are many fascinating insights that can be learned from the Black-Scholes Model. Once you have a better understanding of options, you will start to see that stockholders are option players in disguise and the Black-Scholes Model can be used to value corporate securities, too. If you acknowledge this, you may start to open your eyes to the world of options and create new trading opportunities that you never thought possible.

Answers to Selected Questions
Chapter 10

1) Is there an arbitrage opportunity in the following quotes? How would you perform it? (Hint: Determine which one, using the above principles, is underpriced. Buy the under priced option, sell the overpriced one, and then check to see if it guarantees a profit for all stock prices.)

$60 put = $12
$70 put = $10

Answer: The $70 put should be trading for a higher price relative to the $60 put because it gives the owner the right to sell stock for a higher price, which is more desirable. Because it is trading for less, you could buy the $70 put and simultaneously sell the $60 put for a net credit of $2. At expiration, if the stock is above $70, both puts expire worthless, and you keep the $2. If the stock is between $60 and $70, you will make more than $2. For instance, if the stock is $65 at expiration, you will make $5 on the long $70 put, and the short $60 put expires worthless for a total profit of $7. If the stock is below $60 at expiration, you can sell the stock for $70. But you will be forced to buy it for $60 for a $10 gain on the spread, plus your initial $2 credit for a total profit of $12. You are guaranteed to make at least $2 and could make as much as $12 for no money down, so it is an arbitrage.

2) The underlying stock is trading for $100 with the $110 put trading for $9. Is there an arbitrage opportunity? How would you perform it?

Answer: Options should always trade for their intrinsic value, so the $110 put should be worth $10 if the stock is $100. Because it less than the intrinsic amount and trading for $9, we can buy the $110 put and buy the stock for $109, and then immediately exercise the put and receive $110 for an arbitrage profit of $1. The $1 profit is the result of the option being $1 below intrinsic value.

3) Which option should be worth more, the January $50 call or the June $50 call? Why?

Answer: Assuming all other factors the same, the June $50 call will be worth more since there is more time remaining on it. The more time remaining, the more likely the option will expire with intrinsic value. Because it is more desirable, investors will bid up the price of the June $50 call over the January $50 call.

4) Which option should be worth more, the June $75 call or the June $80 call? Why?

Answer: Assuming all other factors the same, the June $75 call will be more valuable. That's because it gives investors the right to buy the stock for a lower amount, which is more desirable. Because it is more desirable, its price will be bid up higher than the June $80 call.

5) One day you see the following quotes: May $40 call for $7 and a May $45 call for $1.50. Is there an arbitrage opportunity? How would you perform it?

Answer: There is a $5 difference in strikes, so there cannot be more than a $5 difference in prices between the options. However, we see that there is a price difference of $5.50. You would buy the $45 call and simultaneously sell the $40 call for a net credit of $5.50. If the stock is below $40 at expiration, both calls are worthless, and you keep the $5.50. If the stock is between $40 and $45 at expiration, you lose on the short $40 call, but no more than $5. For instance, if the stock is $42, you lose $2 on the short $40 call, which will net a $3.50 profit after accounting for the net credit. If the stock is above $45 at expiration, you must sell it for $40 but can buy it for $45 for a $5 loss, which nets a $0.50 profit.

Chapter 11

1) Which option will have a higher delta: a shorter-term at-the-money or a longer-term at-the-money? Why?

Answer: The longer-term will have the higher delta. This is because neither option is in-the-money at this time; however, there is a much better chance the longer-term will expire with intrinsic value, so it will have a higher delta.

2) The stock is $108, and a $100 call has a delta of 0.75. Volatility in the underlying stock is increasing. Do you expect delta to rise or fall?

Answer: The $100 call is currently $8 in-the-money. Once an option is in-the-money, decreasing time tends to make it more certain to finish that way. Increasing volatility is a form of increasing the time, because it is now more likely for the option to finish out-of-the-money. Therefore, the delta will fall.

3) A $75 call has a delta of 0.30. What would you estimate to be the delta of the $75 put? Why?

Answer: Call and put deltas should sum to one (ignoring the negative sign on the put delta) because that is the total area under the bell curve. If the $75 call delta is 0.30, the $75 put delta should be -0.70.

4) You are holding an in-the-money $100 call with a delta of 0.60 with one month remaining. 20 days later, the stock is the same price. Do you expect your delta to have increased or decreased? Why?

Answer: If an option is in-the-money, then decreasing time, decreasing volatility, or increasing stock price will increase the delta. In this case, the stock price is the same but time is reduced, so delta will increase because there is now a more likely chance for the option to finish in-the-money.

5) A stock is trading for $80. Which do you expect to have a higher delta: the one-month $80 call or the three-month $80 call? Why?

Answer: Neither option is in-the-money at this time, so the three-month option has a better chance of being in-the-money at expiration because of its longer life. Therefore, the three-month option will have a higher delta.

6) What is the approximate delta of an at-the-money option? Why?

Answer: An at-the-money option will have a delta of approximately 0.50. Technically the call delta will be a little higher than this, and the put delta will be a little lower, but they should be fairly close.

7) You think a stock will fall slowly over the next month and want to create an option position to take advantage of your outlook. You should have _____ (positive, negative) delta and _____ (positive, negative) gamma.

Answer: You want negative delta if you think a stock will fall. If you think it will fall slowly, you want negative gamma as well. This could be accomplished by a short call option.

8) You are holding a $75 put option with a delta of 0.70 and gamma of 0.05. If the stock immediately falls 1 point, what do you expect the new delta to be (assuming all else remains the same)?

Answer: The new delta should be approximately 0.75, which is found by adding the gamma to the previous delta: 0.70 + 0.05 = 0.75.

Chapter 12

1) You are holding a $100 strike call option trading for $12 with the stock at $111. The stock is paying a dividend tomorrow, which will reduce the value of your call. Should you exercise early to get the dividend? Why? What is a better strategy to capture the dividend in this case?

Answer: There is still 1 point of time premium remaining on the call option, so you should sell the call in the open market and buy the stock in the open market. You should not exercise early, otherwise you will lose the $1 time premium.

2) You have a $60 call trading for $6. The stock is currently $65. If you exercise the call, what is your cost basis on the stock? What would be a more efficient way to own the stock?

Answer: There is $1 time premium remaining on this call. If you exercise the call, you will pay $60 for the stock but lose the call worth $6 for a cost basis of $66. Because the stock is $65, your cost basis is increased by the sacrificed $1 time premium. A more efficient way to own the stock is to sell the call and buy the stock in the open market. If so, your cost basis is $65 - $1 = $64. The reason your cost basis is not $65 - $6 = $59 is because you are giving up your right to buy the stock at $60 instead of $65, which is a $5 loss and $59 + $5 = $64 cost basis.

3) What is the one condition that should exist if you are going to exercise a call option early?

Answer: The option should be trading at parity (exactly intrinsic) or at best with a fractional amount of time premium remaining. If there is significant time premium on the option, you will be better off selling the option in the open market.

4) Is it ever optimal to exercise a put option early? When?

Answer: Yes, if the put is sufficiently deep-in-the-money (delta is very close to 1), then it can make financial sense to exercise the put option early and earn interest on the proceeds.

Chapter 13

1) You have ten $100 call options near expiration. The stock is $110 and the bid on your option is $9.50. If you want to close out the option, what is the best method? How much more money do you make with this method as compared to a straight sell?

Answer: If you sell your option at the bid, you will receive 1,000 * $9.50 = $9,500. However, if you sell the stock at $110 and then exercise the call, you will receive a credit of $110,000 and can immediately exercise the call and pay $100,000 for the stock leaving you with a $10,000 gain, which is $500 better than the straight sell of the option.

2) Why would a market maker bid below intrinsic value near expiration?

Answer: There is very little activity in the option, and the market maker is having trouble spreading off the risk.

3) You have ten $50 puts bidding $2.50 near expiration. The stock is $47. If you want to close out your options, what is the best method? How much more money will you make when compared to a straight sell?

Answer: If you sell your ten puts at the bid, you will receive 1,000 * $2,500. However, if you buy the stock for $47,000 in the open market and immediately exercise your put, you can sell if for $50,000, making $3,000 on the deal. This is $500 better than with the straight sell of the put.

Chapter 14

Long Puts

1) What is a benefit of owning a call option over the stock?

Answer: A call option costs far less than the stock. Consequently, the option investor has much less at stake. Moreover, the option investor will make point-for-point for every move above the strike price at expiration.

2) Your friend claims that the only way to truly have insurance is through put options. How would you comment?

Answer: Call options provide insurance as well in the sense that the investor has a limited amount of money at risk. In this way, the investor is taking a "deductible" in the amount of the call option premium and not at point-for-point risk below the strike price as is the long stock holder.

3) How do call options provide leverage?

Answer: Call options cost far less than the stock to own but make point-for-point for all stock prices above the strike price at expiration. Therefore, any gain in the stock above the strike price is equally matched by both the option trader and stock trader, but the option trader makes those gains for far less money invested, so he is gaining financial leverage.

4) You are bullish on a stock that is trading for $100. You think it will rise a couple of points over the next few days and would like to make a short-term trade. With all else being equal, which is the better strike to buy, the $90 or the $110? Why?

Answer: The $90 strike. Because it is deep-in-the-money, it will behave much more like the stock, and you will nearly gain the full two points in the stock (assuming you are correct). However, if you buy the $100 call, it is possible for the stock to rise two points yet end up with a loss on the option. This is because the $100 call carries far more time premium and is subjected to the speed component (gamma) of the option far more than the $90 call.

5) You are bearish on a stock and have sold it short. To protect you from upward price moves in the stock, your friend tells you to use a buy stop order to protect yourself from upside moves in the stock. How would you comment? What else could you do to protect yourself from upward stock moves? How does this differ from a buy stop order?

Answer: Buy stops do not prevent losses. In order to truly protect yourself, you could buy a call option, which locks in your purchase price. Buying a call differs from a stop in two ways. One, it guarantees the purchase price whereas the stop does not. Two, it is not path dependent, meaning that the stock price path can wander anywhere it pleases and you are locked into a purchase price. A stop order can easily get triggered only to watch the stock plummet shortly thereafter, leaving you with no position. Call options used in this way are time dependent.

6) Deep-in-the-money call options will move nearly point-for-point up and down with the underlying stock. True or false? Why?

Answer: True. Because they are so deep-in-the-money, they are viewed by the market as being "guaranteed" to have intrinsic value at expiration. Because they will have intrinsic value, the market will price in point-for-point with moves in the underlying stock.

7) You bought a $100 call for $7 yesterday, and the stock is up one point today but the option is trading for $6.75. Is this possible? How would you explain it?

Answer: Yes. That is due to changes in implied volatility. The market priced in some of the move of the stock in the option but also deducted premium for volatility. The net effect is a downward call price even though the stock is up.

8) You recently purchased 300 shares of a stock at $40. It is now trading for $70 and the company is due to release earnings in a few days. You are concerned the stock mayfall sharply if they release an unfavorable report. You do not want to sell your stock yet for tax reasons. How can you protect your position?

Answer: You could buy a $70 put option for insurance. If you were willing to assume some risk, you could buy a lower strike put and pay less money.

Short Puts

1) Is a short put a bullish or bearish position?

Answer: A short put is neutral to bullish. As long as the underlying stock does not fall, a short put will make money. Technically, even a short put can make money with some downward movement as long as it does not exceed the breakeven point. However, the position is generally considered neutral to bullish.

2) Assume the same scenario in question #1. You purchase three $65 puts for $2. What is the total cost not counting commissions? If the stock is trading for $60 at expiration, what is your stock worth? The put? How do you explain the discrepancy between the loss on the stock and gain in the option?

Answer: 3 * 100 * 2 = $600 plus commissions. If the stock is $60 at expiration, the 300 shares are worth $18,000, which were worth 300 * 70 = $21,000 for a loss of $3,000. The put is worth 3 * 100 * $5 = $1,500. The reason the gain in the put did not offset the loss in the stock is because a $65 put was purchased, and $5 of liability was assumed by the investor. This $5 "deductible" on 300 shares makes up the missing $1,500.

3) You just bought 100 shares of a $50 stock and a one-month $50 put for $2. What is your cost basis on the stock? Assume the stock is trading for $45 a few days later, and you're down $500 on your stock position. Why isn't the put up $500 at this point to fully hedge your position?

Answer: The cost basis on the stock is now $52. The put will not fully hedge until expiration. If the delta is less than one, the gain in the put will not offset the loss in the stock.

4) You own shares of a stock currently trading for $75 but are looking to buy 300 more shares if it should fall below $70. You decide to sell three one-month $70 puts for $3.50. How much will you receive from the short put not counting commissions?

You also notice a one-month $50 put trading for $0.25 and decide to buy it. What are your total proceeds from the sale and purchase now? How much have you reduced your down side risk? Compare the risk of the naked put versus the spread. Considering the total credits from both positions, which is more appealing to you?

Answer: You will receive 3 * 100 * $3.50 = $1,050 from the sale of the puts. If you buy the $50 put for $0.25, you will pay 3 * 100 * $0.25 = $75 for a net gain of $1,050 - $75 = $975. In doing so, you have reduced your downside risk by 50 points, because you will always be able to sell the stock for $50 if it should fall below this amount.

The $70 naked put gains $1,050 for accepting 70 points of downside risk, while the spread position gains $975 for only 20 points of downside risk ($70 strike - $50 strike = 20 points). Most would consider the risk-reward to be much better from the spread. However, if you think the chances are slim that the stock will fall below $50, or if you are willing to accept that risk, you may be comfortable in selling the $70 put. But remember, even good stocks can fall; you must ask yourself if it is really worth the risk.

Box Spreads

1) You are thinking of buying a six-month $75 call and selling the six-month $80 call, which is currently quoting a net debit of $3.50 for the spread. You would like to put in a bid at a lower price. How would you determine how much room there is to negotiate? Assume the six-month $75/$80 put spread is trading for $1.88 and interest rates are 5%.

Answer: You could buy the $75/$80 bull spread for $3.50 and also buy the $75/$80 bear spread for $1.88, for a total cost of

$5.38. Doing so would create a box position, which is guaranteed to grow to a value equal to the difference in strikes, or $5. However, you are paying $5.38 and must wait for six months to receive $5, so there is certainly room to negotiate. An asset guaranteed to be worth $5 in six months should be worth $5/(1.025) = $4.87 today and the market makers are asking $5.38, which is theoretically over-valued by $5.38 - $4.87 = 0.505, or roughly 51 cents. Therefore, you could easily shave off half or more of this amount and likely get filled by entering a limit of $3.25 or slightly less.

    2) If you buy a bull spread and buy a bear spread, what is this position called? What is the risk of the position?

Answer: This is a box spread. There is no risk in the position, as it will behave like a zero-coupon bond and grow to a value of the difference in strikes at expiration. Keep in mind that bid-ask spreads will likely make the value somewhat less.

Equity Collars

    1) What is the upside and downside risk of an equity collar position?

Answer: The equity collar is a limited downside and upside risk strategy.

    3) Somebody tells you that you should always enter collars for credits because you receive money instead of paying money to enter the position. How would you respond?

Answer: Receiving credits may be nice but there is a tradeoff. Entering collars for credits increases the downside risk, and you must be willing to accept that risk.

    3) Can collars generally be used in an IRA with option approval?

Answer: Yes, collars are a valid and often highly used strategy in IRAs.

4) Which position is the same as a collar from a profit and loss standpoint?

Answer: A bull spread.

4) You bought stock at $100 per share, sold a $105 call for $3, and bought a $95 put for $2. What is your cost basis on the stock? What is your maximum gain and loss?

Answer: Your cost basis is -$100 + $3 - $2 = $99. The maximum you can make is $105 assigned on the short call for a gain of $6. You can also sell your stock for $95 by exercising the long put if it should fall below $95, which creates a $4 loss. As a check, the gain of $6 and loss of $4 add up to $10, which is the difference in strikes.

GLOSSARY

Abandonment

When a trader allows an option to expire unexercised.

Away from the Market

A limit order to buy below the current market price (the ask) or to sell above the current market price (the bid). These orders are held as either day or good 'til canceled orders and may not be filled if the market does not reach these limits.

Aggregate Exercise Price

The total exercise value of an option contract. It is found by multiplying the strike price by the number of shares represented by the contract. For example, if you hold five $50 calls, the aggregate exercise price is 5 * 50 * 100 = $25,000. This is the amount you would have to pay if you decided to exercise all five contracts. Whenever an option is adjusted (through splits are acquisitions, for example), the aggregate exercise price remains the same. For instance, if the above $50 call splits 2:1, then you would hold ten $25 contracts for an aggregate exercise price of 10 * $25 * 100 = $25,000.

All-or-None (AON)

A type of order restriction that designates that the trader does not want any partial fill. Technically, any buy or sell order is an order to buy or sell *up to* the number of shares or contracts specified in the order. If a trader wants only the entire order filled or nothing at all, then an AON restriction should be placed. Be aware that AON orders greatly affect how the order is traded. It is possible to not get filled with an AON restriction even though the security traded at or through the price. It is not a good idea to use AON on option orders less than 20 contracts, because each option quote is good for at least that many.

American Option

A style of option that allows the holder (buyer) to exercise any time prior to expiration. All equity options are American-style, as is the OEX index. Generally, call options should not be exercised early (except to capture a dividend or other rare cases), and put options should be exercised early once the put is sufficiently in-the-money (where delta = 1). See also *European Option*.

AMEX

An abbreviation for the American Stock Exchange. This is the second-largest options exchange in the world. See also CBOE.

Arbitrage

Any trade that generates a guaranteed profit for no cash outlay. The classic case is the simultaneous purchase and sale of the same security in different markets, such as buy IBM for $100 on the New York Stock Exchange and simultaneously sell it on the Pacific Stock Exchange for $101.25. Because so many traders have access to the quotes, this type of arbitrage rarely occurs. Traders who look for arbitrage situations are called arbitrageurs or arbs, and serve important economic functions in the markets because they help to keep prices fair.

Assignment

When the short option position is notified of the long position's intent to exercise. The long position "exercises" and the short position is "assigned." The long position has the right to exercise; if the trader chooses to exercise, the short position must oblige.

At-the-Money

A term used to describe an option with a strike price equal to the market price of the stock. Because it is rare to see a stock trade exactly at one of the strike prices, the term is loosely used to mean the strike nearest the current stock price.

Automatic Exercise

The process where the Options Clearing Corporation (OCC) exercises an in-the-money call or put without instructions. Generally, equity options are automatically exercised if they are 3/4 of a point or more in-the-money, while index options are exercised it they are in-the-money by one cent or more. If a trader does not wish to have the in-the-money option exercised, he should either sell it in the open market or submit instructions to the broker not to exercise

Backspread

A type of ratio spread having unlimited profit potential. For example, if a trader is short ten $45 calls and long twenty $50 calls, he is long a call backspread. Similarly, short ten $50 puts and long twenty $45 puts is a long a put backspread.

Bear (Bearish)

An investor who believes a stock or index will fall. The term gets its name from the way a bear attacks; it raises it paws and swipes down, simulating a high to low motion. If you think stocks are moving from high to low, you are bearish.

Bear Spread

Any spread that requires the underlying stock to fall in order to be profitable. The basic bear spread, for example, would be to buy a $50 put and sell a $45 put, or buy a $50 call and sell a $45 call (with all other factors the same). Any time the trader is buying the high strike and selling the low strike, with all other factors constant, it is a bear spread.

Beta

A statistical measure showing the relative volatility of a stock compared to the S&P 500 index. If you hold a stock with a beta of 1.3, it is expected to perform 30% better than the S&P 500 index. If the S&P is up 10%, your stock should be up 13%. Likewise, if the index is down 20%, you should expect your stock to be down 26%. High beta stocks are therefore more volatile than the market and low betas are less volatile. High beta stocks will carry relatively high premiums on the options.

Bid-Ask Spread

The difference between the asking price and the bid price. For example, if the bid is $5 and the ask is $5.50, then the spread is 1/2-point, or $0.50. Spreads tend to widen when there is more risk or less liquidity (which is a form of risk). Because of this, it is not uncommon to see far months, out-of-the-money, or deep in-the-money options trade with very wide bid-ask spreads. The market (not the market makers) determines the spreads, which is contrary to what most traders believe.

Big Board

The New York Stock Exchange (NYSE).

Black-Scholes Option Pricing Model

A theoretical option-pricing model developed by Fisher Black and Myron Scholes. It produces the theoretical value of an American call option with the following five inputs: stock price, exercise price, risk-free interest rate, volatility, and time. It is arguably the single most important piece of research in modern finance theory. Myron Scholes was awarded a Nobel Prize in 1997 for his contributions.

Box Spread

A long call and short put at one strike (synthetic long position), along with a short call and long put (synthetic short position) at another. The box spread can also be viewed as a bull vertical spread with calls, and a bear vertical spread with puts (or vice versa). The value of the box position is the present value of the difference in strikes and is considered to be riskless.

Bull (Bullish)

An investor who believes a stock or index will rise. The term gets its name from the way a bull attacks; it lowers its horns and raises its head high. If you think stocks are heading from low to high, you are bullish.

Bull Spread

Any spread that requires the underlying to rise in order to be profitable. A basic bull spread, for example, would be to buy a $50 call and sell a $55 call, or to buy a $50 put and sell a $55 put. Any time the trader is <u>buying the low strike</u> and <u>selling the high strike</u>, with all other factors constant, it is a bull spread. Remember it by the mnemonic **Buy Low, Sell High = BLSH** = Bullish

Butterfly Spread

A spread consisting of at least three different commissions where the trader buys a low strike, sells two middle strikes, and buys a high strike, all equally spaced and on the same underlying. For example, buy one $50 call, sell two $55 calls, and buy one $60 call. The trade can also be done with puts. In addition, synthetic versions of each piece can be used, making more than three commissions.

Another view of the butterfly spread is that it is a bull spread matched with a bear spread either with calls or puts. Butterfly spreads are used primarily by market makers to take advantage of minor price discrepancies between spreads.

Buy-Write

A trade where the investor buys stock and simultaneously sells a call against it. It is a covered call position but the buy-write is a way to enter the trade. Both the stock and call are executed at the same time, thereby eliminating market movement risk called execution risk. See also *Sell-Write*.

Cabinet Bid (CAB)

A clearing trade that allows market makers to clear deep-out-of-the-money option contracts for 1 cent per option (or $1 per contract).

This is a trade you should be aware of because it causes a lot of problems for traders — especially near tax time. Traders holding deep-out-of-the-money options will often want to close it out, even though there is no bid and many brokers suggest placing the trade as a cabinet bid.

The problem arises when traders wish to clear out the option near year-end for a tax loss. In many cases, traders check their accounts on January 1, only to find that the order is still open! There are many reasons why it may not fill, but just be aware that you should place these trades "versus junk," which will guarantee the sale and a confirmation for your tax records.

Calendar Spread

See *Horizontal Spread*.

Call Option

A contract between two people that gives the owner the right, but not the obligation, to buy stock at a specified price over a given time period. The seller of the call has an obligation to sell the stock if the long put position decides to buy.

Cash Market (Spot Market)

The market for the underlying stock (or index). For example, some traders may refer to Intel shares of stock as the "cash market" when talking about Intel options. Because options can be used to defer a purchase or sale, the underlying shares are called the "cash market" or "spot" market (because this is where the asset can be purchased "on the spot").

Cash Settlement

A type of option settlement usually used by index options. These options do not deliver or receive shares in the underlying index. Instead, they are settled for the cash value between the closing of the index (subject to specific guidelines) and the strike price multiplied by the contract size. For example, if a particular index closes at $4,050 and a trader holds ten $4,000 strike calls, that trader will receive $50 * 10 * 100 = $50,000 cash the following business day. The trader receives shares of the index and cannot exercise the call.

CBOE

An acronym for the Chicago Board Options Exchange. This is the largest options exchange in the world.

Class

All call or put options of a particular underlying. For example, all IBM calls are one class of options. All IBM puts are another class.

Clearing House

See *Options Clearing Corporation.*

Closing Purchase

A transaction where an option seller buys the same contract to close. A closing transaction relieves the seller from the potential obligation under the original sale. For example, a trader sells one XYZ March $50 call to open. The trader may be forced to sell 100 shares of XYZ at a price of $50 if the long position exercises. At a later time, the trader decides he does not want to have this obligation, so he can buy one XYZ March $50 call to close. The trader's profits or losses depend on the opening selling price and closing purchase price. See also *Closing Sale, Opening Purchase, Opening Sale*.

Closing Sale

A transaction where an option buyer sells the same contract to close. A closing transaction removes the rights from the original purchase. For example, a trader buys one XYZ March $50 call to open. This trader may purchase 100 shares of XYZ by expiration in March for $50. At a later time, the trader may decide to sell this right to someone else, so he could sell one XYZ March $50 to close. The trader's profits or losses depend on the opening purchase price and closing selling price. See also *Closing Purchase, Opening Purchase, Opening Sale*.

Collar

A strategy where an investor sells calls against a long stock position to finance the purchase of protective puts. From a profit and loss standpoint, it is effectively a bull spread and has limited upside potential and limited downside risk. For example, an investor who owns stock at $100, sells a $105 call, and purchases a $95 put is utilizing a collar strategy. The investor will give up all gains in the stock above $105 but will not take any losses below $95. Also called *funnels, range-forwards, cylinders,* and *split-price conversions*.

Combination

Also known as a combo, this is not a uniquely defined term. Most in the equities market use it to mean a strangle — a strategy where the investor buys a call and a put at different strike prices on the same underlying. For example, a long $50 call and a long $45 put would be a long combo. It has the same basic intention as a straddle with less potential for gains and losses.

Other traders, especially in the futures markets, use combo to mean synthetic long or short position. For example, long $50 call and short $50 put (synthetic long stock) is called a combo.

Condor

A spread involving at least four commissions. The condor trader has similar intentions to the butterfly, except the middle two strikes are split. For example, buy one $50 call, sell one $55 call, sell one $60 call, and buy one $65 call. The condor is a lower-risk, lower-return strategy compared to the butterfly. The condor is really two laddered butterfly spreads.

Conversion

A position usually used by market makers to hedge risk. A conversion is long stock, long put, and short call with the options having the same strike and time to expiration. The trader is long stock and long synthetic short stock, which is why the position is hedged. Because of this, the trader is guaranteeing the sale of his long stock at the exercise price. The cost of the conversion is the present value of the exercise price. See also *Reversal*.

Covered Call (Covered Write)

The sale of a call option against a long stock position. The short call is "covered," because the investor will always be able to deliver the shares regardless of how high the underlying moves. See also *Naked* or *Uncovered Positions*.

Credit Spread

Any purchase and sale of an option that results in a credit to the account. For example, if you buy a $50 call and sell a $45 call, the net will be a credit paid to your account, assuming the two options are traded simultaneously. This is because the lower strike call will always be more valuable and therefore carry a higher price. Likewise, you can buy a $50 put and sell a $55 put simultaneously, which will result in a net credit to your account. With puts, the higher strike will always be more valuable and carry a higher price. With any credit spread, the initial credit is always yours to keep regardless of what happens to the underlying stock. The trade is not risk-free; however, limited losses will occur if the stock lands in a particular range. See also *Debit Spread*.

Day Order

A time limit specification that states the order is only good for that trading day. For example, "Buy 200 shares of stock at a limit of $35 good for the day." If this order does not fill for $35 or lower by the end of the day, it will cease to exist. All orders "at market" can only be good for the day since they are guaranteed to fill.

Debit Spread

Any purchase and sale of an option that results in a debit to the account. For example, if you buy a $50 call and sell a $55 call, the net will be a debit to your account, assuming the two options are traded simultaneously. This is because the lower strike call will always be more valuable and therefore carry a higher price. Likewise, you can buy a $50 put and sell a $45 put simultaneously, which will result in a net debit to your account. With puts, the higher strike will always be more valuable and carry a higher price. With debit spreads, the stock must move in a particular direction to show a profit. See also *Credit Spread*.

Delta

One of the "Greeks" denoting an option's sensitivity to the underlying price. Deltas on calls will always range between 0 and 1 and between 0 and -1 for puts. (Delta can sometimes exceed these ranges but only in unusual circumstances and then only for a short while.) If a $50 call option is priced at $5 with delta of 1/2, the option will be worth approximately $5.50 if the underlying moves up one full point (the option gained 1/2-point to the stock's 1 point). Deltas constantly change and are highly dependent on the strike price, time to expiration, and volatility of the underlying.

Delta Neutral

A trading strategy typically used by market makers where the total deltas of all positions add to zero (or at least very close to it). Because the underlying stock or index moves, traders must continually adjust their positions to remain delta neutral. Retail commissions often make this strategy too costly to use.

Derivative Security

Any financial asset whose value is determined by the value of another security known as the underlying security. Options and futures are probably the most well-known derivatives, but there are many others including Collateralized Mortgage Obligations (CMOs), swaps, swaptions, options on futures, and a host of others. Many bonds are derivative securities because they have embedded call or put features.

Diagonal Spread

A spread where the investor is long a strike at one month and short a strike at another month, with both options being calls or puts and on the same underlying. If the trade results in a net debit (credit), it is a long (short) diagonal spread. For example, if a trader buys a March $50 call and sells a January $60 call, he would be holding a diagonal spread. Quotes are listed in the newspaper with months across the top and strikes down the side. You will see the quotes for a diagonal spread appear on the diagonal of the quote matrix — hence the name.

Ex-Dividend

The day on which a stock trades without the right to the dividend. Say XYZ is trading at $100 and pays a $1 dividend with the ex-date being tomorrow. If you buy the stock today (or bought any time prior), you will be entitled to the upcoming $1 dividend. If you wait until tomorrow, the stock will trade for $99 (because the stock price will be reduced by the amount of the dividend), but you will not be entitled to the upcoming $1 dividend.

Exercise

The procedure where a trader notifies the seller of his intent to buy the stock (if a call) or sell the stock (if a put). The trader wishing to exercise an option simply notifies the brokerage firm, which in turn notifies the Options Clearing Corporation (OCC). The OCC then pairs a short position through random assignment. See also *Assignment*.

Exercise Price

Same as strike price. It is the price where the buyer and seller of the option agree to transact stock. For example, if a trader has a $50 call, he holds a $50 exercise price and can purchase the stock at anytime for $50. The short position must sell for $50. Likewise, the holder of a $50 put has an exercise price of $50 and may sell the stock for $50 at any time. The seller of the put must purchase the stock for $50. With all else constant, lower call strikes will always be more expensive than higher ones, with the reverse being true for puts.

Expiration

Technically, option expiration (for equities) is always the Saturday following the third Friday of the month. If a trader has an October call option, it can no longer be exercised after that point. But for trading purposes, the last day to buy or sell an option will be the third Friday of the month. Equity options can be traded until 4:02 EST and 4:15 EST for index options.

European Option

A style of option that allows the holder (buyer) to exercise only at expiration. Most index options are European-style with the exception of OEX. See American Option.

Extrinsic Value

Same as time value. An option's price can be separated into two components: time value (extrinsic) and intrinsic value. The intrinsic value is the amount by which the option is in-the-money, and the extrinsic value is the remaining amount. The following equation may help: option premium - intrinsic value = time value. See also *Intrinsic Value, In-the-Money*.

Fair Value

The theoretical value of an asset.

Fill or Kill (FOK)

An order time frame (as opposed to the standard "day" or "good 'til canceled" order) where the trader is attempting to have the order filled immediately in entirety or not at all. It's generally not a good idea to use FOK orders. In most cases, the floor traders kill it immediately to avoid making a hasty decision.

Gamma

One of many "Greeks" used in options. It denotes the sensitivity of an option's delta with respect to the underlying stock. It can be viewed as the delta of the delta. Long call and put positions have positive gamma, while the short positions have negative gamma. It measures the speed component of the option and therefore its risk. High gamma positions are riskier relative to low gamma with all other factors the same.

Gearing

A British term used to describe one aspect of leverage of an option. It is not uniquely defined but the two most common definitions are: 1) The price of the stock divided by the price of the option, and 2) The strike price of the option divided by the price of the options. Under the first definition, if the underlying stock is trading for $100 and you purchase a call option for $2, the gearing is $100/$2 = 50. In other words, you are controlling $100 worth of stock for $2, so have leveraged the asset by a factor of 50. The second definition views the options price in relation to the strike price. If the above option is a $110 strike, the gearing is $110/2 = 55. This method says you have potentially committed yourself to a price of $110, but paid only $2 for it, so you have leveraged the asset by a factor of 55.

Good 'Til Canceled (GTC)

An order time limit that specifies to leave the order open until it is either filled or canceled by the investor. The New York Stock Exchange allows for a maximum time limit of six months, but brokerage firms have the liberty to make the restrictions tighter. Check with your brokerage firm for the specific time frame designated by their GTC orders. See also *Day Order, Fill or Kill, Immediate or Cancel*.

Greeks

There are five main Greek letters used to specify an option's price sensitivity: 1) Delta (sensitivity in relation to movements of the underlying stock), 2) Gamma (sensitivity in relation to speed of movement of the underlying), 3) Vega (sensitivity in relation to volatility), 4) Theta (sensitivity in relation to time) 5) Rho (sensitivity in relation to interest rates).

Guts

Any of a number of strategies where the call strike is lower than the put strike, leaving the trader with a built-in box position and a guaranteed minimum value at expiration. One of the basic guts positions, for example, is long $50 call and long $60 put, which is a guts strangle. Because the call strike is below the put strike, the position will always have at least $10 (the difference in strikes) in value; pick *any* stock price and the above strangle will be worth at least $10.

Hedge

Any strategy that is used to limit investment loss by adding a position that offsets an existing position. For example, a long bull spread (buy $50 call and sell a $60 call, for example) is a hedged position. The sale of the $60 call reduces the price (and risk) of the long $50 call.

Holder
The long position or owner of an option.

Horizontal Spread
A spread where the trader buys and sells options of the same type — either calls or puts — on the same underlying with the same strike, but with different times to expiration. For example, if a trader buys a March $50 and sells a January $50, that is a horizontal spread. If the trade results in a debit, it is called a long horizontal, and a short if a credit is received.

Quotes are listed in the newspaper with months across the top and strikes down the side. You will see the quotes for a horizontal spread appear horizontally of the quote matrix — hence the name. Also called a *time* or *calendar* spread.

Immediate or Cancel (IOC)
An order time frame (as opposed to the standard "day" or "good 'til canceled" order) where the investor is requesting an immediate fill or cancellation of the trade. Unlike its Fill-or-Kill counterpart, the IOC order does not need to be filled in its entirety.

Implied Volatility
The volatility necessary to put into the Black-Scholes Option Pricing Model to produce the current quote on the option. It is the forward volatility of the underlying stock that is *implied* by the market price.

In-the-Money
A call option with a strike below or a put option with a strike above the current stock price are said to be in-the-money. This is also the amount of intrinsic value of an option — the amount that would be received if exercised immediately. For example, if the stock is $103.50, a $100 call is $3.50 in-the-money. If the trader exercised the call immediately, he would receive stock worth $103.50

and pay only $100 for a net gain of $3.50. Any amount above this $3.50 figure in the option's premium is called time or extrinsic value. See also *Out-of-the-Money, Extrinsic Value*.

Intrinsic Value

An option's intrinsic value is the amount by which it is in-the-money. See also *In-the-Money, Extrinsic Value*.

Iron Butterfly

A butterfly spread constructed by a bull spread with calls and a bear spread with puts with all options representing the same underlying and expiration date. It can also be viewed as a long straddle paired with a short strangle. A long iron butterfly is equivalent to a short butterfly.

Jelly Roll

A strategy using a long call and short put (synthetic long position), and a short call and long put (synthetic long position) at another date with all options representing the same underlying. If the position is initiated for a debit (credit) it is a long (short) jelly roll. The value of a jelly roll is the cost of carry between months less the present value of dividends received.

Kappa

See *Vega*.

LEAPS®

An acronym for Long Term Equity Anticipation Securities. LEAPS are just longer-term options with expirations up to three years. Because of the time involved, there are many strategies available with LEAPS that cannot be done with regular options.

Limit Order

An order that guarantees the price but not the execution. If a trader places an order to buy ten contracts at a limit of $5 (the limit), the only way the order will fill is if it can be filled for $5 or *lower*. Similarly, if a sell order is placed for $10, the only way it will fill is for $10 or *higher*. Because of these restrictions, limit orders are not guaranteed to fill.

Long Position

A position initiated from the purchase of the security. If a trader buys ten March $50 calls, he is long the position. A long position is one that is owned. Also, long positions will increase (at least theoretically) in value as the underlying increases. See also *Short Position*.

Margin

The use of borrowed funds to purchase stock. If you have a margin account, you are required to pay for only half the position (assuming the stock is marginable) and pay interest on the remainder. For example, an investor can buy $50,000 worth of IBM but needs to deposit only 50% or $25,000 (called the Regulation T or Reg T amount). The trader pays interest on the remaining $25,000. Margin accounts provide additional leverage, which can work for and against the trader. If IBM is up 10%, the margin trader will be up 20%. Most of the popular stocks are marginable, but options never are; they must be paid in full. However, this does not mean you cannot be on margin for an option trade. For example, an investor owns $50,000 worth of IBM outright in a margin account. The brokerage firm is willing to send the investor a check for $50,000 (half the amount) because he is required to have only half the position paid for. This is sometimes called margin cash available. It is this cash that can be used to fully pay for options, but you will have a debit balance and pay interest on it. This is a very basic overview and there are other restrictions, such as minimum amounts that can be margined, so check with your broker before placing your margin trades.

Market on Close (MOC)

An order qualifier that says to buy/sell the position very close to the closing price (usually within the last five minutes of trading) if the limit order does not execute during the day. For example, a trader has an order to sell 100 shares at a limit of $50 MOC. If the stock does not trade high enough to execute the order, it will convert to a market order within the final minutes of the trading day and fill.

Market Order

An order to buy or sell at the best available quote *when the trade reaches the floor* (or market maker). It is guaranteed to execute because the price is allowed to fluctuate. Also, there is no need to designate "day" or "good 'til canceled" with a market order because it is sure to fill (unless it is a short sale with no "uptick"). See also *Limit Order*.

Marketable Limit Order

A limit order to buy at the offer or sell at the bid. For example, if the quote is $5 on the bid and $5.25 on the offer, an order to sell at a limit of $5 is called a marketable limit order. Likewise, an order to buy at a limit of $5.25 is a marketable limit order, too.

Naked (Uncovered)

A short position not covered by an offsetting position. A trader who sells calls to open is short the call. If the underlying stock is not in the account, that call is naked (uncovered). Naked positions are considered to be the most risky because they have unlimited liability (or nearly unlimited for puts) to the trader. Naked positions require margin deposits to ensure performance by the trader.

Not Held

An order qualifier designating that the floor broker or specialist has discretion over how and when to fill the order. "Not held" orders can be useful for very large orders, because they allow the floor broker or specialist to work the order by slowly feeding it into the market. You are designating that the broker is "not held" to time and sales — hence the name. As a general rule, "not held" qualifiers will usually net you a better fill in the long run, but that requires that the trader use them almost exclusively. To casually use a "not held" order once in a while or on smaller orders is probably not really beneficial.

Opening Purchase

A transaction where an option seller buys the contract to open. An opening purchase is initiating a "long" position. See also Opening Sale, Closing Purchase, Closing Sale.

Open Interest

The net long and short positions for any option contract. If a trader "buys to open" and another "sells to open," then open interest will increase by the number of contracts. This is because both traders are opening. If one "buys to open" and the other "sells to close," then open interest will remain unchanged. Finally, if one "buys to close" and another "sells to close," then open interest will decrease by the amount of the contracts.

Opening Sale

A transaction where an option buyer sells the contract to open. An opening sale places the option seller in a potential obligation to buy stock (if short puts) or sell stock (if short calls). The trader receives a premium to the account for this transaction. If the trader desires to get out of this position, he must enter a closing purchase. See also Opening Purchase, Closing Sale, Closing Purchase.

Options Clearing Corporation (OCC)

The organization that acts as a buyer to every seller and a seller to every buyer, thereby guaranteeing the performance of the exchange-traded contracts.

Out-of-the-Money

A call option with a strike above and a put option with a strike below the current stock price. Also, an option with no intrinsic value is said to be out-of-the-money.

For example, if the stock is $100, a $105 call and a $95 put are out-of-the-money. See also *In-the-Money, Extrinsic Value*.

Parity

An option trading with only intrinsic value; the time value is zero. For example, with the stock at $104.50, the $100 call trading at $4.50 is trading at parity. See also *In-the-Money, Extrinsic Value*.

Pin Risk

The risk encountered by the seller of an option that expires exactly at-the-money. The trader is unsure if he will be assigned. This risk is especially critical for market makers using conversions and reversals. Say the stock closes at exactly $50 (or very, very close) on expiration day. If the market maker is long stock, long $50 put, and short $50 call (conversion), he is unsure whether to exercise the put because he is unsure about the assignment of the $50 call. In these situations, you can almost always close vertical spreads for the full spread amount because market makers love to offset this risk for an even trade.

Premium

The amount paid for an option. The option's premium can be further broken down into intrinsic value and time value.

Price Spread

See *Vertical Spread*.

Put Option

A contract between two people that gives the owner the right, but not the obligation, to sell stock at a specified price over a given time period. The seller of the put has an obligation to buy the stock if the long put position decides to sell.

RAES (Retail Automated Execution System)

A proprietary electronic trading system of the Chicago Board Options Exchange. Any retail market order (or marketable limit order) for 20 contracts or fewer is usually filled immediately through RAES.

Ratio Spread

Any spread having unequal long and short positions. Specifically, if the trader has unlimited risk, it is a ratio spread. If the trader has unlimited profit potential, it is a backspread.

Reversal (Reverse Conversion)

A three-sided position used primarily by market makers to hedge risk. A position of short stock, short put, and long call is a reversal. Both options must have the same strike price and expiration. The reversal grows to a guaranteed payment at expiration. The market maker puts on the position when the credit from the interest earned will be higher than the required payment.

Rho

One of the "Greeks" representing the sensitivity of an option's price for a small change in interest rates (usually considered to be a 1% change in rates).

Sell-Write

A trade where the investor shorts stock and simultaneously sells a put against it. It is a covered-put position but the sell-write is a way to enter the trade. Both the stock and put are executed at the same time, thereby eliminating market movement risk called execution risk. See also *Buy-Write*.

Series

All option contracts on the same underlying instrument with the same exercise price and time to expiration. For example, IBM Jan $100 calls are one series of options. IBM Jan $105 calls are another. Likewise, all IBM Jan $100 put options designate another series.

Short Position

A position initiated by the sale of stock or options. Traders who sell options are also said to "write" the contract, so written positions are synonymous with short positions.

Spot Market

See *Cash Market*.

Spread

Any position consisting of a long and short position. If the spread is on the same underlying stock, it is an intramarket spread. If it is over different securities, it is an intermarket spread. For example, long $50 call and short $55 call is a vertical spread. See also *Horizontal Spread, Time Spread, Vertical Spread, Diagonal Spread*.

Stop Order

Previously known as a stop-loss order. A contingency order that becomes a market order if the stock trades at a certain limit. For example, say a stock is trading for $100. A trader placing an order to sell the stock at a stop-price of $98 is instructing the broker to make the order a market order if the stock trades at $98 or lower. Stop orders do not prevent losses! The reason why is that the order will trigger a market order if the stock trades below $98 as well. The stock could open for trading at $80, and the trader will be sold at this price instead of the $98 he was expecting. Because they do not stop losses, the Securities Exchange Commission (SEC) determined that the previous term *stop-loss order* cannot be used. See also *Stop Limit*.

Stop Limit

A contingency order that becomes a limit order if the stock trades at a certain limit or lower. For example, say a stock is trading at $100. A trader placing an order to sell the stock at a *stop-price* of $98 and a *stop limit* of $98 is instructing the broker to sell the stock at a limit of $98 (or higher) if the stock trades at $98 or lower. Notice that two prices must be given: a stop-price and a stop limit. The stop-price activates the order and the stop limit designates the minimum price the trader is willing to accept. The stop-price can be equal to or less than the stop-price (but not greater). Because of this limit, stop-limit orders are not guaranteed to execute even if the stop-price is triggered. Stop-limit orders do not prevent losses. See also *Stop Order*.

Straddle

A strategy using a long call and long put (or short call and short put) with both options having the same exercise price and expiration. The long straddle position is hoping for a large move in either direction, while the short straddle is hoping for the market to sit fairly flat.

Strangle (Combo)

See *Combination*.

Strip

A strategy using two long puts and one long call (or two short puts and one short call) with all options having the same exercise price and expiration. It can be viewed as a ratio straddle as well. See also *Strap*.

Strap

A strategy using two long calls and one long put (or two short calls and one short put) with all options having the same exercise price and expiration . It can be viewed as a ratio straddle as well. See also *Strip*.

Theoretical Value

The fair value of an option based on a known pricing method such as the Black-Scholes Option Pricing Model. If an option trades higher (lower) than its theoretical value, traders will become sellers (buyers) with all else constant.

Theta

One of the "Greeks" that measures an option's price sensitivity in relation to time. Usually it is expressed as the amount of money an option will lose if one day passes with all other factors the same.

Three-Way

Similar to a conversion or reversal except the stock position is replaced with a deep-in-the-money option. For example, a market maker who is long stock, long put, and short a call is long a conversion. If the market maker replaces the long stock position with a deep-in-the-money call, the position is called a three-way. Note too that the market maker in this example could have shorted a deep-in-the-money put, which will also behave like long stock. Three-ways eliminate pin risk to the market maker. See also *Conversion, Reversal, Pin Risk*.

Time Value

The amount of an option's price not accounted for by intrinsic value. If an option is out-of-the-money, its premium will consist entirely of time value. For example, say there is a $55 call trading at $3 with the stock at $50. This option is out-of-the-money, so the entire $3 is time premium. If the stock were at $57, then the $55 call would be in-the-money by $2; the intrinsic value would be $2 and the time premium would be $1.

Tick Value (Tick Size)

The smallest allowable price move in a particular option. For example, an option trading below $3 can usually trade in 1/16th's (5 cents under the new decimalization rule) so its tick value would be 1/16. Options trading at $3 or above generally require 1/8th minimums (10 cents under the new decimalization rules) so it has a tick value of 1/8.

Time Decay

A property of options that states some or all of an option's value will erode with the passage of time, and are consequently known as wasting assets. Time attacks shorter-term options much harder than longer-term. All else equal, an option seller will prefer to sell shorter-term options, while option buyers will prefer to buy longer-term options.

Time Spread

See *Horizontal Spread*.

Triple Witching

Any day where futures, index options, and equity options all expire. Usually this is the third Friday in the end month of each quarter (March, June, September, December). It is of interest to traders, because market makers must buy and sell the underlying stocks to unwind (get out of) their positions. This usually causes great volatility in the market.

Uncovered Position
See *Naked*.

Unwind
Unwind refers to the specific strategy of "undoing" a buy-write position where the investor would sell the stock and buy the call to close. Unwind can be used loosely to mean the reversing of any position.

Vega
One of the "Greeks" (although not technically a Greek letter) denoting an option's price sensitivity for a small change in volatility (usually a 1% change in volatility). Vega is sometimes denoted by the Greek letter, Kappa.

Vertical Spread
A spread where a trader buys options of the same type — either calls or puts — at different strikes with all else the same. For example, if a trader buys a $50 call and sells a $55 call, he would have a vertical spread.

Quotes are listed in the newspaper with months across the top and strikes down the side. You will see the quotes for a vertical spread appear vertically on the quote matrix — hence the name. Also called a *time* or *calendar* spread. See also *Bull Spread, Bear Spread*.

Volatility
Statistically, it is the annualized standard deviation of the price movements in the underlying. It basically measures the amount of expected movement over time. In layman's terms, a stock that has large price swings from one day to the next is volatile. The more volatile the underlying stock, the higher the price of the option (calls and puts) with all other factors the same.

Wrangle

A basic option strategy used primarily by market makers. It is the combination of two long ratio spreads. A long (short) wrangle is a long (short) call ratio spread paired with a long (short) put ratio spread. For example, a long wrangle may be constructed by selling one $50 call and buying two $55 calls (long call ratio spread) and also selling one $55 put and buying two $50 puts (long put ratio spread). The profit and loss diagram for a wrangle is the same as a strangle.

Write/Writing

Selling an option to open. Any time a trader sells an option to open, he is said to have "written" the contract. A call writer is one who has sold calls against stock (covered call position) and is also called a covered-write. Writing is the same as shorting.

About the Authors

Bill Johnson

Bill Johnson started his financial career as a financial analyst for the American Automobile Association's (AAA) world headquarters in Heathrow, Florida in 1993. For two years he designed and analyzed spreadsheets for financial projections, growth rates, and risk assessments for the Association's affinity credit card program. In addition, he researched and reported on interest rate hedging techniques.

It was the financial futures and options that sparked an interest in the brokerage business. In late 1994 he accepted positions with two different regional brokerage firms before being hired by the discount giant, Charles Schwab, where he worked for an active trader team in addition to specialized technical and fundamental analysis teams. He gained invaluable experience while working rotations for Schwab's trade support group, maintenance reports, risk assessment and initial public offerings (IPOs). Bill was also active in training and was selected to write department manuals and teach the corresponding weeklong courses in economics and option strategies, pricing and hedging to advanced brokers.

He received a Master's Degree in Economics in 1996 and an M.B.A. in 1999 both from the University of Central Florida. He is also a Chartered Financial Analyst (CFA) Level II candidate and the author of *The Single-Stock Futures Revolution*.

James DiGeorgia

James DiGeorgia, Publisher of *21st Century Investor*, has been trading since he was a child. An avid rare coin collector, he began buying and selling rare coins while still in high school. By age sixteen, he had found tremendous success as a rare coin dealer.

While still a teenager James expanded his interests to precious metals, currencies, futures, stocks, and options.

After earning BA in economics, James worked for the largest precious metals and numismatic companies in the world. In 1992 he was recruited by largest independent gold service in the world, with subscribers from Abu Dubai to Bangkok. James became a fierce and tireless champion and advocate for individual investors.

In 1997, James decided to pursue another long time passion: The U.S. stock market. James became convinced that the U.S. stock market was presenting investors with the greatest opportunity to profit he'd ever seen. James launched *21st Century Investor,* a newsletter dedicated to profiting from awesome leaps in technology and medicine.

David Nichols

Since graduating with honors from Yale University in 1988, David Nichols has made his living as an investor.

Forecasting the rapid growth and far-reaching impact of high-tech early on, David capitalized on AOL, Cisco, and Sun Microsystems, as well as the surging real estate demand in the Pacific Northwest.

Prior to joining 21st Century Investor Publishing in 1997, David fostered a new technology for building low-cost housing made of plastic, now in use all over the world. He also spent two years in management with a biotech firm, which manufactures human antibodies from corn.

David is recognized for his uncanny ability to forecast underlying technology trends, and has earned a loyal following among tens of thousands of individual investors and financial professionals.

INDEX

Page references followed by *f, t* and *n* refer to
figures, tables, and notes respectively.